CLASSES IN THE UNITED STATES

Workers Against Capitalists

D0170095

CLASSES IN THE UNITED STATES

Workers Against Capitalists

Charles Loren

Cardinal Publishers
P. O. Box 207
Davis, California 95616

Preface

Workers and revolutionaries have been subjected to an enormous amount of capitalist propaganda about class in the United States:

—We are mostly middle class. Workers toil on the assembly line, but office staff are not part of the working class.

—"Worker" is hard to define: big executives get salaries; either they are workers, or typists, who are also on salary, are not workers.

—A large third group, the petty bourgeoisie, stands between the workers and the capitalists.

—According to Marx himself, a worker has to make a *thing;* sales clerks are not workers.

—To be "realistic," it must be recognized that some people who should be' workers from the oppressive nature of their labor simply are not revolutionary proletarians.

This book attempts to clear up such matters. The aim is to state what classes are, to describe their nature, size, and circumstances, and to criticize the appraisal of a person's class by his occupation, income, or other characteristics. The conclusion shows the inseparable connection between the class makeup of a society and revolution.

Part One gives the definition of class and applies it to the United States. Workers, capitalists, and petty producers are identified. The number and economic power of each class are calculated as they stand today and as they have developed historically. The essential relations and antagonisms between the classes are drawn out.

Part Two compares the class outlook with a variety of criteria often substituted in its place: occupation, amount of income, and some sham Marxist theories.

Part Three discusses the objective basis of revolution in class and the question of how a class will come to act in a revolutionary way.

The book stands on its own and should be clear to any interested reader. But for those involved in organizing the working class and studying Marxism, let me indicate one concern that runs through the analysis. Socialist revolutions occurred first in countries where the working class made up a small fraction of the people. What is usually called the petty bourgeoisie was the largest class. In the United States, the working class is the largest, whether one believes that it has a plurality, a majority, or an almost total dominance of the population. But there is still much that is petty bourgeois in the United States. What is the material basis of this petty bourgeois influence? The answer we give to this question will determine the revolutionary goal and the strategy we follow. Friends of China will be reminded of the issue raised in the Cultural Revolution, namely, why are there still classes during socialist society? It is no surprise that the essence of the matter is the same for monopoly capitalism, although many things, including the appropriate strategy, differ in the two kinds of society, which are separated by the historical dividing line of proletarian revolution.

This is only one concern, however; the book starts with basics and works up to the problems of the subject.

CONTENTS

PART ONE: CLASS

> ". . . the human essence is no
> abstraction inherent in each
> single individual. In its reality
> it is the ensemble of the social
> relations."
> —Marx, Theses on Feuerbach,
> VI

1. The Definition of Class

Men satisfy their material needs by social production. They must transform the material world, which they do together in societies. Production by men differs in two ways from the appropriation of nature by animals. First, animals take from the world around them what they need; men put raw materials through a long and elaborate series of changes in order to create food, clothing, shelter, etc. Second, most animals hunt or graze on their own, while men apply their labor jointly. Even when foraging herds cooperate, their activity cannot compare with the deliberate, coordinated labor of men.

The particular way in which a society carries out its tasks is its mode of production. Two aspects of the mode of production are 1) the power that men hold over the world of matter and 2) the relations between men which unite their activities into a single

7

act. These aspects are called by Marx the forces of production and the relations of production.[1]*

The forces of production include the tools, machines, improvements on the land, mines, buildings and other such instruments of production. They are natural objects distinct from men. In addition to these objective forces, there are subjective ones, too. They are the science, technique, art, and strength which the producers keep alive in their brains and hands. Population and culture are measures of the subjective forces of production. Today, we all know something about the growth of man's productive forces, of the passage of man from a rudely clothed, cave-dwelling picker of berries and a hunter dominated by magic to an operator of industry based on science and powered by harnessed forces of heat and electricity, fabricating machines which make machines which in turn make elaborate varieties of goods. We are told much less about the relations of production.

If men are to combine their productive efforts, these must be related in some way and directed to definite, common ends.[2] The relations of production are of several kinds and vary in different societies. Primitive people did not hunt individually. They worked together to flush out, trap, and kill the antelope or the buffalo. When they went out to hunt smaller game one by one, their catch belonged to the community, which provided them with their needs. In contemporary societies, the elaborate degree of social organization between the factory, office, and store and within each of them is obvious to us. Some relations of production spring directly from the needs of work, but others do not correspond to the forces of production in a fixed way. For example, China is industrializing but at the same time putting factory managers on the shop floor one week a month.

We are concerned with a particular kind of relation of production. At certain moments, primitive societies have passed from a stage of bare survival to one of room for development. In the first stage, men must labor continually to obtain what they need, with little or no margin for survival if nature should fail them by a

*Notes will be found at the back of the book.

scarcity of game, fish, wild fruit, etc. In the second stage, the assurance of requirements takes less than the total labor time available to the society. In this case, additional labor yields an extra product above and beyond current needs. The additional time and product are employed in ways that react on the level and organization of the necessary production work. While needs develop continually, the advance of production stays easily ahead of the expansion of needs, so that there exists surplus labor yielding a surplus product. This surplus product is the product over and above that required to sustain the producers and raise a new generation of them. The stage of surplus labor and surplus product was reached as early as 10,000 years ago, being generally connected with the discovery of agriculture.

At first, and usually for centuries, the community disposes of the surplus product in the same manner as it had necessarily distributed the basic product, collectively and without private advantage.[3] As late as 1500 A.D., the Iroquois Indians remained in this stage of enjoying a surplus collectively. They stored corn for a reserve of several years and enjoyed more leisure time in extremely tough and athletic games (that is, part of the surplus labor time was made leisure time). Their institutions of communal living and production and their law of hospitality guaranteed equality and fraternity in their relation to the surplus labor and product.[4]

But the possibility exists that not all members of society will remain producers, and furthermore, that non-producers may come to possess and dispose of the surplus product. After a long period of collective surplus, society divided in this way. Classes appeared. A minority of the population was removed from direct production and gained control over the form of the surplus labor and the disposition of surplus product.[5]

Classes are groups of people which, owing to their different relations to the means of production, differ in relation to the surplus labor of society, generally either providing it to another group, or disposing of the surplus labor of another group, or disposing only of its own surplus labor.

The specific relation to the means of production determines

exactly how one class compels another to perform surplus labor. History shows us a number of classes in a series of modes of production. But if left on their own, all class societies eventually develop into the capitalist mode of production. (Some were not left on their own; incorporated into the capitalist colonial system, they display stultified combinations of their old mode of production and capitalism.) Without going over all the phases between primitive classless society and capitalism, we can study the classes in the United States today, a capitalist society.

In this mode of production, there are three classes: the working class, the capitalist class, and the class of petty producers. The definition of these classes flows from the relations of production under the capitalist mode of production, in particular, from their different relations to the means of production. In a capitalist society, the means of production (the factories and equipment, farms, mines, workshops, offices, means of transport and communication, and all the stocks of raw materials and other goods) are owned privately by a minority, the capitalists. The working class has been freed of ownership of the means of production and therefore offers its labor power, what remains to it of the forces of production, to the capitalists, who employ some of those seeking work. Instead of society as a whole applying the forces of production, both subjective and objective, for social ends, one class by its control of the means of production is able to impose its own ends on production, while the other class can overcome the lack of its material needs only by submitting to the terms of the exploiting class. The constituent parts of production are brought together not in harmony but in antagonism.

There remains a small class for which the union of labor and means of labor has not been broken, although at the penalty of an individual, dwarf scale of both. This is the class of petty producers, who own and operate their own means of production. Small farmers and independent truckers are examples of petty producers. They are working people in the general sense of working in production on nature, but they are not workers in the sense of their relation to the means of production. Instead, they are "propertied" like capitalists, being the owners and disposers of the means and fruit of some production.

The capitalists extract surplus labor from the working class and dispose of the surplus product. The working class also performs its necessary labor and obtains, in wages and salaries, the product necessary to sustain itself, the class of direct producers, and to rear a new generation of workers. The exploitation of workers by capitalists is not apparent at first glance. The process was explained by Marx, who in his book *Capital* has given the scientific explanation of profit and allied forms like interest and rent, all varieties of surplus-value, a category specific to capitalism. But even without this analysis it is clear that we may mentally divide the social product into two parts: one part that the workers are able to purchase with their wage and salary revenues and another part that escapes them and goes to the capitalists. The antagonistic relation between the classes is essentially the same contradiction as that between wealth and value, use-value and value, and paid labor and unpaid labor.

The petty producers are able to keep a portion of their surplus labor, although in a capitalist society they lose a considerable fraction or all of their surplus labor in trade relations of various types. In a society composed entirely of petty producers, this would not be true.

The particular relations of production which define classes in a given society are its class relations of production. They are never the totality of relations of production in a society. They are, however, the dominant relations wherever they exist.

2. Abstract and Concrete Labor

Labor has two aspects, the examination of which brings out the nature of surplus labor and surplus product more clearly. Regardless of the form of society, and in particular whether it is a class society or not, all its labor is concrete: it is labor of a specific type aiming at a particular transformation of matter. The labor of spinning cloth differs from the labor of smelting iron in the operations that spinners and smelters go through, the material on which they work, and the desired result. This is labor viewed concretely, or concrete labor. Change it and the product is changed; we have iron billets instead of yarn. To know what concrete labor someone is doing, we observe his activity or we deduce it from the product.

There are many forms of concrete labor, more or less elaborately distinguished according to the development of the division of labor. No person and no society lives on one product alone; a great variety is required to meet the variety of man's needs. The producers' labor is allocated among the forms of concrete labor. We arrive at the idea of labor in the abstract, apart from its concrete form.

"Productive activity, if we leave out of sight its special form, viz., the useful character of the labor, is nothing but the expenditure of human labor-power. Tailoring and weaving, though qualitatively different productive activities, are each a productive expenditure of human brains, nerves, and muscles, and in this sense are human labor." (Marx, *Capital*, I, p. 44)

This is human labor in the abstract. Concrete and abstract labor are the two aspects of labor; they both go on whenever anyone labors. Concrete labor occurs because a specific product is being made; abstract labor occurs because part of society's fund of labor, its total productive expenditure of brains, nerves, and muscles, is being used up, never to be available for any other work. Abstract labor is measured by time. It cannot be seen in the product of labor. Examine the thread or iron as you wish, you cannot tell what portion of society's labor time went into it. In order to think about abstract labor, not only do we disregard the specific operations performed, but we also measure the labor against the total labor in the society, as a part to a whole.

How abstract labor winds up associated with definite quantities of each type of concrete labor depends on the relations of production in a society. To describe in full the employment of abstract labor is to analyze the relations of production. A society may not be aware of how it distributes abstract labor. For example, it is of the essence of capitalism that there is no plan for the employment of labor in the various branches of concrete activity. The power of employment is distributed among capitalists, who each determine the application of the labor controlled by their capital according to private calculations of profit. Nevertheless, the distribution of abstract labor obviously occurs. At the end of the year, so many shoes, so many machine tools, and so many yachts have been produced. The total actual labor has been determined, too, by the rate of unemployment.[6]

Surplus labor and surplus product come into better view in the light of this double character of labor. The labor of the exploited class, the class which provides surplus labor to another class, must be regarded abstractly. To be a member of the exploited class means precisely to engage, abstractly, in some proportion of necessary and surplus labor. It cannot be all surplus labor, for then the exploited would not survive and reproduce. It cannot be all necessary labor, for the exploiters do not allow production without exploitation. The exploited class as a whole engages in necessary labor and surplus labor. The ratio of their amounts is a ratio of quantities of abstract labor.

Abstract and concrete labor should not be confused. If we try to view surplus labor concretely, we might think the laborer who builds yachts performs only surplus labor while bakers of bread, for example, perform mostly necessary labor. This is incorrect. On the one hand, we have only to remember that the yacht-builder needs bread as surely as the yacht needs sails. On the other hand, the exploiting class controls all of society by its extraction of surplus labor. It extracts surplus labor from the bakers of bread, a much greater mass of it than from the yacht-builders. Furthermore, if we regard labor concretely, we think of the surplus product in such forms as yachts. But the personal consumption of the exploiting class is only a fraction of the surplus product. The expansion of production, and conse-quently the direction this takes, must be accomplished out of surplus labor. In a capitalist society, the manufacture of addi-tional means of production represents thicker bonds on the working class and greater social power for the capitalist class. The replacement of means of production used up in the old ambit of production, however, involves necessary labor; if workers need bread, they need ovens, too, and the productive consump-tion of ovens requires their replacement. Therefore, in the machine building industry among others it is impossible to tell from the concrete form of the labor whether the product is surplus product or necessary product. The magnitude of exploita-tion can only be seen in terms of abstract surplus labor. After that, we can determine how the exploiting class has embodied surplus labor in surplus product. Personal consumption is never the end of a society or class. The appropriation of surplus labor by one class is its seizure of the entire society, of its shape and direction.

3. Other Relations of Production

Class relations are not only relations of production but also relations of non-production. Members of the class that controls surplus labor and disposes of surplus product do not need to work in order to meet their needs. A portion of the exploiting class is idle. Other members protect its interests by choosing and dictating policy in every sphere of social life—economic, political, educational, and religious. This activity is not labor or production; only the outlook that begins from individual consumption regards all activity as labor.

As the rule of an exploiting class and its mode of production mature and then decay, the connection of the exploiting class with production weakens further. Although, for example, capitalists' wives have always been isolated from production, as shown in English novels, the men capitalists in the early days of capitalism were often close to production, playing a role in the workshop or on the factory floor. But the days of the early ironmaster are long past. Today, the Fords, du Ponts, and Rockefellers know very little about the internal workings of automobiles, guns, or oil refineries. They leave such details to

15

hired hands. The growing distance of the capitalists from production is a sign of the decay of capitalism.

The increasing coloration of class relations as relations of non-production does away with neither production nor production relations. Class is a relation of production based on relations to the means of production, but it is not the only kind of production relation. Under the class relation, groups stand in different relation to surplus labor; class might be called the surplus labor relation, except that this is correct only where classes exist, that is, where the community *is* differentiated in regard to the surplus labor. But there are relations of production other than those tied to the question of surplus labor. It is necessary to look at some of them.

a. Collective or Individual

Production is collective or individual, according to the scope of coordination and cooperation. A society composed entirely of petty producers would represent the extreme in individual production relations. Here, each small family produces on its own. In the act of production, none coordinates its effort with that of another family, nor do they cooperate in any way. The petty producers discover what they have wrought only after production is completed, as they take their surplus products to markets.

No such society has ever existed, but Europeans witnessed a relatively high degree of individual production relations in the petty mode of production, which existed between feudalism and capitalism. Here individual production relations were found in harmony with the petty producer's relation to the means of production.[7]

This was a bottom point of descent from primitive communism, whose production was collective. The clan or gens cooperated in production, allocating its labor among hunting, agriculture, and handicrafts, performing each of these as acts of the community. Still, the scope of this collectivity was narrow. It is in capitalism and especially socialism that collective production relations come into their own. The degree of cooperation among workers in a long, complex process of labor leading up to an automobile or a radio is high. Factories operated by hundreds and thousands of workers as a single mechanism appear and become more numerous. The number and variety of semi-finished products used as raw materials in another workshop increase; the labor involved in their production is incomplete except as part of a larger whole. Between the various specialized industries grow many ties. Collective production relations knit the whole economy together as well as grouping large bodies of people in each workplace.

Such production relations necessarily come into contradiction with the essentially individualistic class relations which define the capitalists as private owners of the means of production. The capitalist, reduced solely to a representative of class relations of non-production, becomes an obstruction. The growing opposition between coordinated production and the anarchy and competition of private appropriation of the products become evident in the stagnation and crisis of the capitalist economy.

b. Mental and Manual Labor

Another production relation arises from the division of mental and manual labor. Mental and manual labor are distinguishable because men in the course of production go through a process of acquiring knowledge with three stages or moments to it. First, the world is perceived during activity through the senses. Second, the perceptions are worked up in the brain into a concept reflecting the underlying motion of external matter. Third, action based on this conceptual picture is taken in the world, confirming and modifying the theory. So far, this concerns only the relation between man and nature, not production relations among people. But various relations can arise between people based on the division of labor into mental and manual stages. The separation of types of labor can be extreme, or the two can be closely united in each person in a working collective. The latter situation prevailed in tribal society and reappears under socialism and communism, when the theoretical world is much larger. Class societies separate mental and manual labor. When mental labor is allocated to some and others are confined to manual labor, the latter receive directions for their labor based on plans worked out by others who do not execute them. If all producers were active in the conception of the work, the control of the exploiting class over surplus labor would be much less secure than it is with the separation and specialization of some in mental labor. Still, the production relation between mental and manual labor is not the same thing as the class relation; the lines of division of mental and manual labor do not run along class lines. For the most part, the exploiting class does not perform mental labor, instead creating a group of mental laborers and taking measures to insure their social distance from manual laborers.[8]

With the growth of technique and science, the conceptual stage of knowledge grows in size and in depth of insight into the world. A larger proportion of the work of production consists of manipulating symbols rather than the things themselves. Within the world of mental labor, work rich in conceptual activity separates out from a mass of routine manipulation of symbols, which is today called data processing. Perception undergoes a similar division, creating a sphere of routine acquisition of information and its conversion into symbols, called data gathering. Machines to process symbols are introduced. Mental laborers in data gathering and data processing, represented by keypunchers, file clerks, typists, etc., must be distinguished from those mental laborers who conceptualize, analyze, and plan. In their jobs, the former treat the symbol as a thing, not as a bearer of a concept. What is the difference between many jobs in a computer installation and those in a printing shop? The latter have always been called manual labor; the former have only recently been distilled out of work regarded as mental labor. The guiding principle of the production relation of mental and manual labor is the distinction of the stage of conceptualization versus the stage of execution. The specific boundary is not static, but has to be analyzed as it develops. Except when it would be confusing, we will refer to this production relation as the relation of mental and manual labor.

Regardless of the volume of the scientific heritage that men have accumulated, one general result of extreme separation of mental and manual labor is a decline in the advance of production. The cycle of perception, conception, and execution is never completed but is continually repeated on higher levels. New perceptions arise when we carry out plans. The world reveals new departments of reality to us and makes us study them in practical execution, not in idle, undirected observations on the watch for something novel. One must act on the world to see it. When a problem or vaguely understood opportunity arises in production, only then are fruitful experiments suggested. First men try to smelt large quantities of steel; then we get the science of metallurgy. First men search for oil; then we learn more geology. The separation of mental from manual labor makes theory sterile, because those who embody it suffer from lack of contact with the material world. Manual labor is stultified, too. Magic, craft custom, or directions from above replace alertness and curiosity in the mind of the laborer, at least while he is at work. Yet manual workers are always on the front line with nature and can go only so far astray before brute matter dashes inattention or fantasy into pain. While the advance of production slows, and even slips into retrogression, the source of its renewal always lies among the manual laborers.

c. Authority Relations in Production

Another production relation consists of the relations of authority in production. Management, supervision, and technical direction are necessary functions in any collective work. The labor of a number of persons does not automatically combine and direct itself toward its goal. Management is the planning and coordination of the various sequences and sidelines of production. The inventory of parts must be sufficient, the production rates of feeder assembly lines coordinated, and the allocation of persons to each workshop made in correct proportions. Supervision encompasses the detailed overseeing of production as it occurs, to monitor the operation and to spot and report breakdowns, anomalies, and other problems. Management and supervision also give conscious attention to the various relations of production and the role and position of persons in them—work assignments, training, and so forth. Technical direction from engineers, mechanics, and other technicians is needed on the floor or from the laboratory. They specify the proper conditions (vats, flows, linkages, machines) by which men employ natural laws to transform matter.

Where the production relations are individualistic, these functions do not exist or are merged in the total activity of one person. Therefore, the relations of authority in production are alien and strange to the petty producer. As the scope of production becomes more collective, these functions separate out and are performed by distinct individuals separate from the bulk of actual executors of the immediate process of production.

The specific form of the production relations of authority varies with different modes of production. Under exploiting class rule, these relations take some form of bureaucratic hierarchy. Under socialism, they are revolutionized into democratic centralism, in which operational command is combined with and subordinated to mass supervision at all levels. The necessity of management, supervision, and technical direction does not dictate their form, only saying that somehow the collective must be concerned with them. While the relations of authority in production are distinct from class relations, the latter stamp an indelible mark on the former.

In a capitalist society, the functions of authority are exercised by special workers. The capitalist

"hands over the work of direct and constant supervision of the individual workmen, and groups of workmen, to a special kind of wage-laborer. An industrial army of workmen, under the command of a capitalist, requires, like a real army, officers (managers), and sergeants (foremen, overlookers), who, while the work is being done, command in the name of the capitalist. The work of supervision becomes their established and exclusive function." (Marx, *Capital*, I, p. 332)[9]

Classes are defined by their relation to surplus labor, not by their functions in production. It is a mistake to confuse class relations and other production relations. Yet the content of supervisory labor is twofold. It is labor of coordination required by the fact that individual efforts are pooled, but it is also the task of seeing that surplus labor is performed. Coordinating labor is a particular kind of concrete labor. The capitalist, however, is interested not in the concrete product but in the extraction of surplus labor in the performance of abstract labor, and he makes the supervisory task one of seeing that other labor is exploited.[10]

People who supervise or give technical direction are affected by both class relations and production relations of authority. At the lower and middle levels of the hierarchy of authority, they are workers: they must sell their labor power, in this case, their ability to manage, and they receive a salary in exchange. Still, as carriers of class-imbued authority, part of their function is to increase the surplus labor going to the capitalist class. Either the class relation or other production relations may dominate. It is displayed in supervisors and foremen, some of whom are "red hots" out to extract the maximum of surplus labor from other workers (and in the process from themselves), while some supervisors absorb and cushion the pressure from above. These latter try to concentrate on seeing that the work is performed with necessary quality, both by their own activity of coordination and by the particular direct operations of their subordinates. The conflict of production relations and class relations is also seen in the face that supervisors and foremen present to the capitalists when the issue is the sale of their labor power. From time to time, supervisory workers move toward forming their own unions, as after World War II, or apply to join the existing union.

At the highest levels of management, capitalists hide under this function to masquerade fraudulently as workers. For example,

> "On the basis of capitalist production a new swindle develops in stock enterprises with respect to wages of management, in that boards of numerous managers or directors are placed above the actual director, for whom supervision and management serve only as a pretext to plunder the stockholders and amass wealth." (Marx, *Capital*, III, p. 389)

Besides the directors, the top executives are part of the capitalist class, both by their present position and usually by their social origin. All pretense of any correlation between the "salary" and the price of labor power has disappeared. In fact, the technical intelligence of these men is often quite low. Their forté is the business lunch and the golf session. They guard the interests of the system of surplus labor in the most sensitive positions. Their contribution to production and its relations is nonexistent. They are capitalists because they do not sell their labor power but rather receive a portion of the surplus labor of the workers. They receive it not only in "salaries" of $100,000 or $500,000 per year, but also in bonuses varying with the prosperity of the company, the industry, and the entire capitalist economy. After years in their positions, the top executives have accumulated stocks and other investments which provide significant additional income, again a portion of the surplus labor disposed of and controlled by the capitalist class.

These executives are not petty producers; while their income is dwarfed by that of the monopoly capitalist families whom they serve, the Rockefellers, Morgans, Mellons, du Ponts, and Pews, both groups receive surplus product produced by others, in one or another of the forms of surplus-value. They are capitalists; amount of income does not determine whether one is a petty producer or a capitalist.

The positions of authority in the relations of production are confusing on the surface as to what they suggest about classes. This occurs because class relations color and warp everything in a class society, including other relations of production. It occurs because the ladder of authority in production is one link between opposite classes, the exploited working class and the exploiting capitalist class. Transitions between opposites call for a dialectical treatment. In any case, the importance of the question is qualitative; it is conceptual and political. In simple numbers, as will be seen, the weight of apparently problematical positions of authority is small.

The confusion that follows from ignorance of the basis of class relations combined with superficial awareness of production relations of authority can be seen in N. Bukharin's *Historical Materialism*. Bukharin defines classes as follows:

"It is their different function in the production process that constitutes the basis for the division of men into different social classes." (p. 144)

What is this function? It is, says Bukharin, the role one takes in the production process conceived not from the viewpoint of abstract and surplus labor but from the technical and physical viewpoint:

"A class, as we have seen, is a category of persons united by a common rôle in the production process, a totality in which each member has about the same relative position with regard to the other functions in the production process." (p. 278-79)

Bukharin never mentions surplus labor and surplus product in his definitions of class. As a result, yet another of his vague definitions speaks not about the relation to the means of production but about the "instruments of labor." (p. 276) Bukharin is thinking of the machinery with which the workers work. This is too narrow. The capitalists own not only these instruments but all the means of production, including the buildings and the raw materials. Bukharin's approach is technological, not economic. He thinks of concrete labor but never of abstract labor.

When Bukharin considers relations between persons, the surplus labor relation is still absent. Not knowing about the class relation, he defines classes by the relations of authority in production. To him, class differences are "the differences between the work of those who command and those who obey, the differences expressed in the property relations." (p. 282)[11] Some of the propertyless exercise authority in production, but this does not make them possessors of property and members of a different class than other workers, as Bukharin would have it. He equates the "antagonism between administrators and the administrated, [and that] between the class monopolizing the instruments of production and the class possessing no means of production" (p. 285).

Bukharin does not understand exploitation of surplus labor nor the two aspects of authority. The errors caused by the confusion of class relations and production relations of authority are several. First, the idle portion of the capitalist class disappears, since they never enter the scene to give commands. Rentiers, the political specialists of the capitalists, and all other contingents of capitalists outside the factory are unknown in Bukharin's scheme. Second, Bukharin arbitrarily limits workers to those in manual labor:

> "In the system of class society, the process of production is at the same time a process of the economic exploitation of those who work physically." (p. 285)

It is an extreme position which says that no mental workers, for example, no clerks, are exploited, yet it is the logical outcome of ignoring class relations and substituting other production relations in their place. Those mental workers recognized in Bukharin's scheme can only be a "middle class." Of these supposed "intermediate classes" Bukharin says, "They occupy a middle position between the commanding and exploited[12] classes.

Such are, for instance, the technical mental workers in capitalist society." (p. 283)

The production relations of authority are a bureaucratic hierarchy under capitalism. There are ranks, one above another. It is a frequent error of capitalist theories to conceive of classes, too, as upper, middle, and lower. Class relations, however, are not hierarchies; they are relations of antagonism and polarization of opposites. Yet Bukharin follows the capitalist conception in combining production relations of authority and class relations into a single hierarchical scale: workers, salaried technical staff, higher officials, and owners. (p. 143) It has been seen above how the production relations of authority appear to link opposite classes. Bukharin accepts this picture uncritically; he covers up antagonism in relation to surplus labor.

4. Size of Classes in the U.S.

How large are the classes in the United States today? It would be convenient if we had the results of a survey which inquired of everyone and verified, "Is your income primarily obtained from the sale of your labor power (worker), from working on means of production you own and selling the product (petty producer), or from the employment of workers on means of production they do not own (capitalist)?" Such a survey would require various explanations and solutions for technical problems. For example, someone who needs to sell his or her labor power but has not been able to sell it, that is, an unemployed person, is part of the working class. Or, someone who inherited $50 million and invested it all in tax-free municipal bonds, as Mrs. Dodge of the Dodge motor car family did,[13] would be a capitalist, even though her connection to the ownership of means of production is hidden in a series of financial devices and her receipt of surplus-value takes the form of interest rather than profit.[14] Nonetheless, the survey is conceivable in principle and would give us numbers and percentages for the three classes of developed capitalist society.

The obstacle that deprives us of this survey is nontechnical.

Chemists and physicists who study the elements have no allegiance to iron over sulphur or vice versa. Botanists do not belong to one of the species they investigate. Students of class, however, are members or servants of a class and owe their allegiance to one class over another. Some classes are able to face the truth, in fact, are eager to know the state of classes and class conflict in the society, while other classes want to obscure the whole topic.

The United States government, which is a tool of the capitalist class, presents its statistics so as to hide rather than lay bare the classes of United States society. The task, therefore, is to deduce from the categories of these statistics a good approximation to the true size of classes in the United States.

According to the U.S. Census, we have the following breakdown:

CLASS OF EMPLOYED WORKERS
(AGE 16 AND OVER, 1970)[15]

"Class"	Number of persons
Private wage and salary workers	57,917,538
Government workers	12,320,637
Self-employed workers	5,911,204
Unpaid family workers	404,220
Total	76,553,599

Step 1. Government workers are wage and salary workers, so the first two categories can be combined in one group amounting to 70,238,175 wage and salary earners.

Step 2. Unpaid family workers are "Persons who worked without pay on a farm or in a business operated by a person to whom they are related by blood or marriage. These are usually the children or the wife of the owner of a business or farm. About one half of the unpaid family workers are farm laborers."[16]

In small businesses the line between production work and the maintenance of the family is blurred, and counting such workers is erroneous, unless one is also counting the domestic supportive work in a working-class family. Yet some of the work is undoubtedly unpaid wage labor. The entire category is small in number; one half may be disregarded and the other half allocated to wage and salary workers.

Step 3. Among the "wage and salary earners" the Census Bureau includes those who work for a corporation they own themselves or as part of a group of controlling owners. For accounting purposes, they pay themselves a salary; scientifically regarded, they are petty producers or capitalists, since it is impossible to pay oneself a salary and be a worker and one's own capitalist. To be a capitalist, one must receive surplus labor from others, not oneself. At issue are 1,139,885 persons.[17] These must in the first instance be subtracted from the wage and salary earners and added to the self-employed. This gives:

CLASS OF EMPLOYED WORKERS
(AGE 16 AND OVER, 1970)

"Class"	Number of persons
Wage and salary receivers	69,300,400
Self-employed	7,051,089
Total	76,351,489

Step 4. Workers are workers because of their relation to the means of production, which requires them to work with the means of others in return for a wage or salary and to yield up surplus labor. Class position is independent of the particular kind of work one does, of the industry one works in, and of the public

or private, or profit or non-profit, designation of the employer. Most attempts to eliminate persons from the category of the working class and thereby reduce its size are erroneous, as will be discussed later. For example, performing the function of supervision and administration does not make one a capitalist or a petty producer. Supervision is a necessary part of the process of production, although its nature differs in different modes of production (for example, capitalism and socialism).

One group of persons, however, is not hired for their ability to do mental or manual labor, including the supervision of such labor. Rather, a small group of top executives, nominally paid a salary, actually are assigned to guard the interests of the capitalist class and of capitalism in general.[18] Every mode of production ruled by a minority, exploiting class develops such a group: in the slave system, the slave owners had their overseers; the feudal lords had bailiffs on their manors; and capitalists have their top executives. In the last case, these men (and a few women) must be classed with the capitalist class, obtaining their income through the preservation and expansion of the capitalist ownership and use of the means of production. They do not supervise relations among workers in production, like lower managers; they guard the class relation itself. Their "work" and forms of income have already been discussed (p. 22).

The U.S. Census does not identify this group. The closest approximation is made through study of the earnings of wage and salary receivers. We will assume that with a salary of $25,000 per year or more at 1969 dollar salary levels, the person is such a lieutenant and member of the capitalist class. This level exceeds by 50 percent the earnings of the highest-skilled professionals, illustrated in the table below. If a salary is not a payment for a highly skilled type of labor power, it contains surplus-value; the recipient is not yielding surplus labor but receiving it. The use of the $25,000 cutoff point to discover capitalists on salary has nothing in common with the elaborate division of workers into several income strata to reflect standards of consumption.

MEDIAN EARNINGS FOR WHITE MALES IN PRIME OF WORK
(AGE 35 TO 54) FOR SELECTED OCCUPATIONS[19]

Occupation	Earnings
Aeronautical and astronautical engineers	$17,213
Physicists and astronomers	18,515
College and university teachers	15,107
Airline pilots	22,253

There are 884,023 salaried persons earning $25,000 or more, of whom approximately 93,794 have already been removed from the category of wage and salary earners as employees of their own corporations.[20]

Step 5. It is necessary to divide the category of "self-employed" into petty producers and capitalists. This distinction is the one most obscured by the Census. Data on "class of worker" are submerged within the Census, which emphasizes occupation and income categories. The name "self-employed" taken as a class suggests the petty producer; the capitalists are hidden in the statistics more securely than any other class. "Class of worker" requires the several adjustments made in the first four steps, and still the capitalist class has not emerged into the light of day. The U.S. Census is unwilling to admit that there is an exploiting class in a capitalist society.

To begin, let us turn to the census of farms. Here, among tables of expenditures on equipment and pesticides, there is some data on expenditures for hired labor. Let us assume that a capitalist farmer spends at least $5,000 on hired labor; this figure is probably low. If the rate of exploitation is 100 percent, then $5,000 of his income derives from exploitation, the remainder from the labor of himself and his family. There are 62,050 such capitalist farmers.[21]

For the rest of the economy, we will arbitrarily assume that self-employed workers with earnings over $25,000 are capitalists, deriving most of their income from the exploitation of hired workers. Excluding the farmers, there were 429,622 such capitalists.[22] This yields:

CLASS OF EMPLOYED WORKERS

Class	Number of persons
Wage and salary earners	68,510,171
Petty producers	6,465,623
Capitalists	1,375,695
Total	76,351,489

Step 6. In the above enumeration of capitalists, the distinction between the experienced civilian labor force and those actually employed has been ignored. But among workers there is a great mass of unemployed—at the time of the Census, 3,541,048 persons age 16 and over.[23] These must be added to the working class.

On the other hand, an unknown number of capitalists are not counted in the labor force because they are not "employed," yet they draw a capitalist income from bonds and so forth, like Mrs. Dodge mentioned previously. These persons are classically named the rentier capitalists or coupon-clippers. Let us assume there were 200,000 such persons. These are not dependents of economically active capitalists, but rather persons who hold no salaried post, who are not listed as self-employed in running their business, but who collect property income from businesses, corporations and bond issuers like governments, bridge and port authorities, etc.

Adding these two categories to the table, we finally obtain a picture of the size of classes in the United States.

CLASSES IN THE UNITED STATES

Class	Number of persons	Percent
Working class	72,051,219	90
Petty producers	6,465,623	8
Capitalists	1,575,695	2
Total	80,092,537	100

Spouses and children who depend on someone for their income belong to the same class as the earner.

5. The Ratio of Class Revenues in the U.S.

Because the population is approximately 90 percent working class, eight percent petty producers, and two percent capitalists, it does not follow that the ratio of revenues obtained from the economy is proportional to these percentages. On the contrary, class contradiction demands a separate calculation of opposed economic rewards. Such a computation set against the figures of population will express the antagonism at the core of every class society.

Of the community's productive wealth, its means of production in factories, shops, offices and farms, we know that the working class owns none. Nearly all are in the hands of the capitalists; a few are still held by petty producers. The relation between these latter two classes will be explored later.

With the means of production, worked by the labor of the workers and petty producers, the national income of the United States is produced each year. It must be remembered that this is no cooperative venture of "factors of production," as capitalist economists call them. The laboring people created the means of production in previous generations, but these means have passed into the hands of a nonlaboring minority. As the price of access to the means of production, to make their daily bread, the workers must submit to wage slavery and work beyond the time required to supply their own needs, performing surplus labor for the capitalist owners of the means of production. We are estimating not the share of cooperating groups but rather the numerical expression of the antagonism between classes.

Let us first estimate in dollars the portions at the disposal of the three classes. As with the calculation of population, we must interpret and adjust the categories and amounts reported by the United States government, a capitalist tool.

The Gross National Product (GNP) for 1970 was $977.1 billion, of which $87.3 billion represented the value of machinery and other productive stock on hand January 1 but used up during the year. (See table, p. 39.) In order to account only for newly created value, this amount will be deducted from GNP. In other words, the maintenance of the capital stock of the capitalists will be conceded. This leaves a Net National Product (NNP) of $889.3 billion to be divided among the classes.[24]

The working class received $542 billion in wages and salaries, before deductions to be considered below. Also, payments from private pensions, as a sort of compensation for sacrificing arms, lungs and other bodily parts, powers, and duration of functioning amounted to $32.2 billion. Next, we must add some governmental "transfer payments." Let us assume that the working class received 95 percent of all payments of old age and survivors' insurance and governmental health insurance. This amounts to $36.6 billion. Making the same assumption for veterans' benefits, we add $9.2 billion. All unemployment insurance payments, $3.9 billion, and other transfer payments, $27 billion, will be allocated to workers.

The U.S. government counts as supplements to wages and salaries the various employer contributions for social insurance and for private pension and welfare funds. This is erroneous, for under capitalism the working class can only spend what it receives, and this has already been counted. Workers are familiar with such propaganda from the employers, too, who inform employees from time to time of the huge cost of employing them, including in the total various sinking funds with which the employees have nothing to do. These trusts, such as pension funds, are accumulated, administered, and invested by employers, banks, national trade union bureaucrats, and the state. Only payments made from them to workers can be counted; the building up of these funds is in the hands of the capitalist class.

From the total of $650.9 billion that we have reached we must deduct taxes, both direct and indirect. As a rough approximation of direct taxes, like the income tax, we will assume that the working class share of them is directly proportional to its share of gross personal income. In other words, the fiction that capitalists with higher incomes pay a higher percentage of income in direct taxes will be discarded in favor of the assumption of uniform proportional payment of taxes at all income levels. This deducts $89.8 billion from the working class.[25]

Concerning indirect taxes, we will arbitrarily say that the working class pays 75 percent of them in its purchases, the remainder being paid by other classes in individual purchases or "absorbed" by business. This deducts $70.0 billion from the working class.

Counted as neither direct nor indirect taxes but still deducted from income are contributions for social insurance. We will assume the working class pays 90 percent of them, or $25.2 billion.

The spending power of the working class actually received and at its disposal is thus $465.9 billion. Fifty-two percent of the Net National Product accrues to a class representing 90 percent of the persons in the economy. If we divide the figure by the 72,051,219 workers, this gives an average of $6,500 per working class earner. In reality, there are sizeable variations around this average. Large numbers of workers, because of low wages or unemployment, exist in the meanest circumstances: tenements in the cities without heat or functioning plumbing and clapboard shacks in rural areas through which the weather passes unhindered, food of the starchiest, plainest kind, clothes that mark one's diminished status to all who see them, days and weeks and lives lost to illness that could easily have been prevented or treated, and hours of time to pass without access to the instruction or recreation that help to distinguish human life from animal existence.

To make a rough appraisal of the income of petty producers, let us simply count the $66.9 billion of proprietors' income. This figure, which divides out to $10,400 for each petty producer, is undoubtedly high. Therefore, it is a conservative estimate that the remainder belonging to the capitalists is $356.5 billion.

This divides out to $226,000 per capitalist in the economy, or 35 times the figure per worker. This approximate ratio expresses the antagonism between the working class and the capitalist class.

Not all of this $226,000 is personally assigned to the individual capitalist. Because the capitalist class owns the means of production and controls the state machine, the wealth of the capitalist class can and does take the most varied forms. The capitalists allocate what they wish to themselves for individual consumption. The luxurious estates of the du Ponts in Delaware, of the Rockefellers in New York, and so forth still exist. Consumption, furthermore, may be charged to a corporation instead of to the individual member of the capitalist class who enjoys it.

At Universal American Corporation, a subsidiary of Gulf and Western, the two top offices enjoy "custom-built semi-circular desks, ankle-deep $31-a-yard carpeting, leather lounge chairs and push-button control of the draperies, lights and door locks —for a start.

"The office of the chairman . . . is paneled in rare makassar ebony from Africa." (*Wall Street Journal*, June 1, 1971, p. 1)

For the president of Fabergé, $200,000 was spent decorating his office in the middle of Manhattan. "A hydraulic lift raises and lowers a marble table to cocktail or writing desk height." (*Ibid.*)

This expense is charged to the corporation, which in turn charges about half of it to the government as a business expense. The old stories of fantastic consumption need only be reproduced with a note about the change of accounting. Technical details should not clutter the memory, so it is understandable that "The wife of the chairman of a manufacturing company once dispatched the company plane from Sea Island, Ga. [an exclusive resort island for the capitalists] to fetch a tennis racket she had left at home in Ohio." *(Wall Street Journal,* July 15, 1971, p. 23)

Even with such spectacular and decadent consumption practices, the small capitalist class cannot and does not consume the bulk of its annual income individually. Part of the income is devoted to the expansion of the means of production, to increasing the plant and equipment in which the working class is exploited. Part is devoted to a military machine used to contend for empire around the world and to guard U.S. society from its working class. Part is used to inundate the working class and petty producers with television, films, newspapers, books, and speeches propagating explanations, salves, and orders to guide the working people through the intricacies of life. It is all part of the capitalist world. In a capitalist society, society belongs to the capitalists. While certain expenditures are necessary according to economic law, the division of the national income reflects the effort that the working class is allowed to put into maintaining and feeding itself in ratio to the surplus labor spent on the care, protection, pampering, and enlargement of the capitalist class.

In addition to cash "transfer payments" made to workers, like pensions, there is the question of social services, or various forms of collective consumption, mainly education and health services. In a capitalist society, collective consumption is in the hands of the capitalist class, usually through the state. What will be taught is decided by business and its servants; the emphasis in health on cures of the most elaborate and rare maladies instead of preventive public health is decided by the direction of medical research and expenditure.

The capitalist begrudges these expenses, yet he must make them, since they are largely necessities of continued production. Workers must, usually, be able to read and count, and the occasional repair of human tissue is a necessity as much as upkeep of the machinery. Such expenses are a deduction from the sum available for the expansion of the capitalist system or its enjoyment by the capitalists. Furthermore, these expenditures open up dreadful possibilities, such as that of literate workers realizing more easily that they can master society without having capitalists. Collective consumption in the form of social services is the first, small harbinger of a rational system of collective production, which, of course, the capitalist abhors. He reveals his horror by ordering his welfare economists to allocate these costs as revenue to the working class. Nevertheless, the control and guidance of these social services is in the hands of the capitalist class. Their amount and specific form is an arena of class struggle.

In any case, the amounts are small. As a rough approximation, we may take the sum of expenditures for education ($55.8 billion), health ($3.9 billion) and local parks and recreation ($1.9 billion).[26] If 50 percent of this figure, or $30.8 billion, were allocated to the working class, the relation of the classes would not be materially altered. It would revise the specific weight in society of the capitalist class to 30 times that of the working class.

What it comes down to is that the capitalists are balked in their desire to have capitalism without the working class, an exploiting system without the presence of the exploited. Classes do not exist in two (or three) separate worlds; there is mutual presence and interpenetration of classes as well as contradiction between them, for as long as classes exist. The calculations above reflect this fact, and insofar as quantities can express contradictions, it remains true to say that in 1970, the capitalist class, two percent of the population, extracted surplus labor giving it over 30 times the specific weight in society as the working class.

THE RATIO OF CLASS REVENUES, 1970

Gross National Product	$977.1 billion
Less: capital consumption	87.3
Equals: Net National Product	889.3
Wages and salaries	542.0
Private pensions and compensation for injuries	32.2
Old age and survivors' insurance × 95%	36.6
Veterans' benefits × 95%	9.2
Unemployment insurance	3.9
Other transfer payments	27.0
	650.9
Less: Workers' direct taxes	89.8
Less: Workers' indirect taxes	70.0
Less: Workers' social insurance contributions	25.2
Equals: Workers' spending power	465.9

This is 52 percent of NNP.

$465.9 billion ÷ 72,051,219 workers equals $6,500 per working class earner.

If we assume $66.9 billion for petty producers, then capitalists receive $356.5 billion, or $226,000 per capitalist recipient.

$226,000 ÷ $6,500 equals 35 times.

(Figures from U.S. Census Bureau, *Statistical Abstract: 1974*)

6. The Polarization of Classes

The same method used to calculate the size of classes from government data in 1970 may be applied to earlier censuses. There are differences in detail, however, since capitalist statistics deliberately hide some changes by breaking the continuity of censuses. An analysis given one time is not available for another; money divisions between income groups are not revised properly. Therefore, figures for different years must be compared only approximately. By applying the same steps used in the transformation of census data for 1970, we arrive at the following results:

CLASSES IN THE UNITED STATES, 1940 to 1970

Year	Working class	Petty producers	Capitalists
1970	90%	8%	2%
1960	87	11	2
1950	83	15	2
1940	81	18	1

(Computations are given in the notes[27].)

The figures reveal the steady shrinking of the class of petty producers that underlies the nearly complete polarization of 1970. Where in 1940 there was one petty producer for every four or five workers, in 1970 there is only one for every 11 workers. This means that the entry of a petty producer into the ranks of the working class has occurred more frequently than the opposite movement. Today, the example of the petty producer is far less common to the worker. Overall, the influence of the petty producer over the worker has diminished at least in proportion to this decline of his presence. (As will be seen later, there are other sources of ideas typical of the petty producer, but these bases of ideology do not indicate the existence of a petty producer class.)

The petty producers have seen their number in society contract. They have only 44 percent of the relative weight they had in 1940. This shrinkage appears as the increase of bankruptcy and forced sale of the business, the diminishing frequency of the opening of new businesses, the inability to sell the company on retirement, and the failure of children to take over the operation. In reality, the disappearance of the petty producers is a matter of class.

> "The lower strata of the middle class—the small tradespeople, shopkeepers, and retired tradesmen generally, the handicraftsmen and peasants—all these sink gradually into the proletariat . . ."
> "The bourgeoisie . . . has converted the physician, the lawyer, the priest, the poet, the man of science, into its paid wage-laborers." (Marx and Engels, *Manifesto*, pp. 40, 34)

On the other hand, the figures regarding the capitalist class are too rough to permit any deductions. We cannot say from them whether the number of capitalists has changed by one or one-half percentage point. It matters little. The class is numerically small, and other data must be used to measure the changes of its economic situation.

For the history of U.S. capitalism prior to 1940, we have

figures given by the director of the Census. He estimated the percentage of wage earners among all those engaged in gainful occupations to be 66 percent in 1890 and 65 percent in 1900. (Wright, p. 227) This percent would be raised by counting salary-earning members of the working class and the unemployed, but it would be lowered, though to a lesser degree, by the other adjustments made in this book on later census data. We may conclude that the United States has been a capitalist country with a majority of the population in the working class at least since the end of the Civil War. The principal change in the size of classes has been the steady erosion of petty producers to an insignificant class. The polarization of classes means the disappearance of the class which stood in between, which both labored and owned means of production. The class of petty producers, who neither exploit nor give surplus labor, has practically shrunk to nothing, leaving the working class and the capitalist class face to face.

7. Historical Developments within the Propertied Classes

a. Class Boundaries

The three classes of workers, petty producers, and capitalists are not separate unto themselves. In order to compile statistics it is necessary to set up mutually exclusive, sharply delineated categories. The method is acceptable, provided that the inexact dividing lines and the transitions between the real groups are kept in mind.

The group with the least clear boundaries is the one caught in the middle of the polarization of classes, the petty producer class. The owners and operators of their own means of production are difficult, at their "upper" end, to distinguish from small capitalists, persons who derive most of their income from the exploitation of labor but who also work in the business themselves. We saw this problem in step five of chapter four, when it was necessary to decide when a self-employed farmer is a capitalist and when he is a petty producer. With this farmer, as with the small shopkeeper or craftsman employing an assistant or two, or the operator of a garage factory, the earnings derived from the labor of the petty producer himself and the income derived from the few hired workers admit of a continuous range of proportions. How much labor must the petty producer hire in order to cross into the capitalist class? Does this happen when 50 percent of his income is obtained by exploitation? Or 80 percent? When he leaves the shop floor or the fields for good to move into a new office? This example illustrates a recurring phenomenon in capitalist societies, the working petty producer striving to become a capitalist exploiter. The problem of statistical classification reflects motion in social life.

The transition from petty producers to capitalists is embodied in the term petty bourgeois, the French words for small businessman. The class of small businessmen is called the petty bourgeoisie. These are the petty producers and the smallest capitalists. When the important thing is what petty producers and capitalists have in common, the term petty bourgeois is appropriate. When differences between petty producers on the one side and capitalists on the other side are important, the term petty producer should be used, not petty bourgeois.

b. Monopoly Capital

Within the three classes of workers, capitalists, and petty producers, the members are not all economically the same. It is necessary to look at the differences in economic power between individuals within each class; such differences affect the relations between the classes.

While capitalist apologists focus most attention on real or alleged differences among workers, the working class is least differentiated in economic power. Workers earn different amounts of income, which means that some obtain the necessities of life, some do not and face starvation, and a few enjoy some luxuries of consumption. Such differences in consumption are not differences in economic power. Individual workers in a capitalist society have no economic power. Collectively, their class struggle affects the historical standard of subsistence consumption which is their lot under capitalism.

The place to look for differences within a class is the capitalist class. The economic power of a capitalist is measured by his capital, his command over value of means of production. This quantity, measured in dollars, expresses his place among all capitalists. The variations here are of great importance not only for the strife between capitalists but also for the relations between the classes.

Extreme differences in economic power have developed between capitalists in the United States today. Let us assume that at least $100,000 in active assets was needed in 1970 to be classified as a capitalist rather than a petty producer.[28] Then we find a very unequal distribution of assets among firms. A mere six-hundredth of them, those with active assets exceeding $250 million each, control 59 percent of the assets. On the other end, 85 percent of all firms possess no more than $1 million of assets, so that the specific weight of a firm in the $250 million-and-over range is 4000 times that of each of these lowest-ranking firms. The 200 largest manufacturing corporations alone control 60 percent of the manufacturing assets, up from 48 percent in 1950.[29]

This concentration of capital in large units, surrounded by a fringe of smaller accumulations, has led to the stage of monopoly capital. In nearly every industry, a few companies produce 80 or 90 percent of the output. It is within their power to decide on the amount of production to be released to the community and the corresponding price that may be demanded. This power is routinely and consciously exercised. For example, General Electric entered the refrigerator business after General Motors' Frigidaire division and Kelvinator had established themselves in it. The GE executive in charge, T. K. Quinn, relates how, with a budget to win a market share for GE, he "was given to understand that under no circumstances were we to undersell our large competitors." (Quinn, p. 93-4) When a price war developed in Pittsburgh, the chief of the entire General Electric Corporation stepped in. Gerard Swope brought Quinn to a meeting with counterparts from General Motors. Since Quinn was able to prove with dated newspaper advertisements that Frigidaire had started the price war, its manager was reprimanded at the meeting. Quinn relates how prices were routinely fixed at trade associations by writing them on a blackboard. This is called "price leadership"—in the crusade against the buyer. (Quinn, pp. 97-8, 130) When a handful of firms are so large that they produce a commanding percentage of all automobiles, steel, telephone service, paper, or whatever, then quantity passes into quality: a big business enjoys monopoly control. The main effect is to reduce production below easily attainable levels and to keep up the price of the product. Two major cereal companies can agree that there is greater profit in selling one billion boxes of cereal at 80 cents each for a gross sale of $800 million than in producing one-and-a-half billion boxes but having to set a price of 45 cents per box to sell them all, for a gross sale of only $675 million. In this example, a conservative one, the monopoly price and the monopoly degree of non-production, half a billion boxes, brings a greater total revenue than competitive capitalist levels based on ordinary profit calculations. Keeping down production also reduces the total cost of production, and so less invested capital is required to obtain a greater total and net revenue. The sabotage of production means unemployment. The steadily increasing exercise of monopoly power is the cause of continuous inflation. For example, during the crisis period from the peak of December 1973 to the widely hailed time of recovery in July 1976, the production of steel fell by 12 percent, some 19 million tons per year. At the same time, the steel monopolies raised the composite price of finished steel by over one-half, not only maintaining their gross income but increasing it by 35 percent.[30]

The concentration of capital is approximately reflected in the concentration of employment. Of the 70,238,175 employed wage and salary earners in 1970, the ten largest corporations employed 4.5 percent, the 500 largest industrial corporations employed 21 percent, and the 1250 largest corporations in industry, retailing, utilities, transportation, and banking employed 31 percent.[31] While the working class is still divided up among small firms, a large and decisive section works for and and is arrayed against a handful of employers. This is an inevitable consequence of the concentration of capital in the course of capitalist development. In class terms, as opposed to differences in the amount of personal income or variety in the occupational division of labor, much of the working class has been drawn together into large brigades of an army facing a compact enemy. This fact underscores the polarization into two opposed classes which the measures of the size and income of classes have revealed.

The existence of monopoly capital transforms the economic position of the petty bourgeoisie (the petty producers and smallest capitalists), too. One hundred and thirty years ago, the United States exhibited this petty bourgeoisie; the means of production were dispersed in a myriad of small collections. Today, such a situation is technologically impossible. How can one divide up the coordinated network of large mines, smelters, mills, and warehouses of a steel company among individuals or small groups of individuals?[32] Still, the change has not been a uniform gathering of the means of production into fewer but larger units. Rather, as capital has concentrated, it has left behind a cloud of small units, each little collection of means of production assigned to a petty bourgeois. This necessarily changes the economic power of the petty bourgeois compared to the early, competitive era of capitalism; it reduces their power.

Consider the automobile industry, for example. When it began, it was a collection of small capitalists. From 1903 to 1926, there existed 181 firms in the automobile industry; the maximum at one time was 69. Furthermore, an automobile company only designed and assembled the car. The manufacture of the engine block, the body, the transmission and the other components was carried out by numerous machine shops and carriage builders. Between them and the auto companies approximately equal market relations prevailed. This scene of petty bourgeois prosperity and rough equality did not last long. Even before Henry Ford's engineers laid the technical basis for monopoly-sized firms in the assembly of cars from parts produced on feeder lines, banker-backed monopolists like William Durant were merging willing firms together and driving out the recalcitrant. The individual, of course, is of no great importance. Durant was ousted from his creation, General Motors, in 1920 when a crunch for funds brought in the du Pont family, who control GM to this day.[33]

The petty bourgeoisie in the automobile industry, broadly considered, did not disappear. Only the independent petty bourgeois, producer of engines or bodies contracted for in the open market, disappeared. There are still self-employed men in the industry.

PERSONS IN THE AUTOMOBILE INDUSTRY[34]

Segment of auto industry	Self-employed	Wage and salary workers
Motor vehicles and motor vehicle equipment	3,443	1,029,808
Automotive dealers and gas stations	214,969	1,460,476
Automobile services (mostly repair)	127,387	434,327

The petty bourgeoisie in the automobile industry consists of parts contractors, dealers, and repair shops. None is independent. The parts contractor does not make short-term contracts first with one automobile assembler and then another. He is tied to GM, Ford, or Chrysler, the buyer of nearly all his output, who can and does decide the appropriate wholesale price for the part. The big auto monopolies like to have such parts suppliers. The poor price offered them is transmitted to the employees of the companies in the form of sweatshop conditions, absence of a union, low wages, and lack of overtime bonus. It is a form of contracting out to evade the union. The small producer of parts and his employees absorb the business cycle, too. When the industry is booming, relatively speaking, the small firm stretches its capacity. Machine maintenance is forgotten, and safety levels decline. When business slacks off, orders from the big auto corporations stop. The impact is multiplied on the small producer, for the big three monopolies, often producing most of the supplies of a part themselves, utilize the small producer only for a sharply fluctuating margin of production.

Automobile dealers are not retailers besieged by manufacturers competing for display space. The automobile companies appreciated early the advantages of a network of dealers tied to the exclusive marketing of the cars of one corporation and even of one division. Dealers have long complained of fixed quotas of car deliveries, lack of freedom to set the retail price, forced use of replacement parts from the same company, and arbitrary cancellation of franchises for showing a bit of independence.

Finally, there is the automobile repair shop. The manufacturing is done in three or four giant, coordinated empires of mass production. They deliberately reduce the product below potential quality to a flimsy and short-lived thing. This is not an inevitable characteristic of mass production. It is the result of mass production for profit, which leads to speedup on the assembly line and hence the impossibility of good work, to the sacrifice of engineering design for considerations of salesmanship, and to the substitution of cheap materials for the technically appropriate ones. Once the car is sold, the manufacturer is through with his concern for it. Repair shops then crowd into the industry of doctoring these infirm beings of the world of metal and plastic. Parts must again be obtained from the original manufacturers at exorbitant prices.

Automobiles are an item of individual consumption, and necessarily a large percentage of the customers are workers. They have little sympathy for the dealers and repair men, who utilize every petty trick of trade and swindle to relieve themselves of the economic pressure exerted by the big automobile companies.

The latter stand aside from the exasperation and strife they have caused.

To summarize: if we examine the concentration of economic power, we find an intensification of the opposition between classes. A handful of large firms with monopoly power dominates the capitalist class. The working class is partly gathered into large units facing these employers, but partly scattered among other capitalist and small capitalist employers. The petty bourgeoisie continues to exist in considerable numbers, a small percentage of the population, and under economic ties of dependence on big capital. Both in basic outline and in secondary detail, this is a setting for intense class struggle.

c. Types of Capitalists

When counting the capitalists, we included individuals rewarded with salaries above a certain amount. A somewhat arbitrary dividing line, based solely on income, had to be accepted as a makeshift approximation to distinguish these capitalists from managers and higher mental workers who earn their living by the sale of their labor power. Among capitalists, a capitalist on "salary" is least of all of them an independent owner of the means of production.

This odd appearance is a result of the splitting up and dispersal of functions once united in the capitalist, the decline of some of these functions, and the expansion of others. At the start of capitalism several centuries ago, the capitalist was closely involved in production—more so than preceding exploiting classes like feudal lords or ancient slaveowners and more so than his descendants today. A number of the functions he performed have been delegated to workers, especially to managers and mental workers. But this is not all. Within the capitalist class, different types have appeared. The top executive is one; the owning capitalist is another; the socially and politically active capitalist is another; and the consuming capitalist is still another type.

The top executives manage the class relation within the corporate world, and in this role they make some strategic economic decisions. A group of such men, the Business Advisory Council, told President Nixon after the election of 1968 that the unemployment rate had to go up. The chief executives are at or near the apex of a hierarchy of authority, which gives them qualities not found in independent capitalists. They have mastered bureaucratic politics and palace intrigue, something like the eunuchs behind certain dynasties of ancient China. Yet they understand the limits of their power and learn to consult and coordinate on policy while they promote their individual careers. They know their subordinate position in the capitalist class (unless coming from a monopoly capitalist family), do not aspire to leave their name on things, and can give their children comfort and a head start but not a guarantee of big wealth and power. This is left to the owning capitalists, like John D. Rockefeller, who passed his gains to his sons. The owning capitalists step in and shake things up when there is trouble in the corporation. If a big scandal breaks or the company is going seriously downhill, the overriding power of the owning capitalists is felt, perhaps through the executive committee of the board of directors or an "independent" audit committee chaired by the family lawyer.[35]

Besides these two types of primarily economic capitalists, the top executives and the owning capitalists, other big capitalists specialize in managing the affairs of monopoly capitalist society over a wide spectrum of social departments. In politics, they are usually appointed to office rather than elected. Corporate attorneys knit together industry, banking, and government. Some of these capitalists assemble intellectuals into "think tanks" like the Council on Foreign Relations or the Brookings Institution and oversee their attempts at social engineering. The junior examples of political capitalists resemble executives in their understanding of bureaucracy, their ease of movement in a hierarchy. The socially and politically active capitalists typically move from one post to another every few years. Of all types of capitalists, they have the widest perspective, one that concentrates on their interest as a class—not to the exclusion of a nice deal for their company or family, but in tandem with personal gain.[36]

Finally, some capitalists specialize in consumption, whether cultivating the false elegance of a supposed classical tradition or displaying the open degeneracy of the cafe society crowd or "jet set." They simply spend money on a lavish scale for personal luxuries.

The individual capitalist cannot be designated strictly as one or another of these types. He or she is largely one kind of person at one period of life, but still the characteristics overlap, and in the course of their lives, capitalists may take several of these roles. All of them become increasingly isolated from production itself.

On the grounds that various types of capitalists have acquired a niche for themselves like species within a genus, some have asserted that there are no more capitalists. This is obviously a fraudulent claim. Because each type of monopoly capitalist lacks one of the qualities once joined together in a single individual of earlier days, or because he has developed some new characteristic, it is argued that none is a capitalist and that there is no capitalist class! Mass magazines and publishing houses owned by big businessmen disseminate this nonsense. But for all the differences in roles and functions of various types of capitalists, together they make up a class which does not labor but rather extracts surplus labor from the working class. Overall, there was little difficulty in counting these individuals. Details of the particular social activities of capitalists round out the picture of the class, but the essence of class is the economic forms in which surplus labor flows. Social sketches are an addition to economic science, not a replacement for it.

8. The Invisibility of the Petty Producer Class

Every class has its own mode of production. A class will be found under other modes of production, too, but it always strives to establish its own economy. The mode of production corresponding to the needs of the working class is socialism: the social productive forces are developed by collective production relations; with regard to the class relation, the means of production are owned socially by the working class, so that it can keep and dispose of its surplus labor collectively. Capitalism is the mode of production championed by the capitalists. The means of production are privately owned, each capitalist obtaining some of the surplus-value exploited from the working class. The other production relations tend to become more collective with the development of the social productive forces. Like all exploitive modes of production, capitalism is marked by an irreconcilable contradiction, here seen as the private appropriation of surplus labor by a few from the collective production relations of large bodies of workers.

Is there a mode of production belonging to the petty producers? Yes, there is the petty mode of production, a collection of families of petty producers. It is based on individual ownership of the means of production, individual appropriation of one's own surplus labor, and individual relations of production throughout, not only in the class relation. This mode of production is conceivable in theory and existed to a certain extent in history.

> "Ownership of the land is as necessary for full development of this mode of production as ownership of tools is for free development of handicraft production." (Marx, *Capital*, III, p. 807)

The petty mode of production consists of individual peasants who own and farm their land and of handicraft producers on the same dwarfish scale in the peasant home and craftsmen's shops. The major example of the petty mode of production occurs between feudalism and capitalism; in England, this would be the fifteenth and part of the sixteenth century.

> "This form of free self-managing peasant proprietorship of land parcels as the prevailing, normal form constitutes, on the one hand, the economic foundation of society during the best periods of classical antiquity, and on the other hand, it is found among modern nations as one of the forms arising from the dissolution of feudal landownership. Thus, the yeomanry in England, the peasantry in Sweden, the French and West German peasants." (*Ibid.*, p. 806)

The correspondence of class and mode of production extends to earlier societies, too.[37]
Because of the class struggle and the contradiction in capitalism between its class relation and its other relations of production, capitalism might seem to be the most unstable mode of production. This is not how it turns out, however. This distinction goes to the petty mode of production. It rapidly develops into capitalism or socialism. In England, and wherever history developed spontaneously, variations arising in productive power among the petty producers became entrenched in the

development of a few capitalists and many workers. One family prospers and nurtures the acquisitive habit; another meets with sickness or the ravages of war. The former buys out the latter, whose descendants become wage laborers. The division of labor and the production of commodities for the market spreads, cash must be earned, and self-sufficient farming and home industry for subsistence become impossible. Out of the petty mode of production springs capitalism.

In other countries, landlordism or semi-feudalism is destroyed by a democratic revolution led by the working class through its communist party. Peasants divide the land, creating the petty mode of production. This happened in the Russian revolution of 1917 and the Chinese revolution of 1927 to 1949. But within a few years, the petty producers agree after examples and appeals by the proletarian government to enter the road of cooperation. They voluntarily change the ownership of means of production to more collective forms and pool their surplus labor. Individual petty production disappears, this time yielding not to a few capitalists who exploit a propertyless mass of wage workers but rather to cooperative production for the common good of the producers themselves.

Individual production relations and the small scale of production which necessarily correspond to them cannot survive for long. Collective relations in production are bound to arise. The only question is whether the class relation will remain individual, giving rise to the tremendous contradictions of capitalism, or whether the class relation will develop along with the scale of production and its relations, keeping surplus labor within the hold of the community of producers.

The petty producers under capitalism are the same economic class as the petty producers under the petty mode of production. Their relation to the means of production is individual, and they keep their individual surplus labor, more or less.[38] But under the pressure of capitalist economic forces, the petty producer becomes either a capitalist or a worker. Although the latter process, proletarianization, is more common, the desire, drive, and nature of the petty producer as an owner of means of production is to become a capitalist. We have seen the gradual degrees by which this can happen, giving rise to the term petty bourgeois.

One difference between the classic petty producer and the petty producer under capitalism is the degree to which the latter produces for the market rather than directly to satisfy his own needs. Instead of growing his own food and making most of his own furniture, clothing, and other specific articles of use, the petty producer sells his products, of which one kind tends to dominate (for example, grain), and purchases things to satisfy his various needs. In purchase he is like the worker, but he resembles the capitalist in production of commodities for sale in the market.

Under capitalism, the petty producer hardly has a place in the sun. His individual production is more outmoded each day. He becomes a worker, or he exists under the shadow of bigger property owners, the capitalists. He loses his own name, petty producer, and is called instead petty bourgeois. All of this goes to make the petty producer class the most nearly invisible class in history.

What survives as a rump is the petty bourgeoisie. Capitalism is a contradictory mix of individual and collective elements. The production relations other than class become more and more collective with the growth of large-scale production. The ownership of the means of production remains private, antagonistic to the working class, the surplus labor of ever greater social powers and bodies of production remaining at the disposal of a constellation of ever more narrow interests. The petty bourgeoisie does not want to resolve this contradiction but to suppress it, to retreat to an earlier day. The petty bourgeoisie dislikes big, monopoly capitalists, who crush it methodically. At times, the petty bourgeois proclaims his identification with the worker as a fellow in the ranks of labor. That is, ignoring social relations, he identifies individual labor with collective labor. This was the tactic of the Populists, a political movement of the petty bourgeoisie in the late nineteenth century which rallied itself and workers to demand the breakup of big business and Wall Street finance. It was, however, impossible to break up large-scale production. Once embarked on the road of collective productive forces and production relations, society can only move further into capitalism or on to socialism. The Populist movement achieved the antitrust laws and the various regulatory bodies like the Interstate Commerce Commission, whose effect ever since has been meaningless words or the active preservation of existing monopolies against all challengers.

Capitalism toys with the politics of the petty bourgeoisie. The petty bourgeois demand for individual relations of production other than class is backward and impossible. The petty bourgeoisie also defends individualism in class relations, an attitude fully agreeable to capitalists. In the last analysis, petty bourgeois relations and all reflections of them argue for retarding the development of capitalism, hence for preserving it, hence against socialism. Socialism destroys the old class relation. It resolves the antagonism between collective production relations and forces on the one hand and individual appropriation of surplus labor on the other hand by doing away with the latter.[39]

9. The Bases of the Petty Bourgeois Mentality

It is a general principle of social knowledge that

"The mode of production in material life determines the general character of the social, political and spiritual processes of life. It is not the consciousness of men that determines their existence, but, on the contrary, their social existence determines their consciousness." (Marx, 1904, p. 11-12)

Part of the social existence of men is their ideas, which in turn influence reality. These ideas arise as more or less accurate reflections of a pre-existing social reality, which is a material thing, and their power to react on the world depends on how well they analyze the motion of social and material life and therefore represent and champion the new against the old.

Since workers are exploited of surplus labor by the capitalists, it might seem a logical conclusion that the working class would immediately do away with the class relations of capitalism, reclaim its surplus labor, and develop society in its own interests. At least, as soon as the working class outnumbered the capitalists and any other classes the latter might arouse to oppose socialism, such would be the expected action. Yet it has not happened this way in history. In some countries (for example, China) socialism has been achieved far sooner than the working class became the numerically dominant class, while in others, including the United States, the working class comprises over 90 percent of the population but remains exploited. In these latter countries the working class is not class conscious; too many of its members remain unaware of the nature of capitalism and socialism. They struggle, but within the system.

There must be a material basis for this situation, if the above thesis by Marx is correct. If we examine the material relations of the capitalist mode of production other than its class relation, we find that a number of them foster a petty bourgeois picture of society. They cover up or act against the class conscious analysis of capitalism to which the class relation by itself leads.

a. Wages

The revenue of the working class under capitalism is determined by the sale of its labor power to the capitalist class. The value of labor power is the value of the amount of goods needed to restore and maintain labor power used up in production and to replace one generation of labor powers by the next. This amount, as well as the conditions of the use of labor power in production, are determined within limits by class struggle.

The form of the revenue of the working class, its wages and salaries, does not reveal but instead hides this content. The value created in a working day, which exceeds the value of the goods needed to sustain the worker, is not openly divided into the time needed to produce the value of these goods and the surplus time used to produce surplus product.

"The wage-form thus extinguishes every trace of the division of the working-day into necessary labor and surplus-labor, into paid and unpaid labor. All labor appears as paid labor." (Marx, *Capital*, I, p. 539)

This wage or salary is paid to the individual worker in exchange for his labor power (appearing as an exchange for his labor). Social productive powers seem to belong to individuals, who arrange to apply them in exchange for a wage or salary. The wage form governs the revenue of the individual worker in proportion to his contribution to production—in time if payment is by the hour or month, in number of articles if payment is by piece rate. The principle of relating a person's revenue to his effort becomes fixed in the mind of the wage or salary worker. This is a petty bourgeois conception. The payment of wages

"forms the basis of all the juridical notions of both laborer and capitalist, of all the mystifications of the capitalistic mode of production, of all its illusions as to liberty, of all the apologetic shifts of the vulgar economists." (*Ibid.*, p. 540)

Class struggle still exists, despite the illusion of the form, and workers learn to combine in unions to maintain the rate of pay and to regulate working conditions in the factory or other place of production. Nevertheless, the individual is paid, and this causes petty bourgeois illusions that he or she is rewarded for individual effort, or should be rewarded in proportion to individual effort.

This petty bourgeois conception is recognized in the first stage of socialism, which necessarily operates on the principle, "from each according to his ability, to each according to his labor." It is only in the second, higher stage of socialism (called communism) that the need to reward or bribe the individual for contributing the productive powers endowed in him by society passes away. Then, all give of their powers of labor freely as they are able and needed, and all take for consumption what they need. Labor ceases to regulate individual consumption. Until then, the wage form is necessarily a source of petty bourgeois individualism, appearing in countless different ways. The wage form gives rise, among other things, to erroneous definitions of classes.

The content of the wage relation remains the exploitation of surplus labor. The wage form does not alter this content and its workings. With the given length of the working day, the payment to labor power amounts to what is necessary to purchase goods for the maintenance and reproduction of the worker. Divide the amount by the length of the working day, and the hourly wage is the result. Or divide the amount by the daily production of articles, and the piece rate is the result. The income of the working class is a result of class struggle, which determines the wage rate or piece rate. This income is not determined by first agreeing on rates and then letting workers try to turn out more articles or work much overtime. Overtime is decided by the employer, and if workers drive up production, the piece rate is cut. Underneath the wage form, the apparent payment of the individual for all his working time, lurks the division of the working day into paid labor and unpaid labor, the class relation of the exploited working class and the exploiting capitalist class.

b. The Private Family

The rearing of children, the next generation of workers, exercises an important influence on the outlook of both children and adults. Under capitalism, the private family is universal. This type of family originated with the development of private property, but it was found mainly among the minority exploiting classes of the new class societies.[40] It has spread to the entire society under capitalism, the mode of production of commodities raised to the highest degree.

In the study of the material bases of petty bourgeois ideology, the characteristics of the private family that concern us are the economic dependence of the individual child on individual adults and the transmission of economic position to individual children by adults. The child obtains his or her food and shelter from one or two adults on whom he or she is therefore dependent and from whom the child consequently receives instruction and upbringing. Although the ideal and typical form of the private family under capitalism has been the nuclear patriarchal family (the father, his wife, and children), it is not necessary that the providing adult be the father. Even if both parents work and have potential economic independence from each other, or if the mother or even another relative provides, the child depends on one or two individuals. The providing adult or adults enjoy the power of ultimatum and the supervision, if not always the actual provision, of the instruction and upbringing of the child. If the child's behavior is unsatisfactory, the child may receive less or, more commonly, be threatened with economic sanction. Under this regime, the child acquires an individualist outlook on social relations; the drama of these relations, with all their emotional storms, occurs within the private family, a little solar system of individuals. The child may exchange comparisons with other children regarding treatment received, strategy, and so forth, but the individual setting remains a brute fact.

Also, the economic position of the adult wage or salary earner is transmitted to his or her particular children, or to surrogates like a nephew or grandson. Economic hopes are concentrated on one's own children. Differences among wage earners are transmitted to children as differences in educational opportunities, familiarity with an occupation, and savings. All this reinforces the petty bourgeois outlook in both adults and children; they view social relations as individual capacities and relations, regarding one's economic position as basically a matter of individual endowments, both material and personal.

The influence of schools, mass media, peer groups, and churches may run counter to the influence of the private family. A private family institution which is breaking down under advanced capitalism will produce different results than one which is flourishing in patriarchal form. Despite all this, however, the economic fact of the individual source of necessities for the individual child remains and cannot be overcome completely by other agencies. Only with the return in a classless society to collective provision for children, as existed in the original tribal form of society, will the private family and its effects disappear.

Until then, the private family remains one of the sources of petty bourgeois ideology among the working class.

c. Authority Relations

Some workers occupying positions of management, supervision and technical direction regard their interests as those of capitalists, while on the other hand capitalists try to portray their role as a functional, managerial one that even qualifies them as members of the working class. It must be explained how the relations of authority in production give rise not only to capitalist but to petty bourgeois consciousness as well.

Managerial and supervisory authority in capitalist society is arranged in bureaucratic hierarchies. Those desiring to enter this hierarchy and prosper in it want promotions, that is, a career. Whether promotions are achieved by merit, favoritism, politicking, or other means, the method consists of promoting oneself in order to be promoted. One's situation and progress are seen to depend to a large degree on individual calculations and performances. Bureaucratic hierarchies generate their own brand of petty bourgeois individualism. The influence of the attitude extends beyond the body of actual managers and supervisors to others who nurse hopes of entering the hierarchies. This is more likely to be true in small shops than big factories and among white collar workers who are socially and physically close to their managers and supervisors.

Capitalists reinforce this form of petty bourgeois consciousness by attaching minor privileges to positions of authority. The privileges bear no functional relation to the work of direction and planning, nor do they reward a form of skilled labor that produces value at an intensified rate. Perquisites and slight increments of pay attract the petty bourgeois outlook and give the individual something material to identify as his interest in his individualist actions. This is necessary, because the petty bourgeois operator in a bureaucratic hierarchy must actively push aside and sell out his co-workers in order to further his career. This compounds his fear and loathing of other workers, who in turn identify a renegade from the ranks. This recognition is captured in a number of terms, such as sellout, backstabber, brown-noser and other, more graphic expressions.

While these facts must be recognized politically, the production relations of authority cannot by themselves convert a person from a member of the working class, a yielder of surplus labor, to a capitalist, a receiver and disposer of surplus labor. Instead, we see here one of the means by which the capitalist class infiltrates the working class. In a capitalist society, petty bourgeois consciousness among workers serves the capitalist class. Hatred of renegades afflicted with a petty bourgeois mentality must always be combined with reflection on the subservience of lackeys to their masters in the exploiting class. The lackeys are more visible in daily life, often have to be fought in direct encounters, and earn people's contempt, but the big capitalists are at the headquarters of the enemy camp.

d. Mental Labor

Productive human activity happens in two phases. First, we picture in the mind the action to be taken and the goal to be attained. Then we perform the actual operations, modifying the plan as we proceed. Before a part is turned on a lathe, a blueprint is made. Before cars are assembled, a work flow schedule is written. The entire research of science investigates problems in order to discover laws and theories before the latter are applied.

Where mental labor is separated from manual labor and persons specialize in one or the other, as is the case in capitalist society, the division of mental and manual labor is a basis for petty bourgeois conceptions among those who work with their minds. Those who do this work, especially its higher forms, are called intellectuals. They tend to work alone and to produce a personal product: his or her report, book, performance (acting), artwork, or lecture. The intellectual is similar to the petty producer in working by himself and producing a product clearly identified as his own. The intellectual regards his individual skill and even his individuality as embodied in the product and so thinks, conversely, "that he can attain his aim only by expression of his individuality." (Ahmati, p. 17)

Frequently, the class position of the intellectual corresponds to the qualities of his work, in which case he is a petty producer, for example, the writer who sells his manuscript, the artist his painting, the inventor his patent. Even when the intellectual is a salary earner, however, he retains many of these characteristics. Capitalist bureaucratic organizations are divided into line and staff. The former is the hierarchy of authority down to the actual producers (in a company) or soldiers (in an army). Attached to the higher levels of the organization are staffs, whose job is to investigate problems, plan changes in operations, estimate the outcome of alternative policy decisions, and support negotiations with other bureaucracies. Those who comprise the staff, although integrated into a large organization, share many of the intellectual's qualities in their work. They still undertake specific projects alone or in small teams. Their assignments are made in general terms, the exact shaping of the product (the content of the report) being precisely the substance of their labor. Advancement and distinction in the organization depend heavily on the apparent creativity and insight of the particular person, who regards his individual mental traits as unique and crucial to his welfare. Like the independent intellectual, the staff worker evolves a petty bourgeois mentality.

Staffs have their own bureaucratic hierarchy, with analysts at the base and a series of managers above them. The staff can become large in absolute numbers, although for economic reasons it must always stay within proportion to the line organization. There is an interweaving of the petty bourgeois intellectual mentality and the petty bourgeois thinking that arises out of the relations of authority. Yet the petty producer's outlook develops in the lowest staff analyst, who, even though his unit be attached to the office of the president and even though his investigations take him to various managers who must answer his questions, has no authority. The division of mental and manual labor is an independent source of petty bourgeois thinking.

This thinking is accentuated by the fact that "the intellectual is not in contact with things, but with their symbols." (Ahmati, p. 17) The brute obstacle-ness of matter impresses itself every day on the manual worker—the repairman who cannot get a motor to run even though "everything is like it is supposed to be," the machinist who works to a close tolerance or throws the piece on the scrap heap, the construction worker whose rotary saw cuts wood and also himself unless he is careful, and the miner who moves earth always ready to cave in on him. The thinker and planner writes the proposal; its logic is internally consistent, but it has not been tested in full operation. The author, lecturer, and entertainer convey images that must be persuasive to the audience but still may not conform to reality. Unchecked by matter, the mind of the intellectual can nurture illusions about its power.

Also feeding the sense of personal potency is the fact that the intellectual studies and sums up the work, experience, and deeds of many others. (Ahmati, p. 22) Practice is the source of theory. The sweep and depth of the masses' labor, even of whole historical epochs, goes into the intellectual's work and emerges concentrated under his name. It is easy for him to lose sight of the fact that the power of conceptions is derived from the life of the masses. The intellectual often transposes his work and that of the masses, endowing his personal mental labor with millionfold value.

This kind of petty bourgeois thinking is concentrated most among those who perform the most abstract or highest forms of mental labor. Among teachers, the college professor feels the power and freedom of personally shaping ideas and concepts far more than the elementary school teacher, whose main concern is not developing the subject matter but rather passing it into the brains and muscles of a group of children. The effects of specialized mental labor are most intense where the intellectual charts new conceptual ground in a nonroutine way.

e. The Machinery of Fraud

The wage form of payment for labor power, the private family, the production relations of authority, and the division of mental and manual labor are only four of the many bases in social relations for petty bourgeois consciousness among workers. They are illusions because they lead the worker to think of his or her labor power as individual "capital," to be employed for "profit" strictly on one's own account. Capital, however, is not a thing. Means of production exist in every form of society, but not every society has capitalists. Only when a minority of society owns the means of production and uses them to extract surplus labor in the form of surplus-value do they become capital. To regard one's own person and its capacities for labor as capital is absurd. First, people are a force of production, but not means of production. Second, capital is the expansion of value into value plus surplus-value extracted from others. One cannot exploit oneself.[41] The worker is not a capitalist.

Nor is he a petty producer, for the sale of labor power is not the same thing as the sale of goods or services one produces oneself for a price or fee. The exercise of labor power is one of the constituent elements of the production of things; nerves and sweat must be expended to make something. The petty producer expends this labor, providing the raw materials, tools, and so forth which must be mixed with it. Then he delivers the result to the buyer and collects the price. The worker, in contrast, sells his potential ability to labor to the capitalist. The labor power of the day or month belongs to the latter, who employs the labor, the labor power in use, on means of production the capitalist supplies. The result of production belongs to the capitalist, who intervenes between the producers and the purchasers. He, not the worker, sells the product.

Although the worker may regard himself as a capitalist or

petty producer, that is, as a petty bourgeois, this illusion does not change him into one. The class of workers remains distinct from the bourgeoisie. Consciousness of the class relation means that the worker is aware of his class situation. Consciousness based on subordinate relations gives the worker illusions about his class position.

This false consciousness has its material bases, some of which have been described. An individual worker may pursue secondary interests based on them, forgetting the basic determinant of his social position, the class relation. Or the worker may simply be unaware of classes and have illusions that appearances like the wage form constitute the real vortex of social motion that enmeshes the individual.

Yet the error of thinking does not spring automatically and unalterably from the material bases of petty bourgeois consciousness. Material bases must be reflected in concepts that depend not only on the material bases themselves but also on the thinking brought to bear on them. Ptolemy and Copernicus observed the same stars, yet the framework of comprehension was different. The petty bourgeois illusion among workers requires a material basis, but it also requires continual misinterpretation. This is provided by the various powers of ideology and politics controlled by the capitalist class. In a capitalist society, the worker is subjected to an enormous machinery of ideological shaping, a machinery in service to capitalism. The institutions of education and upbringing, the network of social information both formal and informal (mass media and everyday habits of social thought), and the sphere of explicit deliberation on society, the political sphere, are all dominated by the dominant economic class, the capitalists. It is a machinery of fraud exercised by one class against another. Big capitalists, who own and control this machinery—the newspapers, the television networks, the government, the universities, etc.—have few illusions of a petty bourgeois nature. They are aware of the collective nature of social production, their private ownership of the collective social powers of production, the class antagonism in such a situation, and the need to maintain class rule by active measures of fraud and force. All this is antithetical to the petty bourgeois world outlook.

Just as the petty producers are nearly powerless economically, their ideology can no longer serve them. Petty bourgeois ideology is a tool of the capitalist class against the working class. Someone who pushes this ideology is objectively serving the capitalist class as part of its machinery of fraud. He is not doing any historical service to the petty producers, because it is impossible to revive the petty mode of production. This is why Marxists say that all ideology, including the petty bourgeois outlook, serves either the capitalist class or the working class.[42]

False consciousness is not an automatic reflection of a material foundation. It is a class-determined cognition of some but not all facts. The capitalists do not focus attention on classes, class contradiction, and class struggle. But they are a material reality, the fundamental reality. In ideological and political struggle we can bring out their existence and the necessities that flow from them. (This is discussed in Part Three.)

One area of social thinking is that concerning class itself. It is to the examination of definitions of class peddled by the capitalist class that we now turn.

PART TWO: ANTI-CLASS

10. The Revenue Definition of Class

Bourgeois political economists defined classes by their sources of income. In a capitalist society, "Wages, profit, and rent, are the three original sources of all revenue" (Smith, p. 52). Adam Smith was quite aware that these three forms of revenue are "parcelled out among different inhabitants of the country" (*Ibid.*).

Wages go to laborers, profits go to capitalists, and rent goes to landlords. (Rent always means ground-rent; building rent is another matter.) These are the three main classes of capitalist society defined by Smith, Ricardo, and all adherents of the early period of capitalist economic theorizing. The petty producer was regarded as someone with mixed sources of revenue; he paid himself some wages, earned profit on his stock of means of production, and if he owned land on which he farmed, paid himself rent. [43]

These sources of income were seen in turn to depend on ownership of "things" which were elements of production. Production is possible only if these things come together.

"The produce of the earth—all that is derived from its surface by the united application of labor, machinery, and capital, is divided among three classes of the community, namely, the proprietor of the land, the owner of the stock or capital necessary for its cultivation, and the laborers by whose industry it is cultivated." (Ricardo, p. 1)

Of principal interest to theorists of the revenue definition of classes were the laws governing the magnitudes of the three forms of revenue.[44] They saw that the sources of income were different because the laws determining the quantity of each operated differently. Wages and profits did not increase together under the influence of the same conditions; it was obvious that profits bore a relation to the size of the capital of the capitalist, regardless of how little labor he might perform.[45] Economists also thought that the laws were natural rather than social. Ricardo, for example, saw the proportions of rent, profit, and wages

". . . depending mainly on the actual fertility of the soil, on the accumulation of capital and population, and on the skill, ingenuity, and instruments employed in agriculture." (Ricardo, p. 1)[46]

This last point is a good one from which to begin a critical analysis of the revenue definition. Proponents of natural law expound the way things must be if nature is allowed to run its course, and then they assert without any grounds whatsoever that these natural laws should be allowed to run their course. Immediately after summarizing the natural conditions, such as the state of agriculture, which regulate the magnitude of wages, Ricardo admonishes,

"Like all other contracts, wages should be left to the fair and free competition of the market, and should never be controlled by the interference of the legislature." (Ricardo, p. 61)

It is impossible to repeal the law of gravity. Other natural laws may be utilized to give new effects, such as the laws of fluids employed to design airplane wings with lifting force. Still, the law of gravity remains in force, too. Ricardo betrays a fear, however, that men will try to ignore the natural laws regulating wages. Smith, Ricardo, and other believers in natural laws of classes were really talking about economic laws, a form of social law. It is true that men cannot simply wish for certain states of society and have them; there are laws that govern society. But these laws operate in the actions of men, and by acting in accordance with social law, classes can change society. The fertility of the crops does not determine the workers' fate. The viewpoint of social law is oriented to change; with an understanding of necessity determined by the past, men by revolutionary action can alter the prevailing social order. The earliest capitalist economists ignored basic social change. Capitalism seemed to them eternal; it would always be and really had always been. They felt that wages, profits, and rent had always existed, only emerging more plainly to our eyes with the quantitative growth of the wealth of nations.

The revenues of the classes seemed to be governed by natural laws because they were based on "things"—capital, land, and labor. To the human representative of each type of thing accrued the revenue which really belonged to that thing. Rent was thought to be an inherent feature of land, as was profit of means of production. But these "things" are not things. Capital is not the means of production, the plant and equipment and so forth. Capital is a social relation, the relation which puts some, the capitalists, in a position to control the use of the means of production and to require others, the workers, to yield surplus labor to the capitalists as a precondition of the workers' livelihood. All societies use means of production, but not all suffer this social relation between capitalists and workers. As a socialist country like China builds up more means of production, it does not thereby become a capitalist society.

The revenue definition of class was based on the private

ownership of means of production and of land (and on the free laborer, possessor of the right to sell his labor power). Early capitalist economists did not hide this fact but simply assumed that it was the only possible state of affairs.[47] Ownership, however, was not seen as a social relation between people. Instead, the relations of the capitalist to his means of production, the landlord to his land, and the worker to his labor were regarded as they appear on the surface, as three different, independent relations to unrelated things.

Consequently, the revenues of the three classes were thought to arise independently, too. In the view of these men, capital does not exploit labor. Marx summarized their views.

"Normal average profits themselves seem immanent in capital and independent of exploitation; abnormal exploitation . . . seems to determine only the deviations from average profit, not this profit itself." (Marx, *Capital*, III, p. 829)

In fact, means of production cannot exploit labor; the thought is meaningless. It is true that production requires all its natural elements, both subjective and objective; labor alone cannot make clothes out of air. But looms cannot receive and possess cloth; only their owners can. The capitalist disposes of surplus labor embodied in surplus product because of the relations of production; the ownership of a "factor of production" is an external appearance of this class relation. Because the different revenues appear to derive from independent sources, "they have no inner connection whatsoever." (Marx, 1971, p. 503) Therefore, "they do not stand in any hostile connection to one another" (*Ibid.*). Certainly, the three classes might quarrel over the division of the product to which each has contributed, but there are natural laws governing the division which dictate the only stable distribution. It is an obvious arithmetical fact that a value of annual production, once given, can be divided in one way as opposed to another only by increasing one portion and decreasing another. This, too, is a "natural law." But from the viewpoint of necessary factors of production, this arithmetical truism can never have a fundamental impact. It is entirely different to take the class point of view, to realize that capital is a social relation by which non-laborers dispose of the surplus labor of the working people. Then the inner connection and antagonism are revealed: the working class possesses only its labor power and must sell it because the means of production belong to a small class standing over and against the working class.

The revenue definition of classes divides capitalist society into the same groups as the Marxist definition. It recognizes the petty producer as well as the capitalist and the worker. Its distinction between landlords and capitalists is not important today. The landowners, descendants of feudal lords in many cases, were holding up the development of the industrial phase of capitalism, a position which ran counter to the interests of capitalists, owners of the produced means of production. The struggle between the capitalists and the landlords culminated in England with the repeal of the Corn Laws in 1846, which had increased the rent of agricultural land by imposing a high tariff on imported grain. But while the division of the population into classes is approximately the same, the two definitions lead to opposite results when it comes to the relations between classes, or the basis and nature of a class: one confuses physical objects and social relations, the other gives insight into these relations.

Marx did not claim to discover the concept of classes.[48] The classical political economists, from the Physiocrats of the eighteenth century through Adam Smith to David Ricardo, worked to identify the constituent parts of the capitalist economic system and to trace their action much as one might study an automobile engine. Marx discovered why these forms had developed, and therefore how they tended to develop. This was not a spectator science; men are necessarily involved in the class struggle. Marx understood the difference between society and a physical object like an automobile engine, but he did not redraw the outlines of the classes, which had been pictured fairly accurately by the revenue definition.

The revenue definition of class is still encountered occasionally among Marxist and semi-Marxist thinkers.[49] The most prominent example is Maurice Dobb, once a Marxist but later a capitalist theorist. In his Marxist period he vacillated on the definition of class. In 1937 he wrote that "a class is to be defined in terms of a common source of income, which lays the basis of a common interest" (Dobb, 1955, p. 95). In this essay, Dobb felt that the importance of class lies in its relation to a basic social antagonism, but he never explained clearly how class was bound up with necessary antagonism. This is because he used the revenue definition of classes just quoted. Given independent sources of income in three natural factors of production, no basis for antagonism exists.

In a study of the history of capitalism, Dobb rejected the revenue definition of class: "Nor is it sufficient to say simply that a class consists of those who derive their income from a common source" (Dobb, 1963, p. 15). Instead, the important things are "the relationship in which the group . . . stands to the process of production," "the concentration of ownership of the means of production in the hands of a class," and the use of capital "to yoke labor to the creation of surplus-value in production." (pp. 15, 7, 8) It may be significant that Dobb was clearest on the subject of class when writing about the origins of capitalism but reverted to the revenue definition when speaking publicly about capitalism today.

Classical political economy told the working class that its position was inevitable, that attempts at reform could only make things worse. To the individual worker, there was held out the possibility of his acquiring some capital.[50] After Ricardo's death in 1823, plain, unvarnished statements of at least the appearance of things were not made, and the element of deliberate fraud in economic writing increased. Apologetics and lies took over because of the intensification of the class struggle, such as the Chartist movement of the English workers and the revolutions of 1848 on the European continent. The working class had more economic and social strength than during the French Revolution, for example, so it felt that things could be changed. At the same time, the gulf between classes widened, the minimum requirements to set up shop as a capitalist rose beyond the chance of a worker to save money and start a business, and the examples of individual mobility from working class to capitalist class became too few to support the illusion of opportunity. For awhile, vulgar economists struggled to calm the working class with twistings of the revenue definition of class. But it was no use. The capitalists therefore abandoned the revenue definition of class. This was accomplished by use of a transitional conception, which preceded the modern, completely false definitions of capitalist fraud today.

11. The Transition to Apologetics: Max Weber

Max Weber, one of the fathers of the capitalist discipline of sociology, hated and feared the working class, opposed socialism, and campaigned against Marxism and truth in social science. Born in 1864, the year of the founding of the International Workingmen's Association, Weber was 18 when Marx died in 1883, 25 when the Second International of workers' parties was organized in 1889, and 31 when Engels died in 1895. The field was open for bright young men to distort and "refute" Marxism. Weber was 44 when the 1905 Revolution broke out in tsarist Russia, and 53 at the time of the October Revolution of 1917. He died in 1920.

Although Weber defended the capitalist class in practical politics and took a reactionary stand during the German proletarian revolution of 1918, his principal contributions to the capitalists were ideological. In particular, he offered ideas of groupings to replace class. The revenue definition of the major classes by their respective sources of income (wages, profits and interest, and rent), despite its obscuring of social relations and denial of exploitation, was unsatisfactory to the capitalist class because it still identified the main classes and something of their bases of income. Capitalists needed a picture which drew the lines of division completely wrong and which covered up entirely the economic basis of classes. It took some time to create theories which accomplished these acrobatics of fantasy. Max Weber is an important transitional figure who helped to work out the main lines of the job.

Traces of the old revenue definition of classes survive in Weber's writing. He says, " 'Property' and 'lack of property' are, therefore, the basic categories of all class situations." He speaks of "the entrepreneurial function" and "chances to share . . . in returns on capital" as attributes of "the propertied" (Weber, 1946, p. 182). Here Weber lingers to the old idea that a thing called capital produces its own return and that its human representative supposedly earns income by taking risks and organizing and managing productive activity.

Weber moved away from this picture of the "factors of production." He says, "The economic order is for us merely the way in which economic goods and services are distributed and used." (*Ibid.*, p. 181) Where do economic goods come from, so that they may then be distributed and consumed? The sphere of production does not exist for Weber. The early capitalist often knew something about what was happening in the shop; by the time of Weber, whole sections of capitalists had become largely divorced from production. Goods simply appeared, like wild berries on a forest bush. As an ideologist for the capitalist class, Weber articulated what it saw, and then this world view was imposed on society as a whole, including the working class, through the schools, press, and other tools of intellectual domination in the hands of the capitalists.

When discussing class, Weber therefore ignored production.[51] Also playing down the sphere of consumption, he concentrated on the market. For Weber, one's class situation is one's market situation. " 'Class situation' is . . . ultimately 'market situation.' " (Weber, 1946, p. 182).[52] The specific character of what one brings to the market determines one's "class":

"We may speak of a 'class' when (1) a number of people have in common a specific causal component of their life chances, in so far as (2) this component is represented exclusively by economic interests in the possession of goods and opportunities for income, and (3) is represented under the conditions of the commodity or labor markets." (*Ibid.*, p. 181)[53]

Weber went so far in requiring a market source of income as to deny at one point that slaves were a class!

"Those men whose fate is not determined by the chance of using goods or services for themselves on the market, e.g., slaves, are not, however, a 'class' in the technical sense of the term." (*Ibid.*, p. 183)[54]

These remarks might appear to recognize a social relation. They do, but only a market relation, not a relation of production. The capitalist begins a cycle of production and exploitation with money. He converts it into the constituent elements of production: he buys the instruments of production, the raw materials, the premises of work, and the labor power needed to activate them. All these must be available on the market, including workers who need to sell their labor power. After these elements have been assembled, the process of production and, the aspect that interests the capitalist, the process of exploiting surplus-value occur. The results of production, bearing surplus-value, are then sold by the capitalist, converting these commodities back into money. The capitalist's sole aim is that the proceeds shall be larger than the quantity of money originally converted into elements, both dead and living, of production. The capitalist cycle of exploitation follows the sequence of 1) conversion of money into commodities (M-C), 2) production, and 3) conversion of commodities into money (C-M). In total, the sequence is M-C-M. Two markets are involved. The first market is the one that appears to be reflected in Weber's method of economic grouping. Supposedly, Weber defines a class by what it brings to this market. The worker brings his labor power to it. But the capitalist does not bring means of production to this market. He simply buys with money all the elements of production. He is not a seller on this market at all, but rather a buyer. He buys labor power from workers and he buys machinery and supplies from other capitalists. These latter, however, are realizing the value and surplus-value in the results of production; they are at the second stage, C-M, of the sequence M-C-M.

The worker has only labor power to sell. Under capitalism it is a commodity. He sells it for a money wage or salary, which in turn he spends on the commodities he needs to live—food, transportation, housing and education for himself and his family. The sequence of his life cycle in the market is 1) conversion of labor-power into wages (C-M), 2) labor for the capitalist, and 3) expenditure of his money on the necessities of life (M-C). In total, the sequence is C-M-C. The worker is a seller of labor power on the market Weber looks at. By comparison, we see that in the case of the capitalist Weber is not interested in the same market, for this perspective might lead to an examination of capitalist production. Instead, Weber is interested, despite occasional references to the contrary, in the capitalists' sales of products to realize surplus-value. The things he brings to market determine his class situation. When Weber says, "Ownership or non-ownership of material goods or of definite skills constitute the 'class-situation,'" (Weber, 1946, p. 405), he appears to be speaking about the ownership of means of production in the case of the capitalists. His writing is thoroughly confused on this point. To remain consistent in the market approach to economic groupings, Weber must mean the goods resulting from production, not those brought to it. This is absurd, of course.

So much for the clarity and depth of Weber's "theory." The payoff is the great variety of "classes." In the most abstract terms, Weber had spoken of property and the lack of property as the basic class situations. In a capitalist society we may think of these as capitalists and workers. Weber then differentiates both groups according to their market power. Capitalists who own

buildings are in a different class than capitalists who own factories, and they in turn are different from capitalists who own
mines (Weber, 1946, p. 182). According to Weber, merchants,
shipowners, industrial entrepreneurs, agribusinessmen, and
bankers each constitute a different class (Weber, 1968, p. 304).
Or, "the propertied, for instance, may belong to the class of
rentiers or to the class of entrepreneurs." (Weber, 1946, p. 182)

The capitalist class, owner of all the means of production and
exploiter of surplus labor from the working class, has disappeared. Weber pushes the conflict between industry and banking
over the division of surplus-value to the fore, while obscuring the
extraction of surplus labor in a process of production, of expenditure of abstract labor.

The division of the capitalist class into many "classes" is not the
contribution for which sociologists remember Weber. While
there has been some effort to tell people that the capitalist class is
splitting up, as in talk about the alleged separation of ownership
and control of capital with the extension of management, this
digression has been a minor trail. Sociologists especially like
Weber's division of the working class. Weber puts workers into
different groups "according to the kind of services that can be
offered in the market." (Weber, 1946, p. 182) Acquired or "definite" skills distinguish classes, since workers can sell their labor
power at different rates according to skill. Laborers are divided
according to "varying qualification: a) skilled b) semi-skilled c)
unskilled." (Weber, 1968, p. 304) Then there are classes of
"workers with monopolistic qualifications and skills (natural, or
acquired through drill or training)." (Weber, 1968, p. 304) In the
case of workers endowed with natural skills but unfortunate
enough to have been born to parents without property, we have
the biological determination of class. On the other hand, individual workers wishing to change their class do not need to alter
social relations; they need only acquire a new skill and take it to a
new and entirely different market for this kind of labor power. It
is almost as good as becoming a capitalist.

Weber ends where he began: every individual constitutes a class unto himself:

> "In principle, the various controls over consumer goods, means of production, assets, resources and skills each constitute a *particular* class situation. A *uniform* class situation prevails only when completely unskilled and propertyless persons are dependent on irregular employment." (Weber, 1968, p. 302)

Weber advocates here the idea that proletarians are only those with no skills or job security whatsoever. It is based on an interpretation of labor as pure expenditure of untrained muscle.[55] Labor is conceived in a physiological sense, independent of all social qualities and relations. No such thing exists, of course. Physiologically, all labor is wear on nerves as well as muscles, although not all activity is labor. The wage or salary worker is defined by nonownership of means of production and by forced surplus labor as a result. But if pure muscle power is taken as an extreme case, then Weber can easily assert that most classes are "middle classes," another theme that sociologists repeat with enthusiasm. "In between [such classes as rentiers and paupers] are the various 'middle classes' (*Mittelstandsklassen*), which make a living from their property or their acquired skills." (Weber, 1968, p. 303) By listing property and skills together, Weber causes the dividing line between capitalists and workers to disappear.

Weber carefully distinguished at the outset between class situation and class. Individuals are in a class situation, or market situation as defined above. Then, " 'Class' means all persons in the same class situation." (*Ibid.*, p. 302) Ignoring social relations, Weber begins with the individual and works from there. He obtains only a scheme of classification, perhaps supplemented occasionally by networks of feeling between individuals. Never is he aware that class societies are fundamentally divided into classes, and that individuals only exist within classes. This is a bald petty bourgeois approach.

Weber was quite proud of seizing on market differences, especially skills, to make class vanish. He felt it was a death blow to the science of Marx:

"The unfinished last part of Karl Marx's *Capital* apparently was intended to deal with the issue of class unity in the face of skill differentials." (Weber, 1968, p. 305)

What are we to make of these market and skill variations? Differences in skills do affect the particular jobs workers can compete for, and there will usually be some variation in income, too. If one wants to account for such individual differences in income, one may study these phenomena. This is what interests Weber. He wants to know about the economic determinants of "their life chances," the "probability of 1. procuring goods 2. gaining a position in life and [this is a joke] 3. finding inner satisfactions" (Weber, 1946, p. 181 and 1968, p. 302). We have here a historical root of another substitute conception for class that flowered later, strata defined by amount of income.

Forgotten, or never revealed, in this use of the word class for minor phenomena of the market are the relations to production and the question of surplus labor. No matter at what price and for what particular skill a worker is able to sell his labor power to a capitalist, his labor is still abstract labor as well as concrete, and he yields unpaid labor to the capitalist. The latter hires the former only to exploit him of surplus labor. If it does not happen that way, the capitalist lays him off, regardless of the potential social contribution of the worker's skill. It is to avoid looking at this class relation that Weber applies the term class to minor variations in the market of the class relation. These variations in no way change the basic content of production relations. As variations in the price of a commodity, labor power, they presuppose that labor power is a commodity, that the worker must offer his labor power for sale to a class with interests antagonistic to those of himself and his own class.

After beginning with the distinction of propertied and unpropertied and then approaching the view that every man is a class by himself, Weber regroups individuals into four social classes.

"Social classes are a) the working class as a whole—the more
so, the more automated the work process becomes, b) the
petty bourgeoisie, c) the propertyless intelligentsia and
specialists (technicians, various kinds of white-collar employees, civil servants—possibly with considerable social differences depending on the cost of their training), d) the classes
privileged through property and education." (Weber, 1968, p.
305)

In this list all thinking about relation to the means of production and to the class possession of surplus labor has disappeared.
Two of the four classes, c) and d), do not even have names. One of
them, d), might appear to be the capitalist class, but it is not. At
most, those "privileged through property and education" are the
inheritors of wealth, what is popularly known as the old rich. But
as owners of the means of production and exploiters as well as
beneficiaries of surplus-value, the capitalist class is absent from
this scheme.

Although naming the working class, Weber clearly refers only
to those without special skills or job security. As the class of
laborers who must sell their capacities, whether of muscle or
brain, and work with means provided by a capitalist interested
only in profit out of the operation, the working class includes
many people in the unlabeled category c) as well. Weber, in
regrouping his myriad of individual classes, splits the working
class between blue collar and white collar workers. This is
another of his contributions to capitalist sociology.

What a fine scheme, then, to list four classes, among which the
capitalist is not really to be found and the working class is divided
up, spread about, and misnamed. All sight of class relations has
been banished. Nominally, Weber's criterion for social classes is a
grouping of individual "class situations within which individual
and generational mobility is easy and typical." (Weber, 1968, p.
302) However, no evidence is offered to defend the use of such a
rule, nor to arrive at the particular list and description of four

classes a) to d). The alleged criterion merely introduces the theme of individual migration from one class to another; this is another idea that later sociologists took up and studied while paying no attention to relations between the classes among which a few individuals migrate.

Of course, Weber wrote on other subjects besides class. He tried to submerge the topic among them. After shifting class from the arena of production to the market, to the arena of exchange, Weber moved on to the sphere of consumption. The pattern of consumption, a person's lifestyle, Weber called the basis of grouping by status, which he opposed to class. He tried to assert that social action depended as much or more on status groupings than on class relations. Whatever the influence of status, it is clear that consumption depends on the product of necessary labor (for the working class) or of surplus labor (for the capitalist class). Status can never be more fundamental in a class society than class relations. The detailed examination of Weber's doctrine of status groupings lies outside the scope of this book.

Throughout his discussion of class, Weber drives toward the individual and his position within a given social system. Weber runs away from considering the social system itself and its character as the system of one class against another. In the study of class systems Weber wrongly emphasizes the lot of a class under a mode of production, particularly marginal changes in the fortune of individual members of classes. But the basic thing about the nature and evolution of class systems, given the fact that none is eternal, is the mode of production regarded as the system of one class and the appearance in one mode of production of a class which will replace it with another system. Weber avoided such concerns because they meant in his time as in ours the end of capitalism and the struggle of the working class to give birth to its mode of production, socialism. Therefore, Weber "illustrates 'class action' primarily as struggles within social systems rather than between social systems." (Cox, 1950, p. 227) To define class situation as market situation serves this evasion. Market analysis is concerned only with quantitative changes in prices and in marginal changes in the share of classes in the total product. The origin of this product in antagonistic social relations and its consequent stamp with the sweat of necessary and surplus labor, each in some definite proportion, is hidden. At most, market analysis can measure the share of labor power, its real price. This is the concern of business unionism, the marketing of labor power on business principles. Weber approaches the stance of trade union bureaucrats as his most leftward position. (At the same time this says that these particular labor leaders are Weberians and anti-working class in their theory of classes.) He denies the working class its own social system. Weber explicitly admits lack of interest in the course of social development. The natural law of the revenue theorists is gone. The latter, although regarding the laws of development as physical laws rather than taking social relations of production as their subject, at least tried to project the course of the capitalist system. Weber, particularly in his theory of class, abandons the question. He is a self-proclaimed thinker in the small.

Weber's outlook on classes plays a transitional role. The revenue definition had gone a certain distance, then split into two trends. On one side, the science of political economy continued to develop; on the other side, scientific thinking was abandoned in favor of sophistry and apologetics for capitalism. Weber is a transitional figure in the second, descending path. His writing shows traces of the earlier justification for exploitation, but only as vestiges of a now untenable ideological defense. Weber retained something of the class lines of division but subdivided and regrouped sections of society. He developed for capitalist sociologists a number of conceptions which they were to take up, completely shedding all references to classes as they really exist. In this sense, Weber is a seminal figure, although as clear theorist, penetrating scientist, or sharp polemicist, he holds absolutely no credentials. He made his contribution in the area of confused and fantastic abstractions, removed from both surface appearances and basic currents underlying social life. It is to detailed development of hints in Weber's writing, along with speculation on secondary changes in capitalist societies, that Weber's successors devoted themselves.

A. Occupation

12. The Substitution of Occupation for Class

a. The Concept of Occupations

When the army of workers marches off to set the means of production in motion, they disperse to a great many fronts and perform a variety of tasks. They turn lathes and operate punch presses. They type and file. They drive locomotives, hold down stations on assembly lines, and supply and maintain photocopy machines. They draw blueprints, stack pallets, guide airplanes onto runways, and take X-rays. They put up house frames and they operate computers. They repair automobiles, catalog books into libraries, dig coal, sort tomatoes, cast iron, and ring up groceries. This variety of activities gives workers a number of different occupations.

If one asks a sociologist about class, one is likely to hear about occupations.[56] Sociologists group activities into broad occupational categories. They describe how income, education, mental health, and child rearing practices vary with occupation. Elaborate methods of ranking occupations are worked out and dressed up in statistical symbolism. The principal topic used to divert attention from class is occupation.

Occupation is not class.[57] It is not the economic basis of classes. Occupation and class are related, but still they are independent concepts at their roots. The relation of the two can be studied and understood only after recognizing this independence. To cover over class by talking about occupations and putting class labels on occupational phenomena is a subterfuge of the crudest sort.

Occupations, types of work activity, are principally differentiated by the technical division of labor and the various relations of production. When men specialize in one part of the productive process, they are defining a niche within a technical division of labor. Instead of producing all the items needed for social life, they each produce only some. And instead of producing the product from raw material to completed form, they perform only one act of labor in the series needed to create the product. An intermediate product is received, an operation performed, and a further intermediate product, or a final result, handed on. The steel cube goes into the milling machine, and the operator makes it into a semi-finished engine block. The various places in this technical division of labor are sites of different occupations.[58]

While capitalist thinkers recognize the technical basis of occupation, they generally overlook another one, the relations of production other than class. Some manage and supervise, others are supervised—the relations of authority differentiate occupations. The separation of productive activity into a planning phase and a phase of executing scheduled tasks is not only a technical division of labor, but also a relation of production. The finer technical subdivision of labor into specialized sub-tasks is a consequence of the growing collective work relations, the disappearance of individual working situations. A station on an assembly line arises in this way, while an author may still research, compose, and type his manuscript. Occupations are distinguished in part by the collective or individual production relations.

But the technical division of labor and the relations of production other than class refer only to concrete labor, to labor of a definite and specific type. Regard labor as abstract labor, as labor without reference to any particular characteristics but merely as the exercised power of human muscle, nerves, and tissue in time, and occupation disappears. As laborers drawing down on the labor time available to a society in a given period, a truck driver and a miner cannot be told apart.

Classes are defined with regard to surplus labor, which can be identified only by regarding social labor in the abstract. Only by setting aside the particularities of concrete labor and looking at the flow of abstract labor in a society can we see the existence of different classes, one providing surplus labor to another class, the latter disposing of the surplus labor of the former class. It is impossible to observe both class and occupation at the same time. This fact is obvious in a capitalist society, where two persons may engage in the same concrete labor but stand in different relations to the means of production. A truck driver may own his own rig and be a petty producer, or he may be an employee of a trucking line. The two still drive trucks.[59]

We have, therefore, to trace how capitalist thinkers have confused class and occupation and to observe the real connection between class relations on the one hand and the technical division of labor and other production relations on the other hand.

b. The History of Occupational Categories

In the United States, Census officials have claimed the first social grouping framed around occupation instead of class relation to the means of production and surplus labor. William C. Hunt, a chief statistician for the Bureau of the Census, grouped "gainful workers" into the following "classes" in 1897:

A. The proprietor class
B. The clerical class
C. Skilled workers
D. The laboring class   (Alba Edwards, p. 2n.)

Carroll Wright, Hunt's director, explained the meaning of these groups by enumerating the occupations that comprised each one.

The proprietor class consists of owning farmers, "bankers, brokers, manufacturers, merchants, and dealers," as well as professionals. The clerical class is made up of salesmen and agents, bookkeepers, and clerks. Skilled workers include engineers, metal workers, printers, railroad employees, and textile workers. The laboring class consists of farmworkers, boatmen and fishermen, laborers, miners, messengers, servants, etc. (Wright, 1900, pp. 254-55)

The working class has been made to disappear. Some are in a laboring class, while others, skilled workers, are not even given a definite class name. Still other workers are in a separate clerical class. Along with the change in the basis of grouping from class relation to occupation has come a fragmentation of the growing working class into smaller groups.

Class relations cannot, however, be banished entirely. The "proprietor class" is defined on a mixed basis; Wright lists both occupations and sections of classes. A farmer must be a proprietor to be listed here, while agricultural wage workers are in the "laboring class." The list of four classes has no unified basis of definition; both occupation and class relation are used, neither one systematically.

Within the "proprietor class" are really two classes, capitalists and petty producers. In the era of trusts, jumbling the two served to hide the concentration of capital and the opposition between the petty bourgeoisie and the new monopoly capitalists.

The list of four "classes" introduces a persistent theme of occupational substitutes for class, the notion of rank and hierarchy. Classes properly defined are groups with relations and antagonisms between them. Part of the analysis of classes in a specific mode of production, like capitalism or feudalism, is to investigate and discover these relations and antagonisms. This is what Karl Marx's *Capital* is all about. The specific class relations must be discovered in the actual relations to the means of production; they are not and cannot be contained in the general notion of class. What would the corresponding relations be in the case of an occupational grouping? In the first instance, one could trace the position of occupations in the technical division of labor and in some of the relations of production. The technical position of occupations is of no essential interest for political economy and social science. It is a matter for the student of technology and the industrial administrator, and while the results of their studies contribute to political economy, they are not basic foundations prerequisite to the study of class relations. When the many occupations are grouped into broad collections, these technical relations largely disappear. Relations of production are more important, as we shall see later. But the approach of capitalist ideologists has been another one. All real relations between the groupings are lost, and in their place the vulgar analyst concerns himself with imposing a hierarchy of ranks on the list of occupational categories. Wright refers to the various occupations as "walks of activity," from "the lowest walks of activity" to "the higher walks." There are the "higher stratum" and the "lower stratum." (Wright, p. 254) This ranking of strata has become a fundamental characteristic of capitalist sociology. Sociologists prefer to avoid the term class as much as possible and to speak instead of "social stratification."

The enthusiasm for ranking arises from inability to investigate and discover the actual social relations between classes. Instead, the various occupational collections, between which there are no material connections or antagonisms, are put along some kind of scale of higher and lower. In the particular example by Hunt, it is not surprising that capitalists are at the top and workers at the bottom.

In 1938, Alba Edwards revised the occupational grouping that Hunt had substituted for class. Once again, particular occupations were collected in a set of broad categories and advertised as "a grouping that brings together all of the workers belonging to the same social-economic class." (Edwards, p. 1) Edwards arranged occupations into six main groups:

1. Professional persons
2. Proprietors, managers, and officials
3. Clerks and kindred workers

4. Skilled workers and foremen
5. Semiskilled workers
6. Unskilled workers   (Edwards, p.2)

No concept of social-economic class is given; he defines by enumerating the particular occupations comprising each group.

Comparing the 1938 list with the 1897 list, one can observe both more confusion of class with occupation and some economic developments. Edwards divided the manual occupations, represented as skilled workers and the laboring class in 1897, into three groups by approximate level of skill. The solidarity of the working class is thus further broken up by the magic of categories. The three-part division also reflects the growth of mass production and assembly line methods, which spread throughout industry after World War I.

Professional persons have been separated out from proprietors, conforming to the growth of the salaried contingent of professionals, who can no longer be grouped among owners with any semblance of reality. The proprietors have been combined with managers and officials, also a salaried group to a large extent, and the entire category pushed to a rank beneath professional persons. This is in keeping with the decline of the petty bourgeoisie in both proportion of the population and economic power.

Capitalists are nicely obscured from view in this occupational scheme. The grouping suggests that everyone is a worker. The whole collection is referred to as the "labor force" or the "gainful workers." If everyone is of one class, then classes have disappeared. The six-way division reinforces this impression, for it asserts that the only important difference is a non-class distinction of occupational category. The four-class breakdown by Hunt was obviously constructed unsystematically, reflecting both class and occupation. While a trace of the same problem remains in Edwards' grouping, proprietors are no longer the first group by themselves, but only part of the second group. Proprietorship is not regarded as a property relation but as a concrete form of work similar to management. This achieves greater consistency, at the expense of losing all reflection of class realities in the scheme.

Edwards subdivided some groups, giving twelve in all:

1. Professional persons
2. Proprietors, managers, and officials
   a. Farmers (owners and tenants)
   b. Wholesale and retail dealers
   c. Other
3. Clerks and kindred workers
4. Skilled workers and foremen
5. Semiskilled workers
   a. Semiskilled workers in manufacturing
   b. Other
6. Unskilled workers
   a. Farm laborers
   b. Factory and building construction laborers
   c. Other laborers
   d. Servant classes   (Edwards, p.2)

It is apparent that the basis of subdividing some of the groups is not occupation but industry. In the censuses of the nineteenth century, occupation and industry were not distinguished. Today they are. This is a product of the development of the division of labor, which has destroyed particular crafts and given rise to activities and skills which may be exercised with little change on a variety of subjects of labor. An iron molder had to work with iron or some other metal at most. But an assembly line operative performs a routine and simple operation at his station; whether he is turning bolts (on one of a variety of products), loading and starting a machine, or inspecting, the basic characteristics of the operation—speed, repetition, rhythm—do not depend on the particular subject of labor to a crucial degree. Edwards' introduction of industrial subdivision recognizes the partial separation of occupation and industry in the division of labor.

Edwards commented that the six groups could be even more simply regarded as two collections of groups, the "hand workers and head workers" (Alba Edwards, p. 1). The first three are mental workers; the workers with skill are manual workers. Capitalist ideologists have paid increasing attention to this theme. The division of mental and manual occupations lies at the basis of the contrast between white collar and blue collar, which in turn supports the distinction between "middle class" and "working class."[60] Historically, the appearance of this pair of "class" terms depends on the submergence of classes properly defined beneath an occupational grouping.

The twelve categories of 1938 consolidated the substitution of occupation for class. Since then the changes in census categories have been matters of detail only. The breakdown employed by the 1970 Census was as follows:

Professional, technical, and kindred workers
Managers and administrators, except farm
Sales workers
Clerical and kindred workers
Craftsmen, foremen, and kindred workers
Operatives, except transport
Transport equipment operatives
Laborers, except farm
Farmers and farm managers
Farm laborers and farm foremen
Service workers, except private household
Private household workers

References to proprietors are gone. To be an owner is merely to be one species of manager, a type of worker. Only in agriculture is there still a hint of different relations to the means of production.

Professional persons have been given a more descriptive name in recognition of the large number of occupations which in no way resemble the traditional professions of doctor, lawyer, and minister. Other changes, such as the combination of factory and other nonfarm laborers under one heading, are changes of detail.

Everyone is a worker, and therefore the only meaningful distinctions can be among workers, such as occupational distinctions. This is the message of the table. The monopoly capitalists in particular disappear from view. As the concentration of capital has raised the contradiction between their small numbers and their exploitation of an entire society to the most intense antagonism, the statisticians have simply erased such a handful of persons.

Twelve categories are too many to describe the basic lines of division in a society. They are necessarily recombined into larger groupings.

13. Class and the White Collar Occupations

a. General

There is a middle class composed largely of white collar members of the labor force—this is the main contention of writers who substitute occupation in place of class. They separate the white collar occupations (clerical, sales, managerial, and professional and technical occupations) from the blue collar workers and call them a class. This is not simply a discussion about the facts of occupation; these theories substitute the concept of occupation for that of class. The negative result of this maneuver is the important thing: attention is drawn away from relations to the means of production and from surplus labor and product.

What new "middle class" has appeared under capitalism? In class terms, none. Do white collar employees stand in a different relation to the means of production than workers, petty producers, or capitalists? No, white collar employees can all be accounted for by division among these classes. How do they stand in relation to surplus labor? Those who receive surplus-value in the form of a salary bigger than any payment for labor power have been accounted members of the capitalist class (see chapter four). When that calculation of the division of society into classes was made, no problem arose with occupation in general nor with white collar workers in particular. Those persons in white collar work who operate businesses by themselves are petty producers. A consulting engineer is as much a petty producer as a self-employed plumber or electrician. The great majority of white collar workers are sellers of their labor power, members of the working class. They must sell their ability to labor in order to survive; this is their source of income. They perform both necessary and surplus labor.[61] They cannot go into business for themselves because they lack the means of production—office buildings and equipment, hospitals and equipment, or stores and merchandise.

How to create a new class separate from the working class and diminishing its ranks is the problem faced by the capitalist-minded social theorist. The answer can only be to forget about the criterion of class and to argue from another characteristic. Occupation is the chosen one. Yet there are too many occupations, thousands of them, and even too many broad occupational groupings, a dozen or so. The super-grouping of white collar workers emerges as the vehicle of confusion.

The dividing line between white collar and blue collar occupations is not easily grounded in a theoretical distinction. Their incomes overlap; most clerks earn less than most craftsmen, for example. At one time, the distinction was supposed to be that between a wage and a salary.[62] The blue collar worker was paid for each hour; the salaried person gave his employer not hours but his whole being (often specified in rules that governed socializing and leisure activities). Supposedly, the white collar employee was something of a partner in the business or on his way to becoming a partner in return for this loose and total claim on his time. The illusion has long since gone, and today most biweekly or monthly salaries are essentially wages, as proved by the application of strict hourly equivalent rates for measured overtime.

Education is no dividing line either. Too many blue collar workers have and must have the same amount of formal education as many white collar workers.

Differences have existed between white collar and blue collar workers with regard to secondary attributes like size of income, measurement of labor time, mobility, and education. They remain, although diminished. In any event, these characteristics do not define the division of white collar and blue collar; the definition is supposed to be clear before examining these differences and similarities, on all of which there is considerable overlap between individuals from each half of the divide.

The general distinction most frequently offered as the defining difference between white collar and blue collar occupations is that between primarily mental labor and primarily manual or muscular labor.[63] Yet students of the problem have admitted that

> "it is plainly impossible to draw a hard and fast line between those occupations characterized principally by the exercise of muscular force or manual dexterity and those characterized chiefly by the exercise of mental force or ingenuity" (Alba Edwards, p. 1).

Since Edwards made this observation 40 years ago, the gray area of clerical work has become larger and grayer.[64] Edwards combined muscular force and manual dexterity to get the blue collar grouping. Many clerical jobs require as much dexterity as the average operative job and as little nonroutine use of the brain. Who is doing more mental work, a tomato sorter or a keypuncher?

The difference is not in the worker's use of mind or brute force, but in the subject of labor—the product itself or the accounting symbol. This is perhaps the most nearly solid distinction between blue collar and white collar work. This difference in the subject of labor clearly has little to do with the class relation or even with secondary social qualities of work like pay and working conditions. For various reasons, labor on symbols grows under monopoly capitalism faster than labor on products symbolized. This is the hidden basis of the growth of the white collar ranks, which capitalist writers have seized upon as a new class under capitalism.

Besides occupations working with things or symbols, there is a group of jobs whose practitioners work with people. They are included in the white collar occupations. But to call white collar workers those who work with symbols or people makes it clear what a grab bag the category is. What makes a physicist closer to a politician than to a machinist? A few occupations stand at one pole of the relations of authority or at one pole of the division of the labor of conception from the labor of executing planned tasks—managers, especially higher managers; scientists; etc. The super-grouping of white collar workers associates vast numbers of jobs which do not stand at such extremes with these few exceptional positions. There are also a number of occupations of political and social manipulation found in class society or monopoly capitalist society in particular, such as politician, clergyman, or psychoanalyst, which are placed at the head of the list of white collar occupations for the same purpose of rubbing off their attributes onto many others who do not possess them intrinsically.

In order to understand what the occupation theorists of class are doing, it is necessary to look at the several occupational groupings within the white collar category. This method is historically correct, for capitalist writers have taken up these groupings one after another as the main focus. The commentaries have followed the numerical growth of each grouping to a significant size. "White collar" once meant clerks, when this occupational grouping was expanding. Now professional and technical workers are the prime example. A growing sector received attention as the core of the so-called middle class precisely when its secondary distinguishing qualities, such as greater income, were reverting to the working-class average under the inexorable force of the class relation that opposes capitalists and workers in a capitalist society.

b. Clerks

Clerical and sales employees were 10 percent of all employees in 1880. By 1920 they were nearly 20 percent and together with wage earners they made up 70 percent of the "gainful workers" of all classes. But if they could be classified into a "middle class" with farmers, businessmen, and independent professionals, this newly defined class would comprise 38 percent of the gainful workers and serve as a counterweight to the primarily blue collar wage earners. (Spurgeon Bell, p. 10)

Since clerical employees are nearly all members of the working class by the definition of class, it was necessary to appeal to other conditions and relations in order to argue that they were "middle class." Clerks and others were told that clerks make up a middle class and differ from the (rest of the) working class because 1) their payment was in the form of a salary instead of a wage packet, 2) their earnings were greater than workers' earnings, 3) their jobs were not affected by layoffs during recessions, 4) they enjoyed better hours and working conditions, 5) their work was mental work, of a higher order than manual labor, 6) they worked with management and were entrusted with confidence and responsibility, and 7) they were more likely than blue collar workers to become part of management (in the case of men) or to advance as secretaries when their boss was promoted (in the case of women).

There was some truth to these claims, least of all to the possibility of social mobility into the capitalist class or the petty bourgeoisie.[65] The Horatio Alger myth (marry the boss's daughter) was part of the apologetic material put out by the capitalist class to clerks and sales agents. Employers told clerks that they were "professionals," too. Valid or not, none of these distinctions changed the employee status of clerks, their relation to the means of production, the hidden division of their working day into necessary labor and surplus labor, in short, their class position.

Furthermore, the "middle class" interpretation was based on the combination of two facts that were moving in opposite direction. The number of clerks was growing; this provided occupational theorists with a significant group to classify out of the working class. As the numbers grew, however, the minor distinctions between clerks and other workers shrank to insignificance. This qualitative movement the occupation theorists ignored. The underlying question is this: does class ultimately determine amount of income, working conditions, nature of work, and chance of social mobility, or do these factors exist independently of class?[66] The truth is that class is primary, while the implied answer of the apologists with their vision of a middle class was that class is irrelevant.

Honest observers already by 1930 saw the actual trend:

"Recent studies of wages and working conditions in terms of hours, occupational hazards, economic security and opportunities for advancement tend to show that the shadowy line between many of these clerical tasks and unskilled factory occupations is becoming more and more imperceptible." (Hewes, p. 552)

By 1926, weekly clerical earnings were slightly below those of manual workers (Coyle, p. 29). The difference was that manual workers earned more during relative prosperity but lost ground with the turn of the business cycle and layoffs. It was still probably true that clerical hours and benefits were better. But the gap was narrowing here, too. The principal fact is the direction of movement: from 1890 to 1924, the relative advantage of clerical pay over wages in manufacturing contracted by 15 percent.[67]

Even as regards job security, it was clear 45 years ago,

"As their numbers increase, however, clerical workers are more and more likely to be subject to the incidence of cyclical fluctuations, especially in view of the steadily increasing over-supply of office workers turned out by the schools." (*Ibid.*)

In other words, so long as the number of clerks was small, capitalists could tolerate their minor advantages in pay and conditions. They were even useful. Such differences might be the basis for campaigns to divide workers, hold out hopes to them, and recruit elements to defend capitalism. But capitalists never thought of the wages of clerical employees as anything other than an expense to hold to the minimum. In the 1840's employers used the patriarchal tone of the office relation to hold down salaries. English banks sent their clerks around to customers at Christmas time to solicit donations for a clerks' fund. The bankers did not add the charity to the regular salary, but rather subtracted it from the salary paid for December! In January 1852 the clerks at the London Joint Stock Bank staged a one-day strike. Measured in 1871, real salaries of clerks had fallen during the climactic decades of England's industrial revolution. Capitalists turned to new methods to realize the fixed goal of keeping clerical wages down. As the demand for clerks enlarged, the employing class simply had the schools train more clerks.[68] Typewriters were introduced. Employers hired women at much lower wages, breaking the prevailing wage scales. The tactics worked. By 1900, clerical pay in Britain was down to the level of skilled manual workers' wages.[69]

Today, clerical and sales workers are 26 percent of all wage and salary workers (1970 Census, Report 7A, Table 43). Their median earnings are essentially the same as those of workers in general. There is a division by sex between clerical and sales workers. Among men, sales workers run slightly ahead in median earnings, less than 10 percent, while clerks lag in pay. The position is reversed among women workers. (1970 Census, Report 7A, Table 24) Most salaries are convertible by standard formulas into hourly equivalents for purposes of overtime and the like. Clerical and sales employment fluctuates with the business cycle, although instead of layoffs, hiring freezes may be used, because of sufficiently high rates of turnover. The concrete labor of clerks has been routinized, simplified, and rendered little different from operatives' jobs. The higher mental functions are not called upon in keypunching, typing, sales counter chores, and so forth. There is just enough mental involvement to make the work tedious and exhausting. Finally, offices have become production shops in their own right, with supervisors distinct from general management. The clerk at a station on a floor with 100 fellow workers has no direct contact with management and no real chance to move up into management circles. (This was never a real possibility for most. The main effects of being in a small office with the employer centered on two other points: 1) his shorter office day, not factory hours, became the clerk's hours, too, and 2) individual self-promotion with the boss could be reflected in salary, something not open to a mass of workers paid according to a fixed schedule.)

In objective conditions, the clerical and sales occupations have approached the general working-class level in all secondary conditions and relations of production. The class relation has determined the other conditions and relations, although with some historical lag.

Today, therefore, clerical and sales workers are listed as middle class only under the cover of other confusions. They form a large chunk of the white collar employees—55 percent of white collar wage and salary workers (1970 Census, Report 7A, Table 43)—whose unexamined conditions are glossed over in the drive to construct a middle class. But while the scene of apologetic attention has shifted to professional and technical workers, the method is the same one used 50 years ago to classify clerical employees out of the working class.

c. Professionals

Two occupational groupings, the professional, technical and kindred workers and the nonfarm managers and administrators, were only nine percent of all employees in 1920, but represent 22 percent today (Spurgeon Bell, p. 10, and 1970 Census, Report 7A, Table 43). If class lines could be ignored and these occupations made the vanguard of a middle class containing the petty bourgeoisie and the other white collar workers (clerical and sales workers), then this middle class would comprise over 48 percent of the labor force and would neatly divide the working class in two (1970 Census, *ibid.*). In this way, capitalist apologists could escape the nearly complete polarization of United States society into a numerically overwhelming working class facing a narrow but dominant capitalist class.

The professional, technical and kindred occupations are made up largely of wage and salary workers. As recently as 1950, 13 percent of them were self-employed, but by 1970 the self-employed (and employees of their own corporations) were down to nine percent of all professional, technical and kindred workers. (*Ibid.*) This is roughly the same percentage of self-employed petty producers and capitalists as among the entire labor force. The professional and technical occupational grouping cuts a fairly representative section through the class structure.

Among the professions we expect to find the creative thinkers, the scientists, the practitioners of the higher arts like the author, physicist, and doctor. The work depends on the personal qualities of the individual, who has become competent by a long education or the display and exercise of exceptional ability. These persons are not innately superior—that notion is a myth—but the professions are supposed to represent those fortunate enough to receive the highest cultural and scientific training that society can offer. If this were true, then the growing numbers and percentage of professionals would demonstrate the work of capitalism in spreading civilization and ennobling work.

There are such culturally fortunate persons among the professionals, but they do not represent the bulk of the category, and their weight in it is becoming smaller. Of the professional, technical and kindred members of the working class, 30 percent are teachers. The changes occurring in other realms of the broad grouping suggest that professionalism is mostly an illusion and that "kindred," a vague term the Census uses for unsolved problems of classification, ranks with technical as the typical quality of the occupation.

For example, salaried professional, technical and kindred workers in the health industry can be grouped into the following: doctors, pharmacists, nurses, and technologists and technicians.[70] Their numbers changed from 1950 to 1970 as follows:

HEALTH PROFESSIONALS ON WAGE OR SALARY (THOUSANDS)[71]

Type	1970	Percent	1950	Percent
Doctors	134	10	84	12
Pharmacists	73	5	47	7
Nurses	917	66	497	71
Technologists and technicians	256	19	72	10
Total	1381	100	700	100

While the total number of health professional and technical workers almost doubled in 20 years, the ranks of technologists and technicians multiplied over three and a half times. All other health occupations lost relative weight to make room for them. But nurses as a percentage of the remaining health workers actually increased from 80 to 82 percent. The minority of doctors became a smaller minority. The skilled carrier of the tradition of Hippocrates, Galen, and Pasteur does not perform the bulk of health work. It has become an industry with a routinized division of labor.

There are still many self-employed doctors, more than twice as many as there are doctors on salary. This ratio did not change much from 1950 to 1970. A shift may appear in the next Census, for a polarizing trend is undeniably affecting doctors, too. From being self-employed petty bourgeois, many are becoming salaried employees while a few are becoming health industry capitalists. As with health professional and technical persons in general, the correct perspective on their social development is the class perspective. Occupational groupings that ignore the basic force of class society misrepresent the growing numbers of professionals by ignoring the simultaneous extension of capitalist organization of the work.

The eradication of the characteristics of highly trained professionals can be seen in the engineering field, too. In 1950 the Census listed 496,000 technical engineers on wage or salary and only 26,000 workers in a catchall category of non-health technicians. From 1950 to 1970, encompassing the Sputnik era, the number of engineers increased nearly two and a half times to 1,192,000. At the same time, the "technicians not elsewhere counted" grew to a category of engineering and science technicians numbering 807,000—a multiplication of 31 times.

Engineers no longer enjoy the same salary differential over the wages and salaries of workers in general. From 1929 to 1954 this differential contracted by one-third.[72] Engineers with nine or twelve years experience used to earn nearly three times as much as beginners. This was in 1929; by 1954, the advantage was less than double starting pay (Kuhn, p. 87).

Professional, technical and kindred workers in general enjoy less of a differential over other workers than in the past. Among men, their advantage over operatives dropped from 79 percent more pay in 1939 to 49 percent in 1963 (Sturmthal, p. 361).

Of the professional, technical and kindred workers on salary or wage, 70 percent are health workers, engineering and science workers, and teachers. The classic professionals are the lawyers (one percent), clergymen and religious workers (two percent), and writers, artists and entertainers (six percent). Social scientists, social workers, and personnel workers make up six percent of the professional workers.

In 1900, lawyers and judges were nine percent of all professionals, disregarding class (U.S. Census Bureau, *Historical Statistics*, Series D 123-572). Today, lawyers are less than 2.5 percent of all professionals, but they are still 15 percent of self-employed professionals, as are writers, artists and entertainers together. The old professions are still self-employed petty bourgeois or capitalists in greater than average proportions, while among professional workers in the strict class meaning of the term, they are a small part indeed.

Professional, technical and kindred occupations fall into the three classes of capitalism without forming a new middle class. While in secondary characteristics like income and skill these workers stand above the average of the entire working class, they have lost much of their exceptional position and are moving toward the average as their proportion in the labor force grows. This change confirms their membership in the working class by and large, not their separation out as a new middle class apart from it. The fading aura of the old, highly educated professional shines around those traditional occupations which still have more petty producers among them. This confirms the force of the class relation from the other side.

d. Managers

Managers and officials are divided into classes based on their relations to the means of production and to surplus labor. The percentages are as follows: workers, 75 percent; petty producers, 17 percent; and capitalists, eight percent (1970 Census, Report 7F, Table 14 and Report 7A, Table 43). Petty producers manage their own little businesses. Capitalists are those whose salaries were $25,000 or over in 1969, to approximate a dividing line at which the salary is not a payment for skilled labor but a sharing in surplus-value.[73] Most managers and administrators are working class, but the proportions of petty bourgeois and especially of capitalists among them are above the social average. The weight of managers among the wage and salary earning labor force is small, although it has been growing slowly, from 4.5 percent in 1940 to 6.8 percent in 1970. If managers were equated to capitalists or petty bourgeois, these figures would lead one to conclude that the capitalist class is growing, another erroneous result of substituting occupation for class.[74]

Nevertheless, among salaried managers one in ten is a capitalist, someone who receives surplus product produced by others. This figure takes on added significance because managers are arranged in bureaucratic hierarchies, with subordinates over whom a manager has definite authority and executives who tend to have unlimited authority over him. Within this hierarchy of authority and income, three broad levels may be distinguished, the lower, middle, and top levels.

The lower managers, the workers, are predominantly concerned with the work in hand, both the concrete and abstract labor.[75] This is the manager of the working unit or of a few working units headed by foremen or supervisors (who share many characteristics with lower managers and inflate their numbers greatly). It is required of the manager that he have the work process of the unit in his mind, and that the process occur in the manner he has anticipated it to happen. The distribution of tasks within the unit, potential interruptions and exceptions, the kind of raw material received from inputting units, the quality of the output of the unit, and the scheduling of each chore in sequence must all be the manager's concern.

Capitalism requires these managers because it prevents the rank-and-file workers from being concerned with such matters. The most important reason for this is the antagonism of class interests. Increased productiveness results in greater profits for the capitalist, not in more income or better working conditions for the workers. The manager's responsibility for the concrete labor process reflects the exclusion of the workers in general from "management's prerogatives." The manager is expected to reach the goals of the capitalist, that is, to maximize surplus labor, arranging concrete labor to achieve this goal.

It is also a capitalist practice to subdivide tasks and depend as little as possible on the skill, devotion, or ability of the individual worker. As much as possible, the power of human reason to transform nature is removed from the workers and embodied in plans, schedules, a division of labor, and machinery which appear to belong to capital, standing over the workers and against their interests. The manager has a conscious grasp on the organization of the work so that labor in general is deprived of it. Subdivided, routine, and meaningless jobs are adopted not only because they are efficient and productive (they often are not) but because leaving the powers of production in the hands of the workers would increase their strength in the class struggle at the point of production.

Marx said that "what distinguishes the worst architect from the best of bees is this, that the architect raises his structure in imagination before he erects it in reality." (*Capital*, I, p. 178) This is true of all modes of production. Under capitalism, nine workers out of ten are excluded from this human act while the tenth is required to be the architect of the work.

Another reason for breaking down jobs into a mass of routinized operations on the one hand and a handful of managerial and design positions on the other hand is to drive down wages. By reducing the training needed, a much greater number of workers, whose labor power does not include the cost of much education, are candidates for the mass of jobs. Low wages can be paid.

There is a differential between the earnings of managers and of workers in general. Excluding salaries over $25,000, the managerial bonus was 42 percent in 1970.[76] The robbery of involvement in production leads to a robbery of the paycheck of nonmanager workers. The manager is left with a premium to induce his mind to follow and anticipate the contours of the work. With their low pay, most workers reject these concerns as being of no application to them. They arrive on time and leave on time; in between it is management's job to break the bottlenecks in supplies and so forth. Furthermore, "job involvement" under capitalism can only mean helping capitalists to step up the exploitation of oneself and one's fellow workers.

Most managers are lower level managers, a group of workers. If each middle manager oversees five managers, then 80 percent of all managers are lower level managers.[77] The middle managers may be regarded as the bulk of the capitalist managers on salary, those roughly indicated by earnings in 1969 of $25,000 and over. They coordinate various units which may have no immediate relation to each other in the flow of work. They report to the top, concentrating information and selecting problem areas to call to the notice of their superiors. They receive orders from above and recast them to appropriate form and emphasis for their subordinates. Activities like budgeting occupy much of their attention.

In moving from lower to middle manager, the ratio of concern with concrete labor versus concern with abstract labor and surplus labor swings decisively toward the latter. A middle manager was frequently the head of a business absorbed by a monopoly. This must be the case less frequently today, but the role of the middle manager in class terms is to manage a division or functional service unit within the corporation in capitalist fashion. He applies the criteria of profit accounting, pushes the organization below him to provide more surplus labor, and searches for profitable ways to increase productivity.

The top executives take care of the strategic problems of the owning family or handful of interests to whom the corporation belongs. Sometimes they are members of the family or of the monopoly capitalist class in their own right, that is, independently of holding the position of chairman, president, top corporate vice-president, or division chief.[78] More often they are carefully educated, groomed, and tested middle managers. They serve at the pleasure of the owners, but the latter do not usually supervise them closely.[79] In absolute terms, they are wealthy; a chief executive easily piles up several million dollars during his tenure. In relative terms within the monopoly capitalist class, they never achieve real economic power apart from their office.

These men have never taken over a big corporation from the magnates who own it.[80] Typical of top managers are the 94 chief executive officers (presidents or chairmen of the board) among the top 300 industrial corporations studied by Larner. In 1962 and 1963, their annual salary and bonuses were $158,000, which was increased by $23,000 from their common stock in the company for which they worked (Larner, p. 260; figures are medians). The total remuneration of top executives runs at several times these amounts. Other methods of paying them besides huge salaries and bonuses include stock options for profitable purchase and sale of stock, compensation deferred for several years until separation or retirement, "dividend units" entitling one to dividends on fictitious shares of stock for life, and corporate payment for numerous perquisites. The owners are also afraid that top executives will use their power to extract money from the company by kickbacks and setting up supplier firms with confederates.

The top executives run a system constructed to make the production activities of corporations with tens and hundreds of thousands of employees serve the profit interest of one or a few capitalist families that own the corporation. A pioneer of this system, Alfred Sloan of General Motors, has described its goals and basic methods.

Sloan, son of a capitalist, obtained a degree in engineering at the Massachusetts Institute of Technology and with the help of his father's investment became an independent businessman at the Hyatt Roller Bearing Company. Seeing the inevitability of monopoly capitalism, he combined his interests into General Motors, where he became president and then chairman of the board.

Sloan, neither an industrial nor marketing innovator, contributed a system of organization.

"The General Motors type of organization—co-ordinated in policy and decentralized in administration—not only has worked well for us, but also has become standard practice in a

large part of American industry. Combined with the proper
financial incentives [to managers, not production workers],
this concept is the cornerstone of General Motors' organizational policy." (Sloan, p. xxiii)

By co-ordination in policy, Sloan means that the aim of all actions
must be profit for the capital of the owners, the du Pont family.
The du Ponts own the controlling interest in General Motors,
shared with the Morgan financial group. The system "has worked
well for us," the owners and their chief lieutenants like Sloan. He
wrote a basic organizational study for GM in the early 1920's. "It
distinguished policy from administration of policy, and specified
the location of each in the structure." (p. 55) Specifically, basic
policy resides with powerful committees within the board of
directors: an executive committee which should "confine itself
more particularly to principles which should be presented to it"
from below for its judgment (p. 100) and then a finance committee
to look at whether return on investments would be the most
profitable use of du Pont capital (p. 114).

Operations, however, must be decentralized; it is a mistake to
think that maximum control by a few is achieved by their giving
as many of the orders as possible. Administration, as Sloan calls
it, must be dispersed, so long as it follows policy. Here, Sloan
believed that "only individuals can administer policy." (p. 100)
The problem was to hand out administrative responsibility while
creating the mechanisms that would demand, enable, insure, and
reward the faithful pursuit of General Motors' goal, which Sloan
clearly recognized was surplus-value:

"The primary object of the corporation, therefore, we declared
was to make money, not just to make motor cars." (p. 64)

One mechanism was what businessmen now call the profit
center. For each division of the organization, an attempt was
made by internal accounting rules to measure the capital tied up
in the division and the profit resulting from it. Prior to this setup,

profits flowed on the company's internal books between divisions, giving managers explanations for the performance of their division that amounted to passing the buck. Once profit centers were defined, the du Ponts and Sloans had "an objective basis for the allocation of new investment." (p. 48) Sloan is explicit about the concern with the rate of profit, not its simple magnitude (p. 49). If the figures had indicated that GM should move into importing beef as an expansion of its purchase of natural leather for Cadillacs, and give up making automobiles overnight, then it would be done.

Sloan and GM's owners thus decided that in a capitalist system, capitalist managers had to be motivated and measured by individual profit. Certain advantages of scale were foregone or recognized to be unattainable, while a kind of departmentalism, attention solely to the interests of one's own unit, was encouraged. Then layers of managers coordinated departmental impulses. Sloan himself, for example, received the managers' forecasts of what they could do in the next four months.

"After consulting with the vice president in charge of finance, I approved or modified the production schedule for each division in the light of these forecasts." (p. 127)

That is, Sloan reviewed the overall uses of the capital by checking with finance, then set the goals of the managers. They carried out the work within these limits:

"Thus the division manager still bought the materials, but they were permitted to buy only enough at a time to make the number of cars and trucks specified in their approved production schedules." (p. 127)

This is the relation of policy and administration. I will approve the shopping list personally (policy), but you the manager go to the store and buy the items (administration). And Sloan speaks of these managers as the "men in charge" of "the prosecution of those operations." (p. 140)

It was demanded in this system that innovation be proposed from below. The managers must identify problems and prospects from the actual scenes of work, the only real source of them, and propose solutions and projects. Beneath the finance and executive committees, an operating committee of general corporate and division officers was set up to manage this task (p. 113). Sloan insisted "that the Divisions initiate their respective policies and problems and refer their solution to the Operations Committee for check and approval." (p. 175) If funds were required, then the executive committee of the board of directors decided—on the basis of expected profitability, of course. The committee was familiar with the strategic interests of the du Ponts and the financial groups who own General Motors, and no doubt they took them into account to calculate profit at this higher level.

This is the bureaucracy that top management oversees. Its qualities flow from the nature of monopoly capitalism: an extremely narrow band of owners seeking to hold on to the means of production in the face of ever more socialized and collectivized forces of production. The "complexity of modern organization" and other vacuous evasions do not explain bureaucracy. Bureaucracy is the product of maximizing profit, using capitalist motives and personnel, individualistic and predatory when not watched, to reach the profit goal of the du Ponts or other stars in the oligopolistic firmament. As much as possible, the living activity of production must be removed from the rank-and-file workers and embodied instead in systems, organizations, and machines directed by a few managers and technicians, leaving only motor force, whether of arm or brain, to be exerted by the workers. This system is what the managerial occupation at its middle and top levels represents, the specifically capitalist coordination of social productive activity. It is a way for capital to invade and rob the living powers of labor.

"Managerial decentralization is the almost inevitable corollary to centralization of power to form policy. It becomes more thoroughgoing and uniform in application the greater the centralization. Thus it has become more complete in such firms as the American Telephone and Telegraph Company, the General Motors Corporation, the German Dye Trust, and the German General Electric Company than elsewhere in the capitalistic world. So close and rigid is this connection between managerial decentralization and policy centralization that it can be taken as almost axiomatic that growth of the former is a necessary function of expansion of effective monopoly-type power to enforce uniform compliance with policy decisions from the apex of the pyramid down through all layers to the base." (Brady, p. 355-56)

Here, in the dominance of the class relation over other relations of production, is to be found the key to the white collar occupations.

e. Absurdities of the Notion of a White Collar Class

By examining in turn the occupational groupings within the white collar supergrouping, one finds no new class. Instead, each grouping can be divided into the three basic classes of capitalist society. Today, clerks are overwhelmingly workers, professionals as a whole reflect class sizes in the United States (with variations in specific occupations), and managers have the smallest majority of workers and the largest contingent of capitalists among them. When citing the white collar occupations as the foundation of a middle class, occupation theorists analyze not the class relation, but various conditions of the work and the workers to argue that they are something other than workers in most cases—because of pay, working conditions, nature of the job, and so forth. This change of subject matter while pretending to talk about class cannot be justified.

First, it is up to these theorists to refute the class criterion and to argue that other "factors" should not only supplement it but replace it. This they fail to do. The closest approach that occupation theorists make to a comparison of the class criterion and

other factors is to throw out the relation to the means of production because it does not explain social consciousness by itself.
Lockwood wrote about the clerk that "although he shares the
propertyless status of the manual worker, the clerk has never
been strictly 'proletarian' in terms of income, job security and
occupational mobility." (Lockwood, p. 204) He said this in a book
published in 1958, when the narrowing of differences in pay and
so forth had already gone far. Lockwood included all these
additional influences in the definition of class position (p. 15) on
the grounds that "To explain variations in class consciousness it is
necessary to look for variations in class position" and that "the
definition of class that is adopted can be justified only by its
usefulness in the explanation of particular and concrete events."
(p. 213) Not many writers have dared to be as explicit as
Lockwood, displaying such obvious bankruptcy of scientific
method. To call every outlook a form of class consciousness,
hence the reflection of a corresponding class, is mere playing with
words. One might as well reject the biological criteria for determining the sex of a person and call homosexuals a new sex, since
to explain variations in sexual consciousness it is necessary to
look for variations in sexual position. Although the homosexual
male shares the glandular status of the heterosexual male, he has
never been strictly "male" in terms of marital patterns, preferred
entertainments, and social setting. While occupation theorists in
general are more reticent than Lockwood about their theory,
they share with him 1) the lack of discussion of surplus labor, the
crux of the question of private property ownership, and 2) a
desire to explain immediately items of social consciousness like
voting and opinion polls, which they regard as the only interest-
ing "particular and concrete events."

Second, contrary to the reversal of class relation and secondary
relations which occupation theorists carry out under the name of
class, the examination of specific occupational groupings proves
that class dominates secondary factors like pay, working conditions, and the nature of the job itself. Capitalists exploit workers
of surplus labor, doing away with any special conditions of a

growing "elite" occupation. As a grouping becomes larger within the working class, its income and benefits diminish toward the average, at least for the workers in the grouping, and the concrete work is transformed, routinized, and made less a matter of the worker's ability and more a property of the capitalist machinery, division of labor, and organization of the work. This was seen in the case of clerks, professionals, and managers. The occupation theorist ignores developments within the job while counting the increase of persons in the category. The use of the old name for an essentially new category becomes inaccurate and misleading; yet writers speak of professionals after even the Census has reflected the tension between the name and the fact in the awkward label of professional, technical and kindred workers (mostly kindred).

The general motion of capitalism has been to attack successively more elaborate, more "elite" occupations and subject them to the laws of surplus-value. This is reflected in the search of occupation theorists for new candidates to staff the middle class or its vanguard.

There are countertendencies, to be sure. Technological developments outpace capitalist class relations, for example, when a shortage of computer programmers existed. But each exception pales in comparison with the swelling general tendency. It is also true that some occupational differences in conditions remain; complete uniformity never prevails. The differences are small in comparison with the gulf between classes.

Therefore, when the occupation theorist speaks of a new middle class, the basic questions about class remain to be answered. How is this class different in its relation to the means of production from the three classes of capitalist society? Every class has a mode of production it represents and strives for. What would be the middle class mode of production? Or is this the first class without its own mode of production, a class whose interest is, depending on the fancy of the particular writer, the same as that of the capitalists (capitalism) or that of the workers (socialism)? If capitalism, we have a non-capitalist class whose basic interest lies in capitalism! We have the neat trick by which the growth of a non-capitalist but pro-capitalist class counters the polarization of classes. In real terms this is to say that some workers' basic interest is to collaborate in perpetuating capitalism, an older and more familiar position. On the other hand, "middle class socialism" always turns out to be something other than socialism, something opposed to proletarian interests, as will be seen later.

f. White Collar Occupations and Other Relations of Production

One more fact has emerged in the examination of specific occupational groupings. Although white collar occupations are primarily working class according to class relations, they also contain within them the greatest weight of various other relations of production. In a capitalist society, these relations of production, while distinct from the class relations, are nonetheless colored and shaped by the dominant relation in a class society.

Managers represent at one pole the capitalist influence on the relations of authority in production. Very simply, the work is organized and supervised for maximum extraction of surplus-value. From the aspect of abstract labor, the act of production is the production of surplus-value. The manager represents this capitalist approach to the organization of work; his job is to maximize profits. Even the working-class manager will therefore be the bearer of a capitalist influence on this production relation. This is a contradiction within the working class that reflects the basic class contradiction. It is a real contradiction. One example of it is in the determination of the manager's salary. On the one hand, his individual position, success, and pay depend on his performance of the job, including serving the growth of surplus-value. On the other hand, the pay of the bulk of lower and lower-middle managers is some percentage above the pay of the workers supervised. If their pay rises, so must his. The bulk of managers and their earnings are part of the wage costs of the capitalist, not a sharing of surplus-value.[81] But their role in a production relation of authority also affects their pay.

Salaried engineers, designers, and other professionals similarly reflect capitalist influence on the separation of manual and mental labor. The production process they design aims to create surplus-value, not only specific commodities. Part of their task is to serve this goal. The same contradiction between class position and capitalist influence on another production relation exists here.

Another capitalist influence on the division of mental and manual labor (which is also a relation between persons in work) is manifest in those occupations which are not directly economic. The ruling class is served by a number of theoretical, political, ideological, and literary representatives who think about and formulate plans and culture for the capitalists and push fraudulent ideas, values, political movements and such on other classes. Performing these functions, a certain number of writers, professors, political operatives, clergymen, and so forth are inducted into the capitalist class. The existence of these cultural representatives and servants of the capitalists has an influence on many other cultural workers whose class position is working class. The working newspaper reporter has before him as one path forward the attempt to become a columnist like James Reston. To impress the editor is to demonstrate one's ability and willingness to put service to the capitalists ahead of the duty to make words reflect the truth.

It will be remembered that the relations of authority in production and the division of mental and manual labor also were the basis for petty bourgeois consciousness. In a capitalist society, petty bourgeois tendencies serve to increase capitalist influence. The petty producer spontaneously develops, unless forces counteract it, toward bourgeois life as the natural progress and growth of individualism in the basic relation of production. The successful petty producer becomes a capitalist. All that tends

toward the maintenance of petty bourgeois influence in professional and managerial occupations also merges with and supports
capitalist influence on these relations of production.

These facts change neither the criterion of class nor the objective class position of specific persons. One relation divides people
into classes. Furthermore, the class relation is the dominant one
and determines the evolution of the other production relations.
When looking at occupations, for example, we find that continual
"proletarianization" of secondary attributes is occurring. That is,
the various conditions and relations represented by an occupation
are pressed, for the mass, into line with their working-class
position.

The picture is the very opposite of the one drawn by theorists
who substitute occupation for class. The polarization of a few
capitalists against the mass of workers is increasing, both quan-
titatively and qualitatively. The ranks of the working class are
becoming ever more extensive, comprising a vast legion of workers, blue collar and white collar. The detour of occupational
analysis arrives at the same conclusions about the size and weight
of classes in the United States today. In all walks of life we find
the working class. Everywhere, the workers' lives are shaped
fundamentally by the antagonism between their class and the
narrow capitalist class.

14. White Collar Occupations and the Notion of Post-Industrial Society

In this and the next three chapters we criticize particular authors who set white collar occupations against the working class.

According to Daniel Bell, societies have evolved from pre-industrial to industrial and now, with the United States leading, to post-industrial society. (Bell, 1976, p. 38) These are his names for economies with a large agricultural, machine industry, or modern service sector respectively. "A post-industrial society is based on services." (p. 37) What are its classes? Bell says, "Not only are we a white-collar society, we're quite definitely a *middle-class* society." (p. 38) The basis for this is that "In large measure, occupation is the most important determinant of class and stratification" (Bell, 1973, p. 15).

Although in passing he cites the vulgar Weberian definition of class, "the bare, abstract materiality of 'class' based on market position" (p. 70n.), he makes no use of it. Bell is an occupation theorist.

Not all white collar occupations get Bell's equal attention. He directs our attention to "the scientists and engineers, who form the key group in the post-industrial society." (p. 17) This becomes the broader assertion, "The central occupational category in the society today is the professional and technical." (p. 136) Finally, he adds up all white collar persons and names them the middle class. The aura of the scientist in a white frock amidst the equipment of a modern laboratory is supposed to form a halo around the other white collar settings: the cavernous barn of the aircraft company with hundreds of draftsmen at their tables, the department of women at keypunch machines on the windowless fifth floor of the bank as well as the sales girls, typing pools, and so forth. Let occupation substitute for class, but make one work setting symbolize the variety necessarily included in any occupational aggregation.

In passing, Bell tries a few digs at the notion of class.

"Is the proletariat, or the working class, *all* those who work for wages and salaries? But that so expands the concept as to distort it beyond recognition. (Are all managers workers? Are supervisors and administrators workers? Are highly paid professors and engineers workers?)" (p. 148)

As a first test, the revenue definition ("work for wages and salaries") is far more accurate than occupational schemes. But this is not the essence of class. The working class consists of those who must sell their labor power because they have no other source of income and because they do not own means of production with which they might work in some other way. Many managers are workers, although if we look at whether they work for someone else (petty producers do not) and at whether they are really selling their labor power or sharing in surplus-value, we find that some are not workers. Most engineers are workers, too, and it does not help to borrow their numbers to bolster the image of the capitalist professor, highly paid by a major Ivy League university such as Columbia or Harvard, who has become an ideological spokesman for the monopoly capitalist class, supplementing his salary with consultations, speeches, royalties, and other bonuses. Such a man is a member of the capitalist class, even while he is denying the existence of capitalism and substituting fantasies of a "post-industrial society."

What industries represent the post-industrial mode of life to Bell? "The first *modern* industry is chemistry, because you have to have a theoretical knowledge of the properties of the macromolecules you are manipulating in order to know what to produce." (Bell, 1976, p. 37) Electronics, plastics, and computers are other examples. While there may be more scientists working in these industries than most others, it is not a scientist's service or information alone that produces and delivers a petrochemical like gasoline. He cannot fashion a macromolecule with his bare hands. People in many occupations do the work. They are workers first and members of an occupation second. The electronics industry is known for its exploitation of the unskilled, assembly-line labor of nonunionized women and of workers in low-wage countries like south Korea.

Furthermore, these industries require the most invested capital in capitalist terms. Chemicals and petrochemicals require elaborate refineries and plants—real assemblies of special metals in elaborate piping, valves, measuring instruments, and so on, as well as the raw material, the crude oil. In a capitalist society, the determining group, the "major class of the emerging new society" is not "a professional class, based on knowledge rather than property." (Bell, 1973, p. 374) It is the owners of the refineries and the leases on the oil fields who wield power, the Rockefellers, the Pews, and in chemistry proper the du Ponts and the Olins—in other words, a handful of monopoly capitalists.

So much for "class" changes in the producing industries now allegedly based on professional occupations. Regarding the economy as a whole, Bell emphasizes the theme that the United States today has a large service sector. He has specific services in mind: not the old household and domestic services, nor services auxiliary to production of goods like transportation and distribution, but "such human services as education and health" and "professional and technical services." (pp. 37-38) Yet when it comes to the statistics, Bell moves the old services back in to bolster the figures. Here is his division of industries and occupations into a goods sector and a service sector:

> Goods sector: agriculture, forestry, and fisheries; manufacturing; mining; construction.
>
> Services sector: trade, finance, and real estate; transportation and utilities; professional service; domestic and personal service; government (not elsewhere classified). (Bell, 1973, p. 130)

Only professional service and part of government represent the image that Bell wants to impose on the entire economy. But it helps the statistics to include transportation and utilities from industrial society, as well as the distribution sector of trade and finance, which is partially an outgrowth of industry and partially a feature of monopoly capitalism, not "post-industrial society."

Some services are growing. When food was prepared in the home, it was purchased at the market as a good. Restaurants were part of the "pre-industrial" sector of domestic services. Today, they are being transformed. Fast food service increases while hamburger sales in the market are not holding pace relatively. The meaning of this change cannot be understood in industrial terms alone. The mode of production, in class terms, must be examined. More women must go to work because the husband cannot earn enough or because, the family not surviving, individual women live alone or with their children. While the wages of one earner no longer support a family, the intensity of labor mounts. In every minute at work, more attention is required and nervous exhaustion increases. Child care is unavailable, forcing working women into makeshift arrangements. Consequently, home preparation of food declines. It is too much to do at the end of the day; the wife is arriving home from work just like the husband. Other errands seem to take more time —shopping, medical visits, and straightening out the error of some government or credit bureaucracy. The result: there is only time to grab a fast bite to eat.

In a socialist United States, food service will move into the factories, shops, and offices. Canteens will become integral parts of them, not the bad institutional food services of today. Fast food parlors will diminish. The service aspect grows, but the class character changes entirely.

This is one aspect of the growth of services. Another is that the reproduction of labor power requires more services. These are the education and health sectors of which Bell speaks. As man's power over nature increases, his labor power naturally requires more care and preparation before its application to work.[82] The greater integration of man into production that occurs in this sense, while his muscular involvement decreases, is still part of the total process, part of the alteration of matter which an educated person will help to set in motion.

There is no escape from the class relations of the mode of production. Under capitalism, the education and health of the working class are never equal to the needs of the process of production. The workers fight for every increase of expenditure in these fields and win it only by bitter struggle. Periodic crises and growing general stagnation under monopoly capitalism mean fiercer assaults by the capitalists on the workers' education and health. If there is a temporary boom and bottleneck in educated labor, the capitalists move to break workers' bargaining power. For example, the post-Sputnik shortage of engineers became a glut with the end of the Vietnam war, when these engineers were in the middle of their working lives. At the same time, capitalism tries to make such services into vendible commodities on which a profit can be made. When this happens, services appear in the Gross National Product of a market economy. Part of the growth of services is not a technical development but rather an expansion of activity organized under capitalist and state-capitalist relations.

The notion of post-industrial society has its uses for combating class consciousness with another attempt to look at occupation instead, spinning out cheap philosophy about information versus production and covering up the private ownership of the means of production. Bell writes, "One of the features of an industrial society was the existence of deep conflicts between capitalists and workers" (Bell, 1976, p. 38). Half hoping to dazzle the working class, half believing himself that class conflict can be eliminated from capitalism, Bell speaks of post-industrial society in his service to the monopoly capitalist class. Will post-industrial society be capitalist or socialist? Avoid the very idea of a mode of production with its specific production relations. Was industrial society built under capitalism (for example, England) or can it be built under socialism (for example, China)? Cover up the question with a non-class label. Bell misrepresents the changing character of the forces of production in order to ignore the relations of production. To do this, he employs occupation as a substitute for class.

15. White Collar Occupations and the Notion of a New Working Class

Looking at occupation in place of class, writers who defend capitalism take the growth of professional and technical occupations to mean the creation of a new middle class.[83] Therefore, the anti-capitalist analysis should regard these occupations as a new working class, or so it seems to some theorists.[84]

These writers speak in the name of the new technical, scientific, and cultural workers and their social problems. Aware of the numerical growth of these occupations, they observe:

"But as these occupations have grown they have become proletarianized. Formerly independent professions have become routine and bureaucratized. The pay is sometimes better and the working conditions are usually less hazardous than in factory work . . . But the educated white-collar worker is increasingly powerless, alienated and exhausted by work." (Boyte and Ackerman, p. 46)

The members of the new working class are equipped to make creative contributions to society, but capitalism prevents it:

"And technicians, engineers, students, researchers discover that they are wage earners like the others, paid for a piece of work which is 'good' only to the degree that it is profitable in the short run. They discover that long-range research, creative work on original problems, and the love of workmanship are incompatible with the criteria of capitalist profitability" (Gorz, p. 104).[85]

Since the tyranny and coercion of capital blocks the creative impulse, one requirement of the new working class is liberation from this authority:

"For scientific workers, . . . they cannot exercise their creative praxis unless they bow to the tyranny of capital" (Gorz, p. 113).

" . . . emancipation from the tyranny of capital becomes a fundamental demand." (*Ibid.*)

"It is truly impossible to order around the skilled worker of the pioneer industries [nuclear, chemical, automated factories, etc.]" (Gorz, p. 112).

There are "visions of a qualitatively new society growing out of rebellion against coercion." (Boyte and Ackerman, p. 56)

These writers agree that capitalism has largely provided for the workers' material needs, or at least those of the new working class. The basis of struggle cannot be against material deprivation but must be against constricting authority instead.

" . . . poverty can no longer be the basis of the struggle for socialism." (Gorz, p. 3)

"Capitalism in the United States, and very likely in Europe and Japan, has passed a watershed of sorts; it has attained sufficient material prosperity for a majority of the working class that the revolution can no longer be based solely on rebellion against material deprivation." (Boyte and Ackerman, p. 59)

"This conflict no longer essentially concerns the work situation, nor the exploitation of work, which is often highly paid." (Gorz, p. 112)

" . . . the workers move towards self-management . . . of the means of production" (Gorz, p. 120).

Isn't this narrow thinking on the part of these self-appointed spokesmen of the new working class? It is not enough to say, "But while keeping in mind the continuing importance of the revolt against material deprivation, it is also important to be aware of the rising role of the revolt against coercion, which is of course related." (Boyte and Ackerman, p. 57f.) Poverty still exists for a large number of workers. There are many million more persons in low-paying jobs; black women working as janitors; families broken because the man, unable to support the family, has had to leave while the woman and two children join other welfare mothers in struggle simply to obtain clothing for their children and repairs on rat-infested tenements; "old" workers in their fifties sacked from declining industries and agriculture, unable to get new work; young men of the ghetto, out of high school, college unimaginable, drifting on the streets because the employers have no work for new entrants into the labor force—there are many million more such workers under "advanced" capitalism than there are members of the new working class.

Furthermore, the lot of the impoverished workers weighs upon the entire working class, affecting its wages and working conditions. The employers use them as a threat, an example, a reserve of labor, and a source of insecurity for workers up the line. The steady workers are driven harder, because others are ready to take their places, says the boss. The blue collar worker cannot think about pressing for technical apprenticeship on the job to upgrade his skills; keeping up on wages and job security is enough of a problem. The college-educated white collar workers fear layoff and trim their sails accordingly, because a long period of unemployment may lead to blue collar work and loss of the career. All along the line, the existence of hunger, unemployment, and job insecurity gives the capitalists a weapon against all workers. New working class workers do not live on an economic island that separates them from other workers in this respect; class relations affect all members of the working class, and the theoreticians of the new working class are doing their claimed constituency a disfavor to suggest otherwise.

Poverty alone has never been the basis of the struggle for socialism. Gorz speaks as if once it were but no longer. Poverty testifies to the life-and-death nature of the class struggle. But had it been the basis of the struggle for socialism, revolutionaries would have concentrated on the poorest lumpenproletarians[86] or share-croppers as the vanguard instead of on the working class. It is not poverty, but exploitation of the working class by the capitalist class that has always been and remains the basis of the class struggle and the fight for socialism. Capitalism imposes the struggle for existence, for maintaining a standard of living, and against dangerous and life-shortening working conditions on nearly all workers. Exploitation means that the workers provide surplus labor to the employer, that the capitalist class is receiving the surplus product and using it against the working class. The capitalists make the working class itself forge the chains which bind it, increase the social distance between the classes and, therefore, force the relative lowering of the working class.

Yet Gorz hints that the new working class is not exploited, that the conflict is not over exploitation, for the technician or cultural worker "is often highly paid" (p. 112). The capitalists hire only workers they need to hire. The work force is only so large as maximizes the rate of profit under the given and foreseen conditions. Not one extra technician is hired, and his salary represents his paid labor only, for the capitalist calculates (in inverted terms) the unpaid labor which makes it worthwhile to hire the last technician added to the staff.

For all their blindness to exploitation, these writers seem to have put their finger on something in the alienation of the new working class, the suppression of creativity, the coercion from above, the clash between the instinct of workmanship and the demands of short-range profit, the heavy hand of authority. Work is not only exploited, it is alienated.[87]

The descriptions often reflect experience, but the analysis is wrong. It does not deepen the insight but veers off into a dead end. Alienation can only be understood with a class analysis of exploitation. Taken by itself, or given the primary emphasis, the theme of alienation reflects the stand and outlook, not of the proletarian, but of the petty bourgeois.

First, those who dwell on alienation pit the individual against authority, regarding all authority as coercion.[88] Gorz objects to "the hierarchy of the enterprise" (p. 36), the very existence of direction, supervision, and command. This is the cry of the individual producer who does not want to work collectively, who refuses to submit his work efforts to the coordinated plan of the whole. It is no accident that Gorz portrays the new working class in agreement with the petty producer, like the small farmer, on this point.

"At the bottom, in the technologically most advanced industries—as well as in the professionally qualified sectors of the small and medium peasantry—the workers move towards self-management (cooperative and regional, in the peasants' case) of the means of production" (p. 120).[89]

Authority exists in any mode of production with collective relations of production. This includes both developed capitalism and socialism. In neither society can a small group of workers in one factory go off on its own. In neither do the technicians decide by themselves what they would like to work on and how they would like to do the work. The inferiority of capitalism to socialism is not at all a difference between authority and the lack of it, but between bureaucratic authority and democratic centralism. Bureaucratic authority serves profit and is a necessary system for the exploiting capitalist class. Democratic centralism does not abolish authority but establishes the authority of the entire working class over all spheres of life and work. The individual worker, far from being sent off on his own, is called to join with others in planning for the interest of the entire class, across all lines of occupation, department, enterprise, and local interest. Then this authority is necessarily embodied in institutions, committees, and leaders during the actual performance of the work. Here, too, the entire working class is called on to check up on, watch over, and contribute to this exercise of authority. New ways of mass management appear one after another on the road from socialism to communism. In the theory on the new working class there is not a hint of this. These writers are looking backward to the individual producer, not forward to socialism.

The basic conflict in class societies is between one class and another, not between the individual and society. Exploitation of one class by another is the issue. Alienation, the feeling of isolation from society, of external repression of one's capabilities, being, and so forth, is mostly a concern of petty bourgeois intellectuals.

Second, those who make alienation their theme do not grasp the reality of working conditions in the buzz words of "coercion," "creativity," and "manipulation." These three words with some synonyms fill 90 percent of the discussion of the new working class theorists when they analyze the new workers. This view is, in the philosophical aspect, an idealist one: some spiritual impulse of the new worker is thought to be suppressed by the capitalist's orders. No abstract creativity, however, rests within a person, nor any primal instinct or id (as Herbert Marcuse, whom Gorz praises, would have it). The problems of the technicians and the cultural workers are specific results of their working conditions. The three nuclear engineers who quit General Electric in 1976 over the issue of building more nuclear power reactors quit because the company and the government hid specific findings of their research. Newspaper reporters are cynical not because they are prevented from writing great novels and short stories, but because they are assigned to select remarks from the man in the street that distort the public workers' strike going on, because they must conduct pleasant interviews with degenerate celebrities and turn in favorable stories about them, and because they must transcribe police statements about a police shooting incident but ignore the obvious refutation coming from a framed-up worker or militant. This is not a problem of authority, coercion, or suppression of creativity in general, nor is the solution to "free" the technician or the reporter to do what he individually feels right. Socialism liberates these workers by re-establishing their ties with the rest of the working class and asking them to draw on the wisdom of the masses and learn from them, as much as it requests them to devote their specially developed talents to popular service.

Gorz appears to have a social outlook when he says,

" . . . he [the educated worker] furnishes it [his labor power] as a capital of ability, knowledge, and experience accumulated during a social process of upbringing, education, research, and communication. And this labor power is worthless in itself except insofar as it articulates with the labor power of others in social recognition, collaboration, and interchange." (p. 101)

This apparently social outlook turns out to be the falsely collective theory of the bourgeois social contract, of the free individual who bargains with others for his own good first. Gorz insists that this labor power "has value only by virtue of its own ability to organize its relationships with the forces of others" (p. 111-112). It is not the content of the work, whether it serves capitalism or socialism, that interests the theorists of the new working class. No, it is the process by which the individual grudgingly submits to the collective that they pinpoint as crucial to liberation. Gorz's expressions, if taken seriously as the words of a socialist, are extraordinary on this point. Of the skill and education of the new technical and cultural workers, he declares "that it [this skill] *is* the worker himself, that it belongs to him by right, and that he has the right to determine its social use" (p. 110).

Third, those who make alienation their theme separate the new workers from the working class as a whole. They are elitist about it. Gorz asserts that "qualified workers are no longer (and will become less and less) interchangeable vessels of physical energy" (p. 111). He emphasizes the new worker's individual skill and ability, when the progress of technique proves just the opposite, that anyone under proper conditions can develop a skill, and furthermore, that skills are best exercised under the direction of the collective, who are fully capable of understanding a "genius," of training substitutes, and of rearranging work as necessary. But for Gorz, "They possess it in their own right because they themselves acquired it, because they are in the best position to know how it should be utilized" (p. 111-112).

In this respect Gorz consciously distinguishes between the new working class and the old. Someday the former will be a majority, but the future can be handled later. In the meantime, here and now (and hence with the existing barriers to education), Gorz claims for the new workers a higher sensitivity, higher capacities which in other men are only a potential.

> "For the semi-skilled workers, the dominant contradiction is between the active, potentially creative essence of all work, and the passive condition to which they are doomed by the repetitive and pre-set tasks dictated by assembly line methods, tasks which transform them into worn-out accessories to the machine, deprived of all initiative. For the highly skilled workers, on the other hand, the dominant contradiction is between the active essence, the technical initiative required in their work, and the condition of passive performers to which the hierarchy of the enterprise nevertheless still condemns them." (Gorz, p. 36)

When one worker is denied the chance to exercise the love of workmanship (p. 104), it wears him out and makes him hopeless.

When the new worker meets the same capitalist obstacle, this is a contradiction with his active essence. For the average, semi-skilled worker, his creative essence is only potential, that is, of no real force (only a moral duty to realize in the future), while the highly trained new workers have an active essence being repressed here and now. Why the difference, except to foster elitism and split the working class?

This theme is linked to individual ownership, which the sham proletarian thinker Gorz champions:

" . . . the skilled workers of the leading industries, in the minority today but the majority of tomorrow, possess *in their own right,* unlike the classic proletarians, the labor power they lend. They possess it in their own right because they themselves acquired it" (p. 111-112).

The skill that was the result of a social process of upbringing has suddenly become a private possession!

Writers on alienation take an individualistic approach instead of a class approach; they view the work problems of educated workers in idealist, abstract terms of creativity and coercion instead of identifying the specific problems that capitalism puts into the content of their work; they reinforce elitism based on the distinction of mental and manual labor instead of insisting that the skills of the working class belong to it as a whole and will be disposed of by the working class as a whole under socialism. Alienation, in short, is the catchword of the intellectual holding onto a petty bourgeois outlook.

The writers who parade under the banner of a new working class have selected some occupations in which the secondary relations of production bear more than the average amount of petty bourgeois influence—educated and skilled positions of mental labor, conducted alone and producing a product still closely identified with one person. Yet the class relation puts most of the members of these occupations in the working class. The new working class is part of the working class; it cannot revolt against being workers nor achieve petty producer status. Since the class relation is principal, since it is impossible to convert these workers into petty producers, the contradiction can only be resolved by waging a revolutionary working-class struggle against capitalism and for socialism, where the secondary relations are brought into harmony with the class position of the worker. This is the way to fight capitalist speedup, wreck of the environment, and misuse of technology. But the theorists of the new working class defend the petty bourgeois aspect of the secondary relations of production. This is not progressive but reactionary. When Boyte and Ackerman talk about occupations becoming more proletarianized, they voice the protest of the petty bourgeois or would-be petty bourgeois against proletarian status instead of joining a working-class struggle against capitalist exploitation.

The new working class theorists are not really spokesmen for most professional, technical and kindred workers. These thinkers speak for a few intellectuals among them whose resistance to the working-class situation is greatest. They are most aware of and opposed to authority of any type. Gorz's book is full of classic expressions of anarcho-syndicalism, like his talk about self-management, his praise of Yugoslavia, and his theory of structural reform instead of revolution.[90]

"Be it in agriculture, the university, property relations, the region, the administration, the economy, etc., a structural reform *always* requires the creation of new centers of democratic power . . . a *decentralization* of the decision making power, a *restriction on the powers of State or Capital*" (p. 8n.).

". . . we must firmly reject all attempts to subordinate the union to the party" (p. 14).

"The de facto dictatorship of organized capitalism can no longer be combatted in the advanced industrial countries in the name of an opposed dictatorship" (p. 131).

Identification of all state power with capitalist rule, no leadership by the working-class party, no dictatorship of the proletariat over all that is bourgeois—combined with the elitist view of the educated, this amounts to a demand for a share in capitalist power for these anti-working-class intellectuals. The working class cannot make a socialist revolution: "Seizure of power by insurrection is out of the question" (p. 8). Gorz tries to cover himself by maintaining a utopian approach throughout his "strategy for labor," simply asserting that structural reforms must not be perverted into capitalist schemes that would divert class struggle into participation in management. But it is not enough to put out a warning and a disclaimer. The scheme is still utopian, and it does not serve the interests of the working class, "new" or old.

Gorz winds up with a nonclass view of the highly paid managerial and technical servants of the capitalists, the "technocrats." These are the highest administrators and professionals, yet Gorz will not classify them among the capitalist class. Occupation remains for him more important than class.

" . . . technocracy is not generally the errand boy of the monopolies and does not necessarily wield power as their representative. It is rather the mediator between the particular and contradictory interests of the capitalists on the one hand, the general interest of capitalism on the other, and finally the general interest of society." (Gorz, p. 122)

Technocrats "are rather a 'caste' " who vacillate and are to be won over. This is the classic position of the reformist who wants to serve the capitalists and share power as their servant: the capitalist state is misrepresented as being above class, authority is above class, and we must win it over (that is, we must be allowed to merge into it!). The theorists of a new working class do not speak for the great majority of these workers. They are riding on a petty bourgeois focus on certain aspects of this occupational stratum, on a plausible misinterpretation of its social position, for the place-seeking goals of a few political intellectuals.

We can now observe the essential unity of the notions of the "post-industrial society" and the "new working class." Both frauds are based on the use of occupation in place of class. Both fasten on a period of growth in the professional, technical and kindred occupations. The difference between the two approaches is that the outright servants of monopoly capitalism like Daniel Bell regard these workers as middle class and try to portray monopoly capitalism as something beyond capitalism and class conflict, but not socialist. Those who speak of a new working class distort certain contradictions that these workers run up against, and propose to solve them by various petty bourgeois hopes for admission to a share of capitalist rule. The difference between the two outlooks is minor. Bell accepted some points made by the theorists of a new working class.

> "The engineers, for example, fit many of the attributes of the alienated 'educated worker.' Few of them are allowed to decide how their skills and knowledge will be used" (Bell, 1973, p. 153).

Bell simply felt, as a confident observer from the standpoint of the monopoly capitalists, that the engineers did not think they were workers; therefore, they could not be treated as part of the working class. The writers on a new working class are saying to the monopoly capitalists, make some concessions or you will have serious problems later. Both Bell and the writers on a new working class emphasize secondary aspects of occupations instead of the class relation. They ignore class and the exploitation of one class by another. Both would diminish the strength of the working class and split it.

The underlying identity of the two approaches is not only provable in theory. At least one writer has combined the themes of post-industrial society and the alienated new worker, the monopoly capitalist fraud and the petty bourgeois program. Alain Touraine's book, *The Post-Industrial Society*, appeared in English in 1971, possibly forcing Bell to complicate the title of his 1973 book, *The Coming of Post-Industrial Society*. Like both Bell and the new working class theorists, Touraine agrees that the definition of class should be replaced by market power or occupation.

"In a market capitalism, the wage-earners are the dominated class because they are subject in the labor market to the power of those who hold capital."

"One's trade, one's directly productive work, is not in direct opposition to capital . . . man is no longer involved simply in his occupational role." (p. 54)

While Touraine, a student of standard capitalist sociologists, peddles many of their ideas about post-industrial society, he duplicates the formulations of the theorists of the new working class, too. Instead of class against class, Touraine focuses on the alleged "contradictions between the needs of these social systems and the needs of individuals." (p. 61) The "revolt against a system of integration and manipulation" must lead to the "call rather for self-management" (pp. 74, 75). "We are leaving a society of exploitation and entering a society of alienation" (p. 61).

Touraine believes that plenty is assured to all. With exploitation no longer an issue, he downplays any vestigial capitalist class.

"No longer is it the concentration of available surpluses but the rational organization of human and technical equipment that governs economic development. Under these conditions, the idea of two basic classes that constitute separate milieux, one reduced to subsistence, the other to managing surpluses, loses its importance." (p. 81)

It is not so much that capitalists do not exist; perhaps one or two percent of the population are capitalists. But the exploitation of surplus labor, "the concentration of available surpluses," loses its importance. Touraine has improved on the usual crude, quantitative fraud which simply omits the monopoly capitalist class and its collection of surplus labor from tens of millions of workers. He has managed to deny the importance of exploitation itself.

Only "industrial society" contained classes with an objective antagonism between them. Post-industrial society is based not on surplus labor but on "information," and the conflict in it is a moral one. Touraine is a theorist of social movements without a basis in class. With Bell he has dropped the concept of class. Unlike Bell he is not content to observe some attitudes; he believes there is a politics of social movements, although a moral politics. With this new wisdom Touraine has some advice for the student movement of which he had been a leader in France in May 1968.

> "The student revolt could, for example, give rise to a dogmatic devotion to confrontation which would be as burdensome as conformist integration." (p. 13)

The notion of a new middle class and that of a new working class, besides sharing the theory that substitutes occupation for class, end up with the same political outlook, too: defend capitalism.

16. Class and the Blue Collar Occupations

A blue collar worker belongs to the working class for the same reason as any other: working for a wage or salary, he does not own the means of production and yields surplus labor to the capitalists. It is possible to be classified blue collar and be a small businessman, like a self-employed painter, a construction contractor, or the owner of a janitorial service. But to an even greater degree than white collar occupations, blue collar occupations are overwhelmingly working class. In the white collar occupations, one is more than twice as likely to find a member of other classes.[91] The influence of capitalism and the petty bourgeois mentality on relations of production other than the class relation is concentrated among white collar workers, too. More than them, blue collar workers labor collectively and produce a collective product, are subject to authority without wielding it, and do manual work in closer contact with the material world.

By any measure of numbers, these workers are a sizeable part of the working class. According to the 1970 Census, there were 34 million blue collar workers, or 49 percent of all employed workers.[92] Basic industry pays nearly 30 million workers, or 42 percent of all employed workers.[93] Plants with 500 or more workers employ more than six million production workers.[94] Over 15 percent of the labor force consists of production workers in plants with 100 or more workers. The blue collar workers are a large part of the working class, and they include the workers whose various relations of production conform most closely to the class relation which dominates a class society.

These workers are not to be opposed to the rest of the working class. White collar workers are not a new middle class, nor are professional workers a "new" working class. The logical criticism of views that split the working class leads to uniting workers. It criticizes the use of occupation as a definition of class and explains what determines class: relation to the means of production and to surplus labor.

This approach is not the one taken by blue collarite occupation analysts. These writers oppose the theme of a new middle class or a new working class by dwelling on the position of blue collar workers. They reject the claim that the United States is almost completely or largely middle class, but they accept the criterion of occupation to determine class.

Blue collarite occupation analysts begin by counting the size of the blue collar sector of the labor force, equating blue collar to working class as they make the tallies.

" . . . labor force data for 1970 showed that 57.5 percent of the total non-farm male population was engaged in manual or working-class occupations." (Parker, 1974, p. 38)

Levison counts craftsmen, foremen, operatives and laborers in the working class. He notes that most service workers are blue collar workers, too.[95] Finally, a few detailed occupations within the general category of clerical and sales positions are really blue collar, and altogether he shows, "Thus, three-fifths, 60 percent of America is working-class." (Levison, p. 25)

"Manual or working-class occupations"—this is how these writers define class.

"The gap between the working class and the middle class, between those who work basically with their hands and those who work with their minds, is enormous" (Levison, p. 13).

" . . . blue collar or white collar; working class or middle class." (p. 20)

In other words, these writers claim that everyone works. There is not a capitalist class and a working class. No, there is a middle class (middle between what and what?) which works with its minds, and there is a working class, which works with its hands. This is merely the occupational substitution for class. The type of work activity, the technical division of labor, and various production relations other than class are substituted in place of the class relation. When it comes to classifying a specific stratum of workers, the blue collarite writer, revealing his lack of a stable view of class, draws on any available combination of characteristics.

"In income and education, as well as family background and prestige, they fall well within the ranks of the working class rather than the middle class." (Parker, 1974, p. 38)

Against the claim that the United States is a middle class society, the reminder of these writers that there is a large working class seems to be a positive contribution. But what are the results of their calculations? Accepting their figures uncritically for a moment, we find that between 55 and 60 percent of the population is working class. That means that 40 to 45 percent are not working class, and the only other class that these blue collarite writers impress on our awareness is the middle class. In other words, United States society is divided into two camps, both too large to ignore. Instead of a society sharply polarized into a vast working class facing a narrow capitalist class, with a few petty producers in between, this is a picture of two large classes which had better live with each other, regardless of the difference in their share of man's worldly goods.

Furthermore, what is happening over time to the size of the working class? Levison is reduced to arguing that the working class is not disappearing, citing a slow change in its size from 62 percent in 1950 to 58 percent in 1969 (Levison, p. 27). At this rate, he says, there will be a sizeable working class for a long time. Still, it is a decline. Levison's definition denies the polarization of classes.

Blue collarite occupation analysts play up the differences between blue collar and white collar workers. Levison makes many remarks to incite the anger of blue collar workers at the affluence of white collar workers, or some of them. Blue collarite writers compare the two sectors of the working class on such matters as income, unemployment rates, working conditions, and the qualities of mental and manual work under capitalism. These differences exist. The working class will never become a homogeneous mass under capitalism, so clearly and obviously identical in every detail of social life, standing in such visible contrast to the capitalist class. Such a situation is technologically, economically, and politically impossible. It is probably true, however, that differences are narrowing. The crucial point of comparisons is the trend over time.

For example, if we set the average wage in manufacturing in any year at 100 and compare the salaries of professors ("upper middle class" or "new working class" white collar workers) and elementary school teachers (closer to straight white collar workers like clerks), we find the following narrowing of the gap: the index for professors' salaries declined from 361 in 1904 to 173 in 1953, and the index for elementary school teachers' salaries fell from 159 to 119 at the same time (Keat, p. 590). The comparison is very much an approximate one, but the change, from a gap of almost four to one to differences that are marginal or at most two to one, is clearly demonstrated. One could make other comparisons over time of the differences between the two large sectors of the working class. Statistics would have to be rendered compatible in order to reflect different characteristics of various occupations. For example, unemployment exists among both clerical workers and factory operatives, but the figures show twice as much unemployment for the latter.[96] This gap is undoubtedly overstated, however, for the Census counted persons as unemployed if they had looked for a job in the last four weeks and were available for work. Such unemployment, and layoffs, which are also counted, are more common among operatives, while unemployment created by attrition and by rotation of women out of the labor force who are then discouraged from returning for a long time is more common among clerical and sales workers. Properly measured, this would increase their unemployment rate.

From a class standpoint, relatively minor differences between types of workers can never overshadow the polarization of the working class against the capitalist class. These differences are primary to blue collarite occupation analysts, who define class by occupation and rely on an eclectic jumble of other characteristics to distinguish their working class from their middle class.

Typically, these writers illustrate the middle class by the example of doctors, lawyers, and executives (Levison, p. 21). Having abandoned the class perspective, blue collarite writers ignore the distinction between the self-employed or the petty bourgeoisie and the wage and salary earners. Doctors and lawyers, it will be recalled, are a small part of all professional, technical and kindred workers, but still represent a sizeable chunk of the self-employed professionals. Within the white collar working class proper, the blue collarite writers must distinguish between well-paid professionals and clerical workers. Among white collar wage and salary earners, clerical and kindred workers are 40 percent of the total (1970 Census, Report 7A, Table 43). Levison alludes to them as a gray area. "Some jobs fall in a gray area between these two poles [lawyers versus assembly line operatives]. These are, in general, the lowest level clerical positions." (p. 21) The scheme of these occupation analysts begins to fall apart. In a class society, class sooner or later determines the

position of workers in all occupations. Levison senses this but
does not define class properly. Instead, he assigns the bulk of
clerks to a gray area. His chance remark that "Eighty percent of
the labor force are either manual or clerical workers, with the
majority in manual jobs" (p. 23-24) is not used in his general
theme.

There is more to this treatment of clerical workers, the one
piece that will not fit into the jigsaw puzzle of occupation-as-class.
Clerical workers are disproportionately women, yet these writers measure the relative size of the blue collar sector by counting
men only. Parker took data for "the total non-farm male population"; Levison confined his figures to men, too. The conclusion
that blue collar workers were 55 to 60 percent of all workers was
based on this limitation. If we look at non-farm wage and salary
workers (that is, excluding self-employed workers and employees
of one's own corporation) of both sexes, the blue collar categories
(craftsmen and foremen, operatives, laborers, and service workers outside private households) comprise 49.7 percent of the
total. It is clear why these writers exclude women: by not
counting most clerical workers and by excluding all white collar
women workers in general, the figure for blue collar workers can
be raised from less than half to 55 percent. The halfway point is
an important one emotionally to their scheme, hence the need to
boost 49.7 percent just a little.

These writers claim that the size of the white collar sector has
been inflated by counting women who swelled its ranks after
World War II.

" . . . the 1950s was able to claim a shift or revolution in work
    patterns only by assigning the secretary-wives and waitress-
    daughters of blue-collar factory workers to the white-collar
    group, thereby generating its great hope for a new middle
    class." (Parker, 1974, p. 38)

"In terms of the social class composition of the population,
there has been no significant tendency for the white-collar

proletariat to grow relative to, or at the expense of, the blue-collar proletariat. What has happened is that women from blue-collar families whose husbands work in factories or at similar jobs have left the home and taken jobs, more often than not temporary and frequently changing, as saleswomen and office workers." (Szymanski, 1972, p. 111)

Szymanski joins Parker in deprecating the participation of women in the working class.

"It is generally the occupation of the man of the family that determines a family's social class and concomitant consciousness. The woman's job, at least among manual workers, is generally marginal to the overall family situation. Women tend to work irregularly, change jobs more often than men, define themselves less in terms of their jobs, join unions less frequently, and carry over job experiences to their nonworking times less than men." (p. 105)

Instead of first defining and determining class, occupation analysts draw on all sorts of *ad hoc* arguments for their procedure of measuring class by occupation. This is true even for Szymanski, who differs from Parker and Levison by admitting that he is counting sectors of the proletariat, not different classes. Yet he claims to talk about social class when he talks about these sectors, and his writing contains phrases like "blue-collar in their social class" (1973, p. 113n.) which are telescoped expressions of the theory that occupation defines class.

The allusion to secretary-wives and the discussion of the family in which both spouses work are irrelevant and erroneous. First, this approach ignores the 43 percent of working women who are not married or whose husbands are absent (1970 Census, General Social and Economic Characteristics: U.S. Summary, Table 90). If these women are selling their labor power for necessary income, or are unemployed and trying to sell it, they must be counted as part of the working class. Thus, we are considering only those 57 percent of working women who are married and living with their husbands. Szymanski's arguments were made in a debate with a proponent of new working class theory; the dispute came to center on whether individuals or families should be counted when tabulating classes. This question becomes a problem only when occupation is substituting for class. Under the criterion of class by relation to the means of production, the working class is represented by its economically active members, the employed and those who need to sell their labor power but cannot. Their dependents are part of working-class families, for they depend on the sale of the provider's labor power for their income, upon his or her performance of necessary and surplus labor.[97] Measured either way, the working class makes up the overwhelming majority of the population.

If the wife works, she is a direct participant in the working class. This can only strengthen the class character of the family. The percentage of married women who are working has increased, from 14 percent in 1940 to 40 percent in 1970.[98] This demonstrates the increasing exploitation of the working class, forcing both husband and wife to supply the capitalist class with surplus labor in order to earn the necessities of life. The only problem of classification under the class perspective is the marriage of a member of the working class and one of the petty bourgeoisie.[99] Such instances are necessarily few, because the petty bourgeoisie is small numerically and because marriages tend not to cross class lines.

The very existence of a supposed problem of classifying by individuals or by families shows the non-class character of the occupation definition of class. If our attention is gradually removed from the workplace into attempts to construct a sociology of family life, of interaction between blue collar husband and white collar wife, this is a sign that the analysis of sectors of the working class has led us away from the analysis of classes. There is such a "problem" regarding a visible minority of workers. Of the total labor force, 39 percent are in husband-wife families where both spouses work.[100] Of these, approximately 36 percent are marriages between blue collar and white collar workers.[101] It is roughly one-seventh of all workers over which Szymanski and Stodder are arguing.

These are the results of substituting occupation for class. When Szymanski employs the correct definition of class, the contrast between his outlook and that of Stodder is clear. Szymanski as a class theorist emphasizes "the convergence of the 'new working' with the manual workers" (1972, p. 109). Stodder, on the other hand, is a theorist after the likes of Bell, Gorz, and Touraine, the ideologists of a new middle class or a new working class opposed to a vanishing working class. He follows Bell in talking about a service economy as a new phenomenon (Stodder, p. 100n.), deduces that the key group in the performance of work is the professional and technical workers, "who for the first time can enable the working class to run society without any outside help" (Stodder, p. 105), and concludes with an emphasis on splits rather than unity of the working class.

"The working class in the United States is split . . . based on immediate economic conflict of interest" (Stodder, p. 106).[102]

There is a variety of political orientations open to blue collarite occupation analysts, but they have in common a lack of awareness of class and of the fact that, since a kind of society corresponds to each class, the basic struggle is over the revolutionary change from one mode of production to another. Levison is a reformist.

"Sixty percent of American men still work in essentially rote, manual jobs . . . To anyone who is involved in organizing communities, winning elections, or passing legislation this is the reality they must face." (Levison, p. 26)

He wants an alliance of the trade unions and liberal politicians. At first, they can work for full employment, more meaningful jobs, participation in management, and career ladders offering upward mobility. Ultimately, these require "democratic socialism" (Levison, pp. 289-90).

Parker, on the other hand, has studied the distribution of wealth as well as distribution by occupation (Parker, 1972), making the illusions of reformism apparent to him. Lacking a class analysis, he is reduced to pessimism and mysticism. The United States, he says, needs not a reform of wealth but a new "vision of change."

"The class structure of America depends, in the deepest [that is, murkiest] sense, not on wealth, but on alienation and the isolation of individuals" (Parker, 1974, p. 42).

These inward-turning, quiescent, demoralized words are Parker's conclusion.

17. Evolution of an Analyst of Occupation

Between 1934 and 1945 Lewis Corey wrote extensively about white collar workers. Many points sound very modern, which demonstrates the hackneyed nature of writing today about "the middle class." Trying to use class labels for occupational categories, Corey demonstrates the inevitable confusion of such an approach.

After setting farmers aside for separate analysis, Corey puts *wage* workers and clerks (including salespeople in stores) into the working class. All others—capitalists, petty producers, and white collar workers except clerks—he classifies among various strata of the bourgeoisie. The white collar employees within this bourgeoisie Corey labels the "new middle class." (Corey, 1934, p. 560, 562; 1935, p. 139) Why are "technicians, teachers, professionals" a new middle class? Corey gives all sorts of reasons and never settles on a definite answer.

Sometimes he implies that they are not working class because they receive a salary instead of a wage. (Corey, 1937, p. 139) But why were salaried clerks moved into the working class? Sometimes he says these occupations "are not really a class, merely an

151

aggregation of functional groups" (Corey, 1935, p. 140n.). Sometimes he uses a moral definition, the performance of useful functions. (p. 336) Sometimes he calls most white collar workers "economically and functionally a part of the working class: a 'new' proletariat" (p. 259). The theme of a new working class is an old one!

When Corey alludes to the Marxist criterion of class, it is not clear whether he accepts it as the very definition of class.

> "Lower salaried employees, as much as the workers, are separated from ownership of the means of production and . . . must sell their labor power to earn a livelihood." (p. 259-60)

On the other hand, writing in *Marxist Quarterly*, Corey argues that salaried employees are part of the working class not for this reason but because of a number of changes in their income and conditions. They have become "proletarianized."

> "Security of employment, privileges and differentials in salaries compared with wages have all been undermined." (Corey, 1937, p. 140)

Here proletarianization means low income and job insecurity. True, income and unemployment vary among parts of the working class, but this cannot define class. The exceptional segments of the working class can never be large; as an occupation increases in size, any privileged conditions diminish. We have seen this in the case of succesive waves of white collar occupations. In the strict sense, proletarianization refers to the loss of means of production and the consequent move from the petty bourgeoisie to the working class.

In the first half of the twelve years from 1934 to 1945, his period of evolution, Corey offered an alliance to the new middle class, or new working class, or lower bourgeoisie, or aggregate of functional groups between the proletariat and the bourgeoisie.

He offered them socialism because it needs them and will not demand any changes of them.

> " . . . socialism needs increasingly larger numbers of clerical and managerial and supervisory workers. As economic activity more fully realizes the promise of technology, completely automatic production, it becomes more and more an activity of organization, management and supervision. But when managerial and supervisory functions are stripped of their exploiting capitalist relations, their performance becomes wholly a form of productive social labor." (Corey, 1935, p. 353)

The political allegiance of the new middle class "may be changed by emphasizing that socialism liberates and amplifies the functional services now performed by salaried groups." (Corey, 1937, p. 143) In other words, occupations will not change. Corey had never defined class relations, so he sought an alliance with his new middle class on the basis of not disturbing other production relations, such as the division of mental and manual labor and the production relations of authority. This approach has nothing to do with socialism. The working class, over 90 percent of the population in the United States, can be united to oppose the capitalist class, fight the crises of capitalism, and realize socialism through working-class revolution. But the morning after the working class has smashed the capitalist state machine, set up its own state, and nationalized the capitalist means of production, change does not stop, nor has socialism been completely built. Socialism is a transition to classless society. After the capitalist class has lost its state power and its property, the other production relations still carry the influence of the class relation. The difference is that the remolding of production relations need not be violent and is a joint activity of nearly everyone at both poles of the relations. But to promise managers and technicians that socialism simply brings "the liberation of their craft function" (Corey, 1935, p. 361) is both incorrect and unnecessary. The working class—all parts of it—fights for socialism as the only way out of a capitalist crisis, not because the workers are shopping in a department store of modes of production for the nicest one.

It is no accident that at this time Corey played down the importance of the dictatorship of the proletariat, saying, "The dictatorship is brief" (p. 362).

In 1945 Corey retained the occupation analysis. His tables display the same occupational categories, only now they are regrouped and given different labels. White collar workers are definitely "the new middle class of salaried employees, especially the technical-managerial and professional personnel" (Corey, 1945, p. 68). Corey has decided that they are not part of the working class, and therefore their increase is a growth of the middle class, disproving the polarization of capitalist society.

> "But the Marxists [among whom Corey once numbered himself] were wrong, too, for there is no fulfillment of their prophecy of a rapid, inevitable polarization of classes into proletariat and bourgeoisie, with the virtual eclipse of the middle class." (Corey, 1945, p. 69)

Nor are these new occupations capitalist.

> "In objective functional aptitudes and interests the technical-managerial personnel is not capitalist. It has an instinct for workmanship, which calls for doing a job of production" (p. 78).

The "craft function" has become "an instinct for workmanship," yet these people are not "new" working class (as writers like Gorz were to make them 30 years later) but are still middle class. Why?

> " . . . their occupations, their functions and their potential (if not actual) incomes differentiate them from the workers." (p. 80)

Corey has at last resolved the confusion of his earlier writing, not by finding the definition of class, but by dividing people up according to occupations, income levels, and career prospects. He rejects the criterion of class.

> "Nothing is gained . . . by stretching the meaning of 'working class' and 'proletariat' until they become all-inclusive, meaningless concepts." (p. 82)

For the pragmatist, a category embracing 90 percent of the population is no tool of analysis. Since Corey lacks any idea of the extraction of surplus labor, he finds no significance in the growth of the exploited and the narrowing of the capitalists to the point that tens of millions labor for the benefit of a handful.[103]

Politically, Corey moved from a brief dictatorship of the proletariat to that phony brand of socialism which never socializes anything except the power of the capitalists among themselves. The task is to "break monopoly capitalism and build democratic socialism." (Corey, 1945, p. 86)

Despite the changes of labels and politics, Corey's building blocks throughout are occupational categories. He paints them with different labels depending on which transient phenomena of income and working conditions he wishes to emphasize. As occupations rise and fall, reflecting technological and other changes all within the capitalist system, the political interpretation varies. Semi-moral judgments of functional usefulness add spice. All this was done 30 to 40 years ago. The peculiarity of the analysis then was the lumping of the "new middle class" with an old middle class still of some size, petty producers and small capitalists. Other than that aspect, occupation analysts are still chewing over the same material, whether as new middle class, the heralds of a post-industrial society, or as new working class, champions of the struggle against alienation—all to oppose that "old nineteenth century Marxism!"

B. Sham Marxism

18. Class and Unproductive Labor

Some writers distort the nature of classes by appealing to criteria and restrictions supposedly taken from the theory of Karl Marx. They claim that the working class does not include so many people as we thought and even that Marx predicted the rise and expansion of a new middle class. Among such criteria are assertions that workers are only producers of material goods, that some occupations performing unproductive labor do not belong at all to the working class, that proletarians must produce surplus-value, and that there is a large middle class whose role is to consume surplus unproductively. These claims allegedly derive from the notion of productive and unproductive labor, or they are presented in the atmosphere of this distinction. Therefore, it is necessary to see what productive and unproductive labor were in Marx's time and what they are today.

a. History of Unproductive Labor

The distinction between productive and unproductive labor

was largely developed by Adam Smith, the famous economic writer during the rise of industrial capitalism in England (his *Wealth of Nations* appeared in 1775, and he died in 1790 at the age of 67). Marx studied Smith and all the classical capitalist writers on political economy in depth, critically analyzed and summed up their economic science, and gave us political economy on a completely scientific basis. His treatment of the distinction between productive and unproductive labor was part of this work.[104]

Smith mixed together two definitions of productive and unproductive labor. The first and principal distinction identifies productive labor as wage labor hired with capital and unproductive labor as labor hired out of revenue.

> "Productive labor, in its meaning for capitalist production, is wage-labor which, exchanged against the variable part of capital (the part of the capital that is spent on wages), reproduces not only this part of the capital (or the value of its own labor-power), but in addition produces surplus-value for the capitalist." (Marx, 1963, p. 152)

> "This also establishes absolutely what *unproductive labor* is. It is labor which is not exchanged with capital, but *directly* with revenue, that is, with wages or profit (including of course the various categories of those who share as co-partners in the capitalist's profit, such as interest and rent)." (p. 157)

The capitalist is in business to make money, to expand his capital. He invests in machinery, premises, and raw materials, and he also uses part of his capital to hire workers to operate the means of production. This latter part of his capital, called variable capital, employs wage labor with the intention of making a profit; it hires productive labor. Besides investing, making a profit, and reinvesting, the capitalist withdraws some of his profit for personal consumption. He buys material goods with his revenue, but he may hire servants and cooks and patronize an artist, too.

Revenue spent on unproductive labor is unproductive in the capitalist sense because the money is not going to return, with an added profit yet. It is not producing surplus-value.

Workers receive wages for the sale of their labor power. This income, very rarely converted into capital, remains simply revenue, spent on the needs of the worker and his family to sustain himself, to maintain his energy and skills. Most of the revenue is spent on material goods, but it may be used to hire someone to clean the house, too. The maid is an unproductive laborer, since the worker's revenue is not invested as capital but merely spent to keep up the house.

(Marx is dealing here only with capital invested in production, not capital invested in merchandising or banking, which he treats later (p. 413).)

This definition is concerned with the social relations in which labor is performed. It has nothing to do with the concrete character of the labor.

> *"The same* kind of labor may be *productive* or *unproductive.*
>
> "For example Milton, who wrote *Paradise Lost* for five pounds, was an *unproductive laborer.* On the other hand, the writer who turns out stuff for his publisher in factory style, is a *productive laborer.* . . . A singer who sells her song for her own account is an *unproductive laborer.* But the same singer commissioned by an entrepreneur to sing in order to make money for him is a *productive laborer;* for she produces capital." (p. 401)

> "These definitions are therefore not derived from the material characteristics of labor (neither from the nature of its product nor from the particular character of the labor as concrete labor), but from the definite social form, the social relations of production, within which the labor is realized." (p. 157)

Since occupation reflects the concrete character of the labor, we cannot under the social definition include or exclude whole occupations as productive or unproductive labor. Nor is any judgment made about the use-value which the productive laborer produces for the capitalist to sell. A capitalist may hire lab workers to distill cocaine, heroin, and other debilitating drugs which he will then market with the aid of a network of gangsters and the protection of the Central Intelligence Agency. Still, the employees are productive laborers under the capitalist definition.[105]

The social definition is not the only one in Smith's writing. Eager to reflect the new phenomena of capitalism, Smith was not too particular about definitions. It is characteristic that "Jumbled together in his presentation we find two definitions of what he calls productive labor" (p. 152). Smith slips from the social relations of labor to a physical characteristic of it. Under the second definition,

". . . a productive laborer is one whose labor *produces commodities*. . . . His labor fixes and realizes itself '*in some such vendible commodity*' " (p. 164).

What is a commodity here?

"A *commodity*—as distinguished from labor-power itself—is a material thing confronting man, a thing of a certain utility for him, in which a definite quantity of labor is fixed or materialized." (p. 164)

"The *commodity* is the most elementary form of bourgeois wealth. The explanation of 'productive labor' as labor which produces 'commodities' also corresponds, therefore, to a much more elementary point of view than that which defines productive labor as labor which produces capital." (p. 173)

Under the material definition, "*unproductive labor* is such as produces personal services." (p. 173)

There is some question about where to draw the line between someone who produces a commodity, a material thing, and someone whose service leads to the production of a commodity. Smith and Marx drew the line narrowly in order to reject contentions

that everyone is a productive laborer in one sense or another.
Still,

> "Included among these productive workers, of course, are all
> those who contribute in one way or another to the production
> of the commodity, from the actual operative to the manager or
> engineer (as distinct from the capitalist)." (p. 156-57)[106]

A factory manager on salary is a productive laborer under the
material definition; his counterpart in a trading company is not. A
scientist in the laboratory of Shell Oil Company developing
petrochemicals is a productive laborer. If he leaves to do research
at a university on the theory of the carbon bond, he is no longer a
productive laborer. Under the second definition as under the
first, it is impossible to categorize whole occupations as productive or unproductive labor.[107]

Before examining the relation of these two definitions of productive and unproductive labor, we must look at the historical
meaning of the distinction for Adam Smith. For capitalism to
grow, unproductive labor should be kept to a minimum. Smith
pulled no punches identifying unproductive labor. His words on
the subject have become famous.

> "The labor of some of the most respectable orders in the
> society is, like that of menial servants, unproductive of any
> value. . . . The sovereign, for example, with all the officers
> both of justice and war who serve under him, the whole army
> and navy, are unproductive laborers. They are the servants of
> the public, and are maintained by a part of the annual produce
> of the industry of other people. . . . In the same class must be
> ranked . . . churchmen, lawyers, physicians, men of letters of
> all kinds; players, buffoons, musicians, opera-singers, opera-
> dancers, etc." (quoted by Marx, 1963, p. 160)

These people are maintained out of revenues. Instead of being yoked to capital by an exchange of their labor power against variable capital, they live off revenues, the private consumption funds of various classes. In particular, when Smith was writing in 1775, unproductive laborers were the minions of landlords and banking capitalists. Behind the criticism lay Smith's attack on their revenues. He stood for the industrial capitalists driving to accumulate, to increase capitalist production, to exist solely as human representatives of the urge of capital to expand itself, to add surplus-value to itself.

> "This is the language of the still revolutionary bourgeoisie, which has not yet subjected to itself the whole of society, the State, etc. All these illustrious and time-honored occupations . . . are *from an economic standpoint* put on the same level as the swarm of their own lackeys and jesters maintained by the bourgeoisie and by idle wealth—the landed nobility and idle capitalists." (p. 300-01)[108]

Here is the class content of the distinction between productive and unproductive laborers. The landed nobility were leftovers from the ruling class prior to the English bourgeois revolution of 1640. In 1688, the bourgeoisie compromised and brought the nobles back as junior partners in order to subjugate the petty producers and workers. As a rule, the landed nobility did not engage in production, its management or development. Instead, their rent withdrew funds from capitalist accumulation. Living in idleness, they and the coupon-clippers spent their income as revenue. The unproductive laborers they hired represented social power for the maintenance of this state of affairs and resistance to the demands of industrial capital. Their men of letters apologized for stagnation, social and economic. State officials weighed on industry as a burden. The unproductive laborers were so many persons not working to expand capital. In this respect, they were no different than the hordes of menial servants whom the idle rich employed primarily to display their wealth. The intent of distinguishing between productive and unproductive labor was to criticize this system from the standpoint of industrial capitalists. Smith spoke not for narrow occupational interests but for the class he defended in the realm of economic theory.

What was the relation in this period between Smith's two definitions? First, the definition that reveals the superiority of capitalism to previous modes of production and calls for expanding it is the definition based on social relations.

> "A coat is a coat. But have it made in the first form of exchange [against variable capital], and you have capitalist production and modern bourgeois society; in the second [against revenue], and you have a form of handicraft which is compatible even with Asiatic relations or those of the Middle Ages, etc. And these *forms* are decisive for material wealth itself." (p. 296)

What counts for capitalism is not only that goods rather than services are produced, but that goods are produced in the capitalist factory rather than in workshops attached to priests' temples, for example. In turn, early capitalism developed production at the highest rate then known in history.

Second, the greatest rate of development of capitalist production can be achieved by reducing unproductive labor, in the sense of labor hired out of revenue, to a minimum, setting free the maximum amount of labor for productive employment, in the sense of labor that produces surplus-value.

> ". . . the greater part of the revenue (wages and profit) that is spent on commodities produced by capital, the less the part that can be spent on the services of unproductive laborers, and vice versa." (p. 158)

When capitalism was champing at the bit, this important demand

was served by the definition of productive labor according to
social relations.

Third, the two definitions tended to coincide in Smith's time.
More and more production of goods was capitalist production.
Being more powerful than individual, petty production because it
is more socialized, capitalism was winning this battle. Material
production was becoming capitalist production. On the other
side, capitalist relations were concentrated in the production of
material things. Services were still purchased primarily by the
revenue of idle classes without going through capitalist inter-
mediaries: footmen hired for display, state and church officials
sucking taxes and tithes out of the economy, and men of letters
preserving the culture that justified this order. If the labor
power was not purchased for production of material things, it was
unlikely to be labor power exploited for a profit.

During the rise of the industrial capitalist, therefore, the social
definition of productive labor reflects the victory over pre-
capitalist production and spurs the development of capitalism.
But the two definitions did not seriously diverge at the time.

By the time Marx wrote, the situation had changed, and he
took note of developments. Having established its complete
domination over society, the capitalist class no longer wanted to
discuss social relations. The social definition of productive labor
was ignored. Furthermore, the bourgeoisie discovered its own
need for state, religious, and ideological servants to glorify
capitalism and ward off the demands of socialism. As justification
for their own position, these ideological servants attacked the
material definition of productive labor and asserted that all kinds
of activity were productive labor, necessary, good, and part of
this best of all possible worlds.[109] In attacking the distinction
between labor producing material goods and other kinds of labor,
these sycophants attacked the primacy of material production
over "spiritual production." In a long, brilliant discussion which
cannot be duplicated here, Marx showed the utter bankruptcy of
this outlook. "Smith does not at all deny that these [spiritual]

activities produce a 'result,' a 'product' of some kind." (p. 266)
But if one ignores the social relations of material production,

> "If material production itself is not conceived in its *specific
> historical* form, it is impossible to understand what is specific
> in the spiritual production corresponding to it and the recip-
> rocal influence of one on the other. Otherwise one cannot get
> beyond inanities." (Marx, 1963, p. 285)

These apologists of the mature bourgeoisie argued that if a
country were under attack, then the soldier helps the peasant to
produce the harvest and is equally as productive.

> ". . . that is not true. Smith would say that the soldier's
> protective care is productive of defense, but not of the corn. If
> order was restored in the country, the ploughman would
> produce the corn just as before, without being compelled to
> produce the maintenance, and therefore the life, of the soldiers
> into the bargain. The soldier belongs to the incidental ex-
> penses of production, in the same way as a large part of the
> unproductive laborers who produce nothing themselves,
> either spiritual or material, but who are useful and necessary
> only because of the faulty social relations—they owe their
> existence to social evils." (p. 288-89)

One writer argued that a magistrate who provided justice for the
peasant was a productive laborer, as shown by the necessity for
order and justice if production is to go forward in peace. Of
course, the magistrate's labor is still, in the material sense,
unproductive. "Otherwise we would have to say that since the
magistrate is absolutely unable to live without the peasant,
therefore the peasant is an indirect producer of justice! And so
on. Utter nonsense!" (p. 293-94)

Neither Smith nor Marx argued that all labor should produce
material things. There must be other activities.

"Smith never denied this, as he wants to reduce the 'necessary unproductive laborers like State officials, lawyers, priests, etc., to the *extent* in which their services are indispensable. And this is in any case the 'proportion' in which they make the labor of productive laborers most efficacious." (p. 289)[110]

Still, the difference between productive and unproductive labor

"must be kept in mind and the fact that all other sorts of activity influence material production and vice versa in no way affects the necessity for making this distinction." (Marx, 1971, p. 432)

In any society, the distinction between material production and other activity is valuable because it allows us to ask of ideological, social, and political activities whether they are 1) purely unnecessary for the development of production, 2) necessary only because of the class contradictions in society, in its social relations (such as the example of the soldier above), or 3) necessary to material production, revolutionizing man's powers and forces of production or the relations within which production is carried out. Under socialism, for example, the first type of activity is abolished, such as the play of the idle rich, the second type continues to the extent needed to defend the dictatorship of the proletariat, and the third type of activity increases (natural science, permanently; political activities, for a historical period; and conscious arrangement of social relations, permanently).

On the question of hiring labor out of revenue, of the social definition of productive labor, the capitalists reversed themselves, too, between the times of Smith and Marx. There was a period in the middle of the nineteenth century when the number of menial servants was large, retained more often by capitalists than landlords.[111] The bourgeoisie was no longer purely an agent of capital in its drive for surplus-value; it was also learning to consume surplus product and enjoy.[112] The capitalist class, not having developed its own luxuries, copied the feudal pattern of consuming wealth in the form of a contingent of servants.

At this time, the working class began to point out that the capitalists themselves were no longer a contribution to material production. The workers asked, who contributes to the production of material things? We do, from laborer and operative to manager. But the capitalist is unnecessary. His role as an organizer of production, always partial, is now minor. He sits in an office, does not supervise in the plant, and makes business deals. Such had the capitalist class become. Now "the real productive laborers rise against it and moreover tell it that it lives on other people's industry" (Marx, 1963, p. 301). The capitalists do not want to hear about productive labor. They send out apologists to claim the productive power of labor for the name of capital. Formerly, the industrial capitalists attacked the landlords and idle rich. Now their apologists turn around and assert against the working class that "in fact *the industrial capitalists* are the *sole productive laborers* in the higher meaning of the word." (p. 279) The retreat to the higher meaning of words admits that the workers were correct, "that the. industrial capitalist becomes more or less unable to fulfill his function as soon as he personifies the enjoyment of wealth, as soon as he wants the accumulation of pleasures instead of the pleasure of accumulation." (p. 282-83)

What is the overall result of historical changes on the two definitions of productive and unproductive labor? Their changing position reflects the role of capitalism as a mode of production in history, an advance on previous modes but an exploitative mode of production, certain to die and give birth to a new system. To introduce such definitions, to praise productive labor and criticize unproductive labor, is a historical advance. "Aristotle and Caesar would have regarded even the title 'laborers' as an insult" without even asking whether they were productive or unproductive (p. 287). At its birth capitalism proclaimed that it would develop man's power of production, demanded the right to do so, and attacked all obstacles left over from previous social systems. The two definitions of productive labor tended to coincide: capitalist social relations went hand in hand with the development of material production. But as soon as they conquered society, the capitalists decided that social relations were no longer to be questioned; this is best enforced by suppressing the concept itself. On the other hand, the critical attack on the feudal or absolutist state, the church, and ideology as a waste should now be explicitly reversed, to glorify spiritual service to capitalism. The bourgeoisie split the two definitions by suppressing the social definition and reversing its position on productive labor with regard to the material definition.

It should be noted that these categories underwent changes within the life of capitalism, in the 75 years from Smith to Marx. This is unlike the category of class itself, which reflects the essence of a society. The definition of classes and the list of basic classes remain so long as capitalism exists. The category of productive labor primarily served the early capitalists in battle against survivals of previous ruling classes. With the development of capitalism first to maturity, then to decay in the era of monopoly capitalism, the meaning of the concept falls apart. Socialism will make its own social definition of productive labor. It will obviously not be the same as the capitalist criterion, labor that produces surplus-value. It will be a call to develop socialist production—something that can be done only under socialism, not under capitalism.

b. Class and Productive Workers

From the start it smells a little fishy when writers use the notion of productive versus unproductive labor to define the working class in the United States today. The definition of the working class must be the same throughout capitalism, if we are penetrating to the essence of this system. The size and qualities of the working class can and certainly do change within the life of capitalism, but the class criterion remains. Yet some writers attempt to make productive labor, with its great changes under capitalism, a requirement to be a member of the working class.[113] Supposedly, there are a large number of unproductive laborers, who are not members of the working class or the proletariat.

For example, the assumption that the industrial proletariat is the only "true" proletariat is often based on or alludes to the definition of productive labor as labor which produces commodities, material things. This is the second and poorer of Smith's two definitions. Never was it a definition of class. As we have seen, the class content of the distinction was to mark off both workers and industrial capitalists from landlords, the idle rich, and their retainers. Later, the capitalist class attacked this distinction and tried to equate mental activity and the production of material things. Capitalism needed its own ideological apparatus. Today, many workers properly defined—dependent on the sale of their labor power and dispossessed of means of production—do not produce material things. This does not change their class position; it only tells us that in late capitalism the two definitions of productive labor have separated. The drive to extend capitalist relations formerly coincided with the expansion of material production. Now these relations encompass even more than material production and grow even when material production stagnates. This is a sign of the decay of capitalism in its monopoly stage, but it would be absurd to think that capitalism dissolves its principal antagonist, the working class, in the course of its decline. The industrial workers have certain characteristics to be considered later, but they are not the only workers, because of some notion of productive labor which helped the capitalist class take over society from the landed nobility.

Adam Smith did not have a clear conception of labor power, only of labor, which is labor power in use. "Commodity" to him did not include labor power, although it is a commodity under capitalism of a very special type. Marx discussed the classification of teachers under the definition of productive labor as labor which produces commodities. For the worker, Marx said,

". . . what he pays out for education is devilishly little, but when he does, his payments are productive, for education produces labor-power" (Marx, 1963, p. 210).

"Productive labor would therefore be such labor as produces commodities or directly produces, trains, develops, maintains or reproduces labor-power itself. Adam Smith excludes the latter from his category of productive labor; arbitrarily, but with a certain correct instinct—that if he included it, this would open the flood-gates for false pretensions to the title of productive labor." (p. 172)

The teaching of basic skills of literacy and all vocational education, a concept which broadens with the application of science to production, is productive labor in this sense.

The principal definition of productive labor is different. It refers to wage labor hired by variable capital as opposed to revenue. The classic example of unproductive labor hired by revenue was the menial servant. The lords consumed part of their income by employing hordes of these servants. Early industrial capitalists attacked this unproductive labor as a limit on the pace of accumulation, of the growth of capital, since what is spent as revenue cannot be laid out as capital. Later, there was a period in which the capitalists, imitating the lords, hired servants. This phenomenon was not a basic feature of capitalism but only a passing moment, when the capitalists had a surplus, were aping the nobility, and spent their revenue on unproductive labor rather than on commodities sold by fellow capitalists. Today, private household wage workers are only 1.7 percent of the wage and salary workers; the craftsmen, operatives, and laborers alone are a group 22 times as large.[114] When a capitalist consumes revenue today, he buys luxury goods, such as a yacht, a jet plane, or a large house.[115] He purchases these commodities from another capitalist, who has exploited labor hired with variable capital and who makes a profit in this business. These laborers are productive of surplus-value. A few unproductive laborers are hired to operate these luxuries, such as the pilot of the plane.

They are only a handful of the total laborers and even of the laborers involved in the production and consumption of luxury goods.

These results are the ones we expect if we remember the history of the distinction between productive and unproductive labor. Some persons, however, want to use an old issue to make the ever growing body of antagonists to the capitalist class vanish. Strictly examined, there is nothing to this theme. The twist, therefore, is to abuse the distinction and argue by metaphor and vague analogy.

Whatever productive labor is, it does not run along lines of occupation. Production of material things includes every member of the collective laborer which produces them. And in many cases, one may engage in the same occupation as an employee or a petty producer (and hence an unproductive laborer by the social definition). When a writer calls a whole occupation unproductive, this represents a lack of understanding of the idea of productive labor in any of its senses. This is the case when we meet with a list of *"other than productive workers. . . .* e.g. bookkeepers, clerks, secretaries, lawyers, designers, engineers, salesmen, etc."* (Nicolaus, p. 39) When designers and engineers are part of the collective labor of production, they are laborers involved in the production of material goods. They are productive in the capitalist social sense, too, assuming they are on salary. The same is true of clerks and bookkeepers. Under either definition, some of them are productive laborers.

The example of clerks raises another question, that of the definition of workers as those who produce surplus-value. Commercial clerks, unlike clerks attached to a factory, are engaged not in producing surplus-value but in realizing it for the capitalist. Are they members of the working class?

1. commercial clerks

In the analysis of capitalism or any other mode of production, the first thing to examine is the process of production itself. This

is the essence of a system. But many other economic activities go
on in a mode of production: its specific way of distributing the
products, its method or lack of it for planning future production,
and so forth. The first and basic volume of *Capital* is subtitled,
"A Critical Analysis of Capitalist Production." The later volumes
study "The Process of Circulation of Capital" and "The Process of
Capitalist Production as a Whole."

Marx followed the same procedure in his discussion of productive and unproductive labor. At the end of the basic material on
the subject, Marx noted,

> "Here we have been dealing only with *productive capital*, that
> is, capital employed in the *direct process of production*. We
> come later to capital in the *process of circulation*. And only
> after that, in considering the special form assumed by capital
> as *merchant's capital*, can the question be answered as to how
> far the laborers employed by it are productive or unproduc-
> tive." (Marx, 1963, p. 413)

After the capitalist has produced commodities and extracted
surplus-value, he still has to convert the surplus-value into
money. The commodities have no use to him, either by their own
nature or as a vehicle for extracting still more surplus-value. The
value including the surplus-value in them must be realized in
money, so that once again the capitalist can convert his capital
into the specific forms needed to extract more surplus-value—
—means of production and labor power. The activity of buying
and selling is necessary for the capitalist, but it does not create
surplus-value. Surplus-value is created only in production.

At first the capitalist sells the product himself, often in
wholesale lots to a merchant capitalist, who in turn divides up the
product and sends it out through the arteries and capillaries of
circulation.[116] Soon, both capitalists hire commercial clerks to do
this work for them. What is the class position of the clerks in the
sales office of manufacturers, in the office of the wholesaler, and
at the counters of merchandisers like Wards and Safeway? Do

they belong to the working class, or do they make up a new class in the history of classes and class societies?

Marx's answer was always very clear: 1) they do not produce surplus-value, 2) they do provide unpaid labor to the capitalist, and so 3) they are members of the working class.

> "Whatever his pay, as a wage-laborer he works part of his time for nothing. He may receive daily the value of the product of eight working-hours, yet functions ten." (*Capital*, II, p. 132)

> "The commercial worker produces no surplus-value directly. But the price of his labor is determined by the value of his labor-power, hence by its costs of production, while the application of this labor-power, its exertion, expenditure of energy, and wear and tear, is as in the case of every other wage-laborer by no means limited by its value." (*Capital*, III, p. 300)

If you do not own means of production and have to sell your labor power in order to obtain an income, you are a member of the working class. This is true "whatever the pay," says Marx. The capitalist takes advantage of the fact that he pays you, if he pays for labor power at its value, the product of so many hours of labor, enough to produce the things a worker needs to survive and reconstitute the ability to work. Once you enter his workplace, he drives you for a full working day. Nothing forbids this day from containing more hours of labor than are represented in the wage. Labor power was paid for at its value. Now the capitalist uses it like the buyer of any commodity, to its full capacities. This is the essence of the relation between capitalists and workers. The commercial clerk is bound up in it as much as any worker.

> "What he costs the capitalist and what he brings in for him, are two different things. He creates no direct surplus-value, but

adds to the capitalist's income by helping him to reduce the cost of realizing surplus-value, inasmuch as he performs partly unpaid labor." (*Ibid.*)

The labor power of the commercial clerk

> "is bought with the variable capital of the merchant, not with money expended as revenue, and consequently it is not bought for private service, but for the purpose of expanding the value of the capital advanced for it." (p. 292)

> "The unpaid labor of these clerks, while it does not create surplus-value, enables him [the merchant] to appropriate surplus-value, which, in effect, amounts to the same thing with respect to his capital." (p. 294)

Marx is talking about the commercial clerk who works for the capitalist specializing in trade, the merchant capitalist. His words apply, for example, to the many thousands of employees of Sears and Wards. Capital is invested in these corporations to make a profit. This is done by performing the work of realizing the value of commodities, or rather by having workers perform this labor while minimizing their wages and salaries. Except for some transportation, warehousing, and service functions, Sears and Wards do not create surplus-value. They only capture part of it by realizing for the manufacturing capitalist the value of his commodities. They do not perform this service for their fellow capitalists out of comradeship. On the contrary, they extract as much of the surplus-value created by the manufacturer as possible. The owners of Sears and Wards measure the worth of engaging in this business instead of in manufacturing on the basis of what profit they can obtain on the capital used to hire clerks, build stores, etc.

As we have seen, the wages of commercial clerks are ultimately governed in their magnitude by class relations like those of all workers, regardless of occupation, sector, industry, etc.

"The commercial worker, in the strict sense of the term, belongs [in the 1860's] to the better-paid class of wage-workers—to those whose labor is classified as skilled and stands above average labor. Yet the wage tends to fall, even in relation to average labor, with the advance of the capitalist mode of production. This is due partly to the division of labor in the office, implying a one-sided development of the labor capacity. . . . Secondly, because the necessary training, knowledge of commercial practices, languages, etc. is more and more rapidly, easily, universally and cheaply reproduced with the progress of science and public education. . . . With few exceptions, the labor-power of these people is therefore devaluated with the progress of capitalist production." (p. 300)

The requirement that to be a member of the working class one must produce surplus-value is imposed only by those who understate the size of the working class. They oust some workers from the working class, usually into a vaguely defined, amorphous "middle class."[117] Yet these workers bear no different relation to the means of production. They must sell their labor power to a capitalist for a wage or salary. They perform unpaid labor for his business. They are part of the working class.

The analysis of commercial clerical workers is important not only for the correct classification of millions of workers in a prominent industry of monopoly capitalism, but also because it shows us the way to analyze other alleged exceptions to the general criterion of membership in the working class.

2. government workers

Are government employees part of the working class? Those who distort the notion of productive labor say no. First, they argue, government workers do not produce surplus-value, and second, did not Smith and Marx denounce state servants as unproductive laborers?

Smith branded employees of a state that served the landed nobility as unproductive laborers. Neither part of this proposition applies to the question. Today, the state is firmly in the hands of the capitalist class; when this happens, the question of unproductive labor changes completely. And the question of being an unproductive laborer has nothing to do with membership in the working class, as the example of commercial clerks demonstrated.

Let us look at a functional classification of government and state employees.

Function[118]	Percent of government employees
1. Education	42
2. Health, parks and recreation, and welfare	13
3. Postal, highway, fire, sanitation and sewage, and natural resources	16
4. Military and police	12
5. Financial, general government, and other	17
Total	100

Productive and unproductive labor are defined in two ways, according to economic relations and according to production of material things. When capitalism was a rising mode of production, the two definitions tended to coincide. The functions of government bring home strikingly how much they have diverged and even become opposites. The great bulk of education and of health and other recuperative work are obviously directly productive of labor power and its capabilities. As we have seen, Marx would have classified such labor as productive in the material sense. Production depends more than ever on the characteristics of labor power. Capitalism has always recognized this fact reluctantly, partially, and grudgingly. Education and health-work for the workers have been won only through bitter class struggle by the working class. For while these activities are necessary to production and consequently for the production of surplus-value under capitalism, they do not create surplus-value themselves. Furthermore, profit-oriented education businesses have so far not been very practical, so that not even profit garnered in the way that bankers and merchants appropriate surplus-value is available. (All school construction and supplies are purchased from private business, but we are counting government workers here, not the government budget. The latter is a big pork barrel of enrichment for businessmen.)

Postal, highway, and property protection and management services are clearly necessary activities for the production of material things. Capitalists allocate the functions to government because a single agency must carry each one out or because a higher level of business activity overall is possible if profit-making is forbidden in these activities. The question of whether the postal service should be public or private illustrates this consideration. If it is subsidized, then business activity as a whole benefits from speedy and cheap communication. If private business ran the postal service for a profit, the price of service would seriously hurt the whole game of extracting surplus-value. Postal workers are obviously productive in the sense of moving material goods. It looks now as if monopolies may find it worthwhile to set up their own postal services and electronic communication systems, calling on an expensive public or quasi-public system only for non-routine letters. Let the workers and smaller businesses hang. If this occurs, it will be another expression of the decay of monopoly capitalism, of its sabotage of production. But it has nothing to do with the definition of classes.

The first three categories in the table account for 71 percent of the employees. They do what the capitalist class has them do, and the capitalists have them do what the maintenance of capitalist production requires. These workers are obviously not being paid out of revenue consumed privately by idle lords. They are wage and salary workers.

Education of the workers is controlled by the capitalist class. The schools teach workers more than productive skills like literacy and vocational training. They are a social and political indoctrination system in the reactionary ideology of monopoly capitalism, too. Here the capitalists have hired some workers, in a vast bureaucracy, to develop the miseducation imparted to the workers' children. This does not remove these specialized workers from the working class. They are a species of mental worker. Like other mental workers and like managers, their activities bear much capitalist influence, although the mass of teachers are, along with clerks, least of all white collar workers an elite. The class relation is primary.

It is necessary to distinguish between government and the state. The state is the machinery of repression—the police, army, jails, courts, and the officials who control them. The state proper is essential to the preservation of the capitalist system, to the very existence of surplus-value. Government refers to collective social functions stemming from production, not directly from class rule. In a capitalist society, the capitalist class controls both state and government. The state, the highest instrument of class rule, must be smashed in its capitalist form. A new state, set up as the dictatorship of the proletariat, will eventually wither away. But government functions will remain and grow in a socialist and communist society, although the people themselves, not a separate bureaucracy, will carry them out. Within the military and police functions and, although less so, in the general government function, are contained the institutions of the state. The personnel of the state proper cannot be counted as part of the working class, although economically they are wage and salary earners.

As distinguished from the personnel of the state, government workers are wage and salary earners and part of the working class. The growth of government functions reflects the ascent of production to a higher, collective level despite capitalism. The growth of the state reflects the decay and defense of the capitalist system. Socialism will mean a great change in the activities of many, not only in government. The expansion of an institution under capitalism, however, does not do away with class. On the contrary, every institution under capitalism reproduces its basic class contradiction and requires a class analysis to be understood. Only those who objectively serve the capitalist class in its last days diminish the size of the working class by twisting a question of early capitalism versus feudal holdovers, the question of productive and unproductive labor, into an allegedly Marxist criterion for membership in the working class. The confusion can be seen in the contention that

" . . . to Marx, the proletariat meant *productive* workers only. If the proletariat is defined to include all those who work for wages, then many corporation executives and managers are proletarians too." (Nicolaus, p. 49)

No, Marx never defined class by the criterion of productive worker, neither in the sense of being productive of surplus-value (commercial clerks are workers) nor in the sense of being productive of material goods (the singer in the entrepreneur's troupe is a worker). Furthermore, because the writer is not aware of unpaid labor, he makes a problem out of the question of executives and managers, who can be divided among classes by quite definite criteria flowing out of the relation of classes to surplus labor. It is exactly wrong to say,

"This class of unproductive workers . . . is the middle class." (Nicolaus, p. 46)

c. **The Notion of Consumers of Surplus-Value**

So far the category of productive and unproductive labor has been misused to represent a number of workers as not really workers. The distortions hold that only those who produce material goods are workers, a confusion of the two definitions of productive labor; that entire occupations are unproductive, a plain confusion of occupational boundaries with the notion of productive versus unproductive labor; or that only those who produce surplus-value are productive and therefore workers, an attempt to judge capitalism in decay by the standards of early capitalism. When this magic has been used to narrow the ranks of the working class, the implication is that the persons involved must be part of a new middle class.

On the other side, some argue that capitalism today contains a large number of unproductive workers whose importance lies not in what they do for a living but in their consumption of the surplus.

"The second reason why there must be an increase of non-productive workers is that an increase in the surplus product requires an increase in the number of people who can afford to consume it . . .; the system would collapse if there were not also a class which consumed more than it produced." (Nicolaus, p. 40)[119]

The idea is not new, and it is a service of Martin Nicolaus, a representative advocate, to bring out its heritage. Over 150 years ago Thomas R. Malthus scribbled out the classic statement of the necessity for a class of unproductive consumers. Marx examined this claim in detail in his *Theories of Surplus-Value*. It is well known that Marx rejected another theory of Parson Malthus, his theory of overpopulation, the view that people cannot produce what they must consume, so the growth of population, being the growth of unmet consumption needs, must lead to hunger, famine, war, and other fine ends. What did Marx think of Malthus's more properly economic views?

The root of Malthus's economics is his theory of the origin of surplus-value or profit. Marx showed how capitalists extract surplus-value from the workers in the course of production.

When the capitalists sell products at their value, surplus-value is included. Malthus had a different view.

"What Malthus does not understand is the difference between the total sum of labor contained in a particular commodity and the sum of paid labor which is contained in it. It is precisely this difference which constitutes the source of profit. Further, Malthus inevitably arrives at the point of deriving profit from the fact that the seller sells his commodity not only *above* the amount it costs *him* (and the capitalist does this), but above what *it costs;* he thus reverts to the vulgarized conception of profit upon expropriation" (Marx, 1971, p. 20).

The seller cheats the buyer—this is Malthus's theory of profit. It may explain how an individual dealer makes money, but it cannot explain how surplus-value is created.

"It is in particular difficult to understand how society as a whole can enrich itself in this way, how a real surplus-value or surplus product can thus arise. An absurd, stupid idea." (*Ibid.*)

"Thus Malthus, instead of advancing beyond Ricardo, seeks to drag political economy back to where it was before Ricardo, even to where it was before Adam Smith and the Physiocrats." (p. 16)

Malthus's and Nicolaus's idea that a class of consumers of the surplus is needed to realize the prices set by the cheating capitalists follows directly from Malthus's theory of value and surplus-value.

"Malthus's theory of value gives rise to the whole doctrine of the necessity for continually rising unproductive consumption which this exponent of over-population (because of shortage of food) preaches so energetically." (p. 40)

"This nominal price increment represents the profit . . . . how is this price to be realized?" (p. 40-41)

"What is *required* therefore are *buyers who are not sellers,* so that the capitalist can realize his profit. . . . what follows from this is his plea for the greatest possible increase in the unproductive classes in order that the sellers may find a market, a demand for the goods they supply. . . . [Malthus] preaches continuous overconsumption and the maximum possible appropriation of the annual product by idlers, as a condition of production." (p. 22)

Workers work hard. The capitalists add profit to the cost of goods, and unproductive idlers are needed to consume them, to provide the additional demand for this added-on surplus-value. Three classes, each with its role. Marx thought this was a stupid, absurd idea. He showed how surplus-value, extracted in production, is part of the value of the commodity. The capitalists can and on the average do sell commodities at their value. Marx showed how markets clear, how accumulation proceeds, all based on the exploitation and the limited consumption of the working class. The problem of realizing profit, in the sense of completing a possible circuit of transactions, does not exist.

Malthus's idea has been refurbished for the era of monopoly capitalism. Since Marx lived, the productivity of labor has gone up enormously; for any given quantity of goods, less and less labor is needed to produce them. Therefore, the consumption theorists say, if the system is not to collapse, capitalism develops a class of consumers of the surplus, an alleged new middle class.

Marx's theory did not work only up to a point and then fail to explain things after a certain level of productivity. On the contrary, as far as accumulation is concerned, capitalism might go on forever. What Marx explained remains valid today. The changes in capitalism are not changes in its essence, but rather the maturing of new contradictions on top of the basic ones, the appearance of monopoly capitalism. With the formation in one industry and country after another of a handful of corporations dominating the market, the drive to expand production slows and even reverses. Firms now have the power to limit production, raise prices, enlarge profits this way, and exclude newcomers from undercutting the lovely arrangement. Capitalists exercise this power. It is not smoothly exercised, and crises of over-production (at given price levels, which must always be upheld) do appear. But more and more the gap between potential and actual production enlarges. This is a trend of secular stagnation. Monopoly saps the drive to expand production in the course of accumulating surplus-value. Of course, the capitalists do not hand out the surplus to a class of unproductive consumers num-bering millions upon millions: This would not be capitalism. With rising productivity and stagnant output or very slowly growing levels of output, poverty and unemployment grow. Unemployed workers and poverty of consumption among them—this, and not the rosy affluence of a new middle class, is the result of capitalism in decay.

Quoting Rousseau, Marx says,

" 'The more monopoly spreads, the heavier do the chains become for the exploited.' Malthus, 'the profound thinker', has different views. His supreme hope, which he himself describes as more or less utopian, is that the mass of the middle class should grow and that the proletariat (those who work) should constitute a constantly declining proportion (even though it increases absolutely) of the total population. This in fact is the *course* taken by bourgeois society." (p. 63)

Marx then quotes Malthus to this effect. It is a sign of the bankruptcy of writers like Nicolaus that they take Marx's ironic paraphrase of Malthus to represent the considered views of Marx. This would not be simply one conclusion that Marx con-ceded to Malthus, for Malthus's views flow directly out of his garbled ideas of surplus-value and value itself. That is, to make Marx and Malthus agree, it is only necessary to argue that Marx abandoned fifteen years of economic research. And this to arrive at the conclusion that the proletariat will continually diminish as a percentage of capitalist society, while the middle class grows, living idly off the surplus, while the capitalists devote themselves to pushing this machine faster. This theory portrays the gradual, quantitative disappearance of the basic class contradiction of capitalism.

Nonetheless, if one is at all a revolutionary, one might suppose that even as it shrinks in size, the industrial proletariat, bearing the weight of society on its back, would be a revolutionary agency. One might suppose this, but Nicolaus does not. He abandons the concept of antagonism between classes as the dominant feature of capitalism as of all exploiting societies, along with the pretense to be a follower of Marx.

"The advance of capitalist society has not meant increasingly sharp conflict between capital and labor. The most industrially advanced capitalist nations typically have the most quiescent, noninsurrectionary proletariats—witness the United States; and in every capitalist country there has arisen a broad, vocal and specifically new middle class to thwart Marxist theory and to stifle and crush Marxist action." (Nicolaus, p. 29)

"It was Marx's captivation with this choreography [Hegel's dialectical movement], I shall argue, which led him to the prediction that capitalist society must inevitably become polarized into two directly antagonistic classes, and that, in this polarization, the industrial proletariat must play the role of successful negation.

"That this prediction has proved to be mistaken . . . has been apparent for some time." (Nicolaus, p. 23)

These words were published in 1967. One year later in France, ten million workers, practically the entire working class, went on general strike. From manufacturing plants to the staff of the state radio and television monopoly, they stopped work and ripped the cover off the class antagonism in an advanced capitalist country. Revolutionary situations in advanced capitalist countries, confidently expected by Marxist theory, became a reality none could ignore. Apparently, the French workers had not heard of their mistaken captivation with a hypnotic dance of dialectic.[120]

C. The Amount of Personal Income

19. Class and the Amount of Personal Income

For everyday propaganda, capitalist apologists most often substitute the amount of income that a person receives in place of his or her class. Instead of looking at the division of society into classes which, based on relations to the means of production, perform surplus labor or control and receive it, they look at strata or layers defined by dollar ranges. There is the "class" receiving $2,000 or less, the "class" receiving from $2,000 to $4,000, the "class" receiving $4,000 to $7,000, and so on. This is the basis for the definition of class in popular newspaper sociology. Middle class means middle income according to this conception.[121] For example,

"In absolute terms, the middle class has greatly expanded since World War II. The median income has risen steadily and is now near $13,000. . . . Americans in the broader range of $10,000 to $35,000 do three-quarters of the nation's buying." (Barbour, p. 1)

185

Many sociologists can think of no other way to measure class than
by amount of income or by occupation.

"If class is taken to refer to stratification in the economic
realm, conceptually distinct from prestige status and political
power, then financial rewards and occupation become obvious
candidates for the role of class indicators." (Haug, p. 447)

"Most studies in stratification have, explicitly or implicitly,
used income as the decisive factor in indicating economic
power." (Gordon, p. 240)[122]

As with the grouping of people by occupations, the switch from
classes to income strata is found in Max Weber, too.

"Present-day society is predominantly stratified in classes,
and to an especially high degree in income classes." (Weber,
1946, p. 301)[123]

Of the three phases of economic life—production, distribution,
and consumption—production determines the others. It is obvious that what there is to distribute and consume depends materially on what is produced. More importantly, the relations in
which men carry on production determine the relations of distribution among them and their various patterns of consumption.[124] Class relations are a type of production relation;
to study classes is to study relations among persons in production. Categorizing people mainly by the amount of income they
receive abandons the sphere of production. Furthermore, when
attention wanders from looking at tables of income to anything
qualitative, the drift is almost always toward consumption not
production. Students of the income definition of "class" ignore
production and concentrate on what and how much people are
consuming.

"Differences in modes of living and consumption, dictated by differences in income, create a sharply stratified social order and a distinct social structure." (Kolko, 1964, p. 126)

"From them [differences in income] stem great variations in health and wealth, knowledge and experience, wisdom and happiness." (Mayer, p. 1)

These writers conceive the essence of men to be formed by what and how much they consume. Hence Mayer's contempt for the wisdom of the masses, the assertion that the wealthy are the wise.

Gabriel Kolko gives a typical picture of income distribution. He divides all income recipients into ten groups, each containing 10 percent of the total recipients. The highest tenth receive the highest incomes, the second tenth receive the next highest incomes, and so forth. His unit of recipient is the " 'spending unit,' consisting of all related persons living in the same dwelling who pool their incomes" (Kolko, 1964, p. 12).[125] Kolko then calculates the share of personal income received by each income tenth.

PERCENTAGE OF NATIONAL PERSONAL INCOME RE-
CEIVED BY EACH INCOME TENTH BEFORE TAXES,
1959[126]

Income tenth	Percentage of income
Highest	28.9
2nd	15.8
3rd	12.7
4th	10.7
5th	9.2
6th	7.8
7th	6.3
8th	4.6
9th	2.9
Lowest	1.1

The table is constructed strictly according to amount of income received; no other considerations intrude: Since different sources of income are not distinguished, surplus labor is hidden. Some persons receive wages and salaries only on the condition of providing unpaid labor, surplus labor, to others, who receive various forms of surplus-value without working. This opposite and antagonistic relation to surplus labor, either providing it to another class or receiving it, is dissolved into quantitative differences in the amount of income received. An engineer who makes three times the salary of a typist but who like the typist works for an employer is presented in the same light as the capitalist who gets three times what the engineer makes but by exploitation. We know that most capitalists must be in the highest income tenth, but this knowledge brought to the table does not change its form: a ladder of unequal incomes, without regard to class position. Class boundaries disappear.

Kolko's table covers only personal income, ignoring the rest of the surplus product. Kolko makes corrections for some unreported personal income, such as expense accounts for top executives, intercorporate gift giving, and club memberships paid for by the company. He also notes the prevalence of tax evasion at higher income levels and the corporate retention of profits to avoid personal income taxes. Showing this hidden personal income would increase the percentage of total personal income received by the highest income tenth from 29 to 36 percent on a conservative estimate. (Kolko, 1964, p. 23)

These corrections do not challenge the non-class view based on income received for personal consumption. Kolko never discusses the surplus product that the capitalist class disposes of outside the channels of personal income. When Rockefeller and other capitalists built the World Trade Center, a $600 million pair of 110-story buildings in lower Manhattan, this was not declared as personal use of surplus labor. Yet it is a material expression of the capitalist receipt and control of workers' surplus labor. The capitalists chose to give themselves this grand monument, to displace homes and small businesses, and to build this project rather than hospitals and schools. The World Trade Center is an expression of class rule and an allocation of surplus labor flowing to the capitalist class as surely as the Egyptian pyramids were the same for a priestly ruling class headed by the pharoahs. Even school children hear about the tremendous amount of labor enslaved to build monumental graves for the privileged of Egypt, but when it comes to this capitalist society, the statistics on personal income hide the same thing.

The surplus goes to many things, from office buildings to new plant and equipment to military machines. These things may be necessary under the capitalist system, so capitalists may cry that it is unfair to count them. But of course, the income statisticians do not define and measure only discretionary income, so the excuse is irrelevant. Surplus labor is transferred from one class to another, regardless of the laws that govern the system in which this transfer occurs.

By obscuring the division of society into classes and shifting attention to levels of income, theorists of a middle class come into their own. No definition of the middle class could be more immediate than this one, those with middle incomes, neither the greater nor the smaller incomes. This profound outlook has two variations. The first regards nearly everyone as middle class.

"Americans in the broader range of $10,000 to $35,000 do three-quarters of the nation's buying. When they feel bad, the nation feels bad." (Barbour, p. 1)

"At one extreme [of the income distribution] will be the very poor, who have drawn a blank in life; at the other, the very rich. The vast majority fall in between." (Samuelson, p. 109)

These writers do not realize, or do not want their readers to realize, that by counting persons and not income, nearly everyone can be included in a middle income range. If one arranges all incomes on a scale from lowest to highest and chooses appropriate boundary lines to mark out all but the extremes of the scale, it is both easy and trivial to display a large middle income group. Samuelson tells us that if we exclude the very poor and the very rich, the vast majority will fall in between, a statement well worth a Nobel Prize. Barbour, to include three-fourths of the personal consumption spending, had to extend the upper limit of his middle class to $35,000. This "middle class" undoubtedly thins out considerably toward its upper limit; yet the limit must be set high to include a few families with large incomes who represent so much of the nation's buying.

The second variation on the income approach to the middle class grants that a sizeable "lower class" is not receiving middle incomes—but a numerous group does fall in this range. The result is to split the working class in two. These authors usually relate variations of income to differences in occupation. Kolko refers to "the middle-income classes," which becomes "the middle class (the higher-income white-collar workers, professionals, and managers)" (Kolko, 1964, pp. 106, 114).[127] Levison and Parker incite antagonism between semiskilled manual workers and the "affluent" middle class defined by somewhat higher incomes or by craft and white collar occupations. When 20 percent or 40 percent of the population becomes the target, this is splitting the working class, not concentrating on the truly exorbitant incomes obtained not by holding better jobs but by exploitation.

So much for the nonclass picture of the distribution of income, of claims on the product of labor. The next task is to explain the inequality of income, an inequality which exists not only between classes but within them. There are at least five causes of inequality of income. The first reason is class itself. The amount of income depends strongly on its form. Kolko is aware that the highest income tenth of the population receives most of the dividends and that wages and salaries are unimportant forms of income to them. (Kolko, 1964, p. 22) As shown earlier, the capitalist class, comprising two percent of the population, disposes of 40 percent of the national income. Kolko's statistics give a pale reflection of this fact, showing the highest income tenth receiving over one-third of the personal income.

At the other end of the scale, a second cause of unequal incomes makes itself felt, unemployment among the working class. Workers must sell their labor for a wage or salary in order to receive an income. But monopoly capitalism never offers a job to every worker seeking one. Capitalism in general never achieves full employment for very long; it requires the existence of a reserve army of labor, the unemployed workers, or it will face a fully employed working class able to push wage demands successfully and defend working conditions. In the course of accumulation, of the conversion of profit into capital and the extraction of surplus-value at a higher intensity and on a broader scale, this reserve army of labor is created.[128] Whenever a survey of income distribution is taken, there will be a group of unemployed workers, along with their helpless or abandoned dependents, whose income is practically nothing. They may live on savings or credit. Crime and charity may provide them with a pittance. These people fill the lower reaches of the income distribution, a sizeable group which receives a tiny percentage of the total income.

A third cause of unequal incomes appears among the employed workers as well as being reflected in the unemployment just discussed. This cause is the set of capitalist-maintained inequalities among workers such as racism and sexism. Seizing on one or another historical opportunity, capitalists divide workers and engage in the superexploitation of one portion of them, for example, black people and women. The unemployment rate among these groups is always higher than average, too.

Where there would otherwise be two workers earning the same wages, say $10,000 per year, we find that one, the worker subject to this discrimination, earns only $6,000, being forcibly retarded in the worse job and denied training, seniority and promotion. Consequently, there is a well-known spread in the income of workers, with the average income of nonwhite and women workers falling well below that of white and male workers.

This cause of inequality reacts on the basic gap between classes to strengthen it. The difference in wages accrues to the employer, not to the one worker. More importantly, capitalists use their own practices of superexploitation as a basis for encouraging division among workers, lack of unity in class struggle, and consequently a lower wage level. The general wage level is the outcome of the struggle between labor and capital, between the working class and the capitalist class. If disunity in the workers' camp undercuts the struggle, by refusal of some workers to support others, by prejudices and fears seeking to maintain wage differentials between races and sexes, then the capitalists can hold down the wage level of all workers, regardless of color or sex. In the example above, instead of both workers earning $10,000 per year, one earns $6,000 while the other earns $8,000. A differential exists, but this does not erase the fact that both wages are below the potential realizable by united class struggle.

Racism and sexism are maintained solely by the capitalist class. Capitalists, and exploiting classes generally, have fostered and maintained distinctions of skin color, sex, religion, or whatever. In the absence of capitalists, workers of different skin color and sex would have identical average incomes, just as workers of different hair color and lefthandedness or righthandedness have identical average incomes. Socialism will eliminate racism and sexism. Perhaps two generations will be required to complete this task. During this time racist and sexist phenomena will diminish both steadily and in spurts. The lack of progress under capitalism is shown by statistical inquiries made a few years after every wave of small concessions to nonwhite and women workers; the gaps always reappear and widen.

A fourth cause of unequal incomes is the difference in wages for different occupations and levels of education. Under capitalism, labor power is a commodity; like all commodities, its varieties command different prices. The use-value of different capabilities to the capitalist, namely the amount of value each can create, attracts from him a willingness to pay different prices for them. These are phenomena of the market, specifically, the various markets for different kinds of labor power. Of course, the capitalist only buys labor power so long as it serves him as a use-value of a peculiar kind, as something that produces surplus-value for him. There is no need to re-examine here the the power of the capitalist class to hammer occupational markets into shapes and sizes to its liking.

Capitalist apologists give this cause of unequal incomes the most weight. Economist Paul Samuelson concentrates on them, as shown by section headings in his text: Income Differences Among Occupations, Is College Worth While?, and Differences in Ability and Incomes. (Samuelson, pp. 113-115) The United States government's official writer on income distribution, Herman P. Miller, analyzes the same points. A large chunk of his book is concerned with these differences in workers' incomes: Wage and Salary Trends for Major Occupational Groups, for Detailed Occupations, and by Skills for Selected Manufacturing Industries, and finally, Income and Education. (H. Miller, 1966) These authors do not discuss the buyer of the varieties of labor power, the capitalist, and what use-value the commodity serves him. They assume the permanence of capitalism and the unchangeable course of the evolution of its needs. The writers seek to impart to their readers only a practical knowledge of the markets for which the worker might prepare himself or herself. All these markets are simply departments of one social relation, the class relation which plunges workers into the sale of their labor power as a necessity of life.

A fifth cause of unequal incomes consists of the discrepancy between the role of producer and consumer. The individual worker goes through a life cycle of varying activity as a producer. At the same time, he or she is a member of a family, the unit of consumption under capitalism.[129] Individuals move through different positions in the family, from dependent, consuming child through the phases of family head and provider, to the conclusion of consuming, non-earning old age. The aged, without families, not earning, but still needing to consume, are disproportionately at the lower levels of the income distribution. Families, being units of consumption, have different incomes depending (among the working class) on the number and type of labor powers they sell to the capitalist class. There are varying numbers of consumers and earners in families. As Marx put it,

> ". . .one worker is married, another not; one has more children than another, and so on and so forth. Thus, with an equal performance of labor, and hence an equal share in the consumption fund, one will in fact receive more than another, one will be richer than another, and so on."[130]

Among married working men, some will have working wives and others will not. How is the income to be measured? If we look at the family, or the "spending unit," which is nearly the same thing, then a working couple may well earn more than another couple of which only the man works. But if we show a distribution of income by earners, the pattern of equality or inequality will be different, depending on how much the wife earns. Finally, if we measure income per capita, that is, dividing the family income by the number of persons in it, then a wealthy family with many children will add entries to the lower middle portion of the distribution while both members of a working couple with no children appear to be higher on the income scale. We say, "appear to be higher," for one family may be smaller because the couple cannot afford to have children.[131] It is like squaring the circle: the family is a unit of consumption, but income is determined by production, and there is no way to combine the two relations in one expression of inequality.

The inequality displayed in a distribution of incomes is the result of numerous causes: class form and size of income, capitalist refusal to enter all workers into the employment relation, relations of superexploitation like racism and sexism, occupational differences in the price of labor power, and contradiction in the units of production and consumption under capitalism.

These causes are basically social relations of capitalism, either class relations or determined by the dominant class relation of capitalism. The amount of income does not define class; rather, class relations determine the facts of income.

20. Equality

Out of the study of income distribution arises the demand for equality of income. If a number, the dollar income for the year, is attached to each individual, then the abstract possibility exists of making it the same for everyone. The present inequalities of income are clearly unjust and unjustifiable, even as described by capitalist apologists.

> "If we made an income pyramid out of a child's blocks, with each layer portraying $1,000 of income, the peak would be far higher than the Eiffel Tower, but almost all of us would be within a yard of the ground." (Samuelson, p. 110)

The demand for equal incomes is often "the spontaneous reaction against the crying social inequalities, against the contrast of rich and poor" (Engels, 1966, p. 117). But the demand can go no further than the theory behind it. Distribution and consumption cannot be taken in themselves. What exists to be distributed and consumed has been produced; the relations of production among people determine the patterns of distribution and consumption.

196

Conservatives ask, what causes inequality of income? Superficial answers about occupations and educational levels lead back to economic rationales for inequality and demonstrations of its eternal necessity. Yes, says the conservative, it would be admirable to equalize incomes, but then people would not take certain jobs, there would be tremendous crowding into others, and so forth. That is, if the radical has not challenged the existence of classes, the capitalist market in labor power, and other facts of production relations, then the conservative disposes of the plan for equality with sham science. And indeed, individuals will never be exactly identical with respect to consumption.

The field cannot be left to income theorists. Long before the academic servants of the capitalist class had put across the amount of income as a substitute for class position, Marxists were aware of the unequal, unjust distribution of buying power and the consumption of goods. While the ditchdigger's baby died for lack of heat and food, capitalists were filling swimming pools with champagne. Displacing the class perspective by the income perspective, however, income theorists asserted that production relations are unimportant, advanced a peculiar picture of the division of society, stressed other causes of social infanticide and robbery of life in place of class antagonism, and "defended" the goal of abstract equality by opening it to easy defeat.

The problem is not one of individuals but of classes. The "real content of the proletarian demand for equality is the demand for the *abolition of classes*. Any demand for equality which goes beyond that, of necessity passes into absurdity." (Engels, 1966, p. 118) The issue is one class's exploitation of surplus labor from another, the appropriation of surplus product. Abolish classes, and the class determination of income is abolished, too. The abolition of classes encompasses not only the end of the class relation itself, but also the reshaping of all production relations to free them from the dominance of the class relation. Distinctions between mental workers and manual workers have to be overcome, as well as those between direct producers and managers. These relations have been created during thousands of years of class society. With their gradual reshaping, with the appearance of people who do both mental and manual work, who both labor and manage, the needs of consumption change, too. The level of consumption of culture, for example, is raised and equalized.

Particular reforms that would redistribute income or enable individuals to approach equality in various conditions of life are not rejected. Depending on its exact content, a scheme may be worth fighting for. But some income theorists go beyond this. For example, Kolko asks us to join him to "evaluate the structure of the American economy and decide whether it has, in fact, achieved the equalitarian goal set forth by Jefferson." (Kolko, 1964, p. 7) Jefferson believed in a society of small producers and small capitalists. Petty bourgeois are typically aware not of classes but individuals, so that egalitarianism is a natural trend within the petty bourgeoisie.

Those income theorists who call themselves socialists really have nothing socialist about them. The social democrats, particularly the British school descended from the Fabian Society, conceive of socialism in terms of income redistribution.

". . .even a modest redistribution [of income and wealth], together with the general rise in incomes, the expansion of social services, and greater security of employment, would clearly bring about an important change in the position of the working class in society. It seems no longer possible in this second half of the twentieth century to regard the working class in the advanced industrial countries as being totally alienated from society" (Bottomore, p. 23).

Not the revolutionary change of capitalism to socialism, but a change in the position of the working class in . . . society in general, society in nonclass terms. Never questioning the production relations, these social democrats, or socialists of distribution, want to equalize incomes without challenging capitalism; they want capitalism to provide a general rise in incomes, more social services, and secure employment for workers.

In "practical" legislative terms, there is a radical approach and a liberal approach to the achievement of income equality under capitalism. The radical solution is to demand the legislation of income redistribution itself, by progressive taxation, closing tax loopholes, large cash welfare payments, and guaranteed incomes. Such "radicals" are unaware of what determines the inequality of income; they do not act from an understanding of the laws of the subject. The liberal solution is to introduce a number of bureaucratic programs that should give individuals more nearly equal chances to earn an average income, such as programs of education, programs of managing the job market, and programs for health, family planning, and other services. Liberals do have a theory of distribution and consumption. Following mainly those authors who regard income as determined by occupation and education, by place on the job market, liberal theorists attack a cycle of income and consumption: one's income determines what life chances one can purchase for oneself or one's children, and purchases of education, health, and so forth determine one's ability to earn an income. Therefore, the government should subsidize these means to an income for the poor. Instead of rallying the producers to change class and other production relations, to fight for socialism and then build it, these theorists design bureaucratic schemes that will endow individuals with the proper attributes and attitudes with which they can earn average incomes under capitalism.

Neither cash grants nor government programs for passive clients can eliminate class privilege, unemployment, racism, sexism, occupational differences, and the disparities of families. Only class struggle by the working class, culminating in socialism, can alter class relations and their effects.

21. Class and Stratification

This chapter and the next are technical and may be skipped by the general reader.

"Middle class," especially when defined as middle income, implies the theory of stratification.

> "The very term 'middle classes' implies the notion of a society divided into classes, and at least suggests a main division into three—upper, middle, and lower." (Cole, 1950, p. 277)

The theory of stratification regards society as a bonding of layers each above some and below others (except at the top and bottom).[132] Groupings by amount of income are the basis of the theory. But classes, properly understood, are not above and below each other. In specific qualities, one class is superior to another. For example, as the source of knowledge, the motor of production, the agent of social progress, and the embodiment of moral and cultural vigor, the working class is far higher than the capitalist class. But classes stand in specific relations and antagonisms to each other. There is no scale underlying them on

200

which each class sits at a certain point. When income theorists drop attention to class and bring income groupings to the fore, then there is a scale of ranking. Annual incomes can be compared, grouped, and ordered into greater or lesser, higher or lower. Even the distinct strata melt away into a continuous spectrum of dollar incomes.

While the income grouping is the basis of the theory of stratification, sociologists present the idea in universal terms.

"There is still much controversy among sociologists about the theory of social class, and more broadly, of social stratification. The latter term may be used to refer to any hierarchical ordering of social groups or strata in a society" (Bottomore, p. 9).[133]

Thus begins a book on classes in modern society and a chapter on the nature of social class. Right away, the author abandons class in favor of the concept of stratification. "Class" reappears as one way of social ranking. Class relations disappear; surplus labor is never mentioned.

The specific content of stratification theory, its pictures of income and occupation groupings, has already been presented. It remains to contrast the philosophical approach of stratification theory to real science. In place of social relations between classes, stratification theory arrives at correlations between different scales and indexes. Studies of "class" according to stratification theory typically measure the correlation between income levels or occupations somehow arranged in rank order to other phenomena, such as years of education, tendency toward permissive or strict practices of child rearing, amount of illness suffered, number of voluntary associations belonged to, etc., etc.

Such correlations are not science but positivism. Positivism makes our concern not the world around us but mathematical or other patterns. Instead of being used as tools of description and calculation, the mathematical or logical schemes become, for the positivist, the seat of reality itself. The material world becomes unknowable. So long as it displays certain correlations, we may make practical use of them, but knowledge of the laws of matter in motion, of real causes and effects, is held to be impossible. As Lenin said, "positivism is agnosticism and . . . it denies the objective necessity of nature, which existed prior to, and apart from, all 'knowledge' and all human beings." (Lenin, 1968a, p. 168) Positivists say of themselves, "modern positivism regards the law of causality only as a means of cognitively connecting phenomena into a continuous series, only as a form of co-ordinating experience. . . . Laws do not belong to the sphere of experience" (*Ibid.*, quoting the positivist Bogdanov). Therefore, classes do not exist. There are only certain patterns of observations we seem to find recurring, if we define our scales in certain ways. Instead of real relations between classes, the subject matter of the study of class, there are only correlations. As for the origin, development, and necessary consequences of class relations, these do not exist for the positivist. He says that objective laws, causes and effects, are not to be known because they do not exist. In place of class relations there are only inexplicable mathematical facts.

"...according to the materialists, sensible phenomena are due to *material substance...*; according to Hume and the Positivists, their origin is absolutely unknown, and we can only generalize them inductively, through custom, as facts." (Lenin, 1968a, p. 32)[134]

The distinction between positivism and science may be illustrated in the area of physical science. The planets are physical bodies in motion. This motion is not arbitrary nor is it conventionally summarized by equations; the laws of motion of the planets exist, their paths are necessary. Mathematics serves as a language for expressing, approximately, these laws of motion. We say "approximately" because we have attained some knowledge of the motion of the planets but not an exhaustive, total knowledge. Although this is unachievable, our knowledge of matter and its motions becomes deeper all the time. For example, the Einsteinian laws of motion deepen and extend but do not wholly replace the Newtonian laws of motion. If we ever make the mistake of thinking that differential equations are the substance of reality itself instead of a representation of our grasp on material laws of motion, then some observation of the planetary revolutions will awaken us. We do not say that the planets disobeyed the equations but rather that the equations are not sufficiently accurate conceptions of the planetary motions. Then we deepen our knowledge of this motion; we do not merely fish about for another convenient summary of it, as the positivist would have us believe.

Men are part of the material world, and their basic relation to it is the process of production. The social relations of production, as well as the connections between man and nature, are material, objective, and developing. The study of class relations is a science, a department of our knowledge of the real world just like astronomy. Stratification theory, a resort to positivist philosophy and methods, denies the reality of classes and confuses the understanding of them. It is opposed to science. Just as astronomy has been burdened with astrology and its charts, the study of classes has been burdened with stratification theory and its correlations based on income groupings.

22. The Combined Notion of Occupation and Amount of Income

a. Practical

Although some capitalist-minded writers emphasize an income basis of grouping and others an occupational basis, the two methods are often merged and called "class."[135] Kolko, for example, switches back and forth, combining the two criteria in a rapid and loose manner.

"the middle-income classes"
"major differences exist in the economic positions of the occupational classes"
"a visible class structure . . . each income class"
"income and occupational classes"
"the middle class (the higher-income white-collar workers, professionals and managers)"
"the highest income classes"
"the blue-collar class" (Kolko, 1964, pp. 106-15).

Lines can be drawn pretty much as one pleases by using occupation and income in an eclectic way. After a major division into blue collar and white collar, some members of each group can be moved up or down the ladder of stratification based on variations in income. Skilled craft workers may be moved up, while clerks are shifted down. Mayer, for example, concludes his chapter on class in American society with a section on "the hierarchy of classes." The term hierarchy identifies a writer who thinks in terms of a stratified ranking of layers of people rather than classes in relation to each other through the relations of production. Mayer distinguishes a large working class composed of manual occupations, a small upper class of big businessmen and top executives, and a grab-bag middle class of white collar workers and petty bourgeois. (Mayer, p. 40f.) But craftsmen, foremen, and skilled mechanics are hard to classify, partly because of values and beliefs (an irrelevant subjective criterion), more because their "high wages nowadays exceed the salaries of many lower middle class white collar employees" (p. 41). The line between the two groups "has become increasingly blurred in recent years." (p. 42) Still, Mayer holds to large occupational groupings ranked by average income. He does not move fully to an income criterion, in which occupation would be forgotten and each individual ranked by earnings. On the other hand, Mayer insists on some distinctions within the broadest occupational groupings because of differences in income. It is like ranking Detroit's automobile models basically by length but sometimes by style of tail light, so that a car owner can shift his model up a notch or two by emphasizing one or the other. And no one can dispute him. This exercise is nothing but the reproduction of unsystematic opinions about conglomerate social status in fancy academic terms. We learn nothing of the necessity of the rankings, because there is nothing to learn.

Some writers combine occupational criteria with the amount of income by asserting that occupation is a source of income.

"First, the *economic* dimension stratifies modern populations according to the amount and source of income, which is usually derived from a set of occupational activities, the ownership of property, or both. [Such] Differences . . . divide the members of modern societies into several strata or *classes.*" (Mayer, p. 23)

Mayer thinks of classes as strata, with no conception of class relations. This makes his allusions to the source of income and the ownership of property dead letters. What remains is the assertion that income is derived from occupation, at least in the case of the working class. This goes beyond the correlation of income variations with variations of occupation. Occupation, according to such writers, does not merely influence the size of the income but constitutes the source of it.

Any wage or salary worker who knows that the employer might lay him or her off or pass him or her over for promotion regardless of performance on the job knows the absurdity of this theory. The worker's income is derived from a class relation between men, not automatically from the performance of certain tasks in the division of labor.

With the merged view of income and occupation as the basis of "class," the practical sociology of the individual career comes into full bloom. Instead of large classes in relation to each other, there is a finely graded stratification of rankings. Occupation earns one an income, and income is convertible into advantages for oneself or one's children in the pursuit of better occupations. For example, those who would insure a middle class occupation are advised to purchase a college education. The possession of this amount of income and other factors, such as motivation to attend college, to learn to be a careerist, to prefer words to things, and so forth, are correlated with the occupation of the father. Occupation is inserted into the cycle of income and consumption; all factors determining economic position seem to be present. In place of the relations and antagonisms between classes, the individual is related to "society," as if this were something above men which the individual bows to and maneuvers within. According to whether the writer is giving advice to careerists or explaining the necessity of contrasts of prosperity and poverty, he emphasizes the opportunities of sound calculation and individual effort or the "hard facts" of statistical correlations. The class actions of the capitalists are ignored; it would not be scientific to talk about mean class interest and conscious action to realize it. The class action of the working class is ignored, too, in the hope that what is not mentioned will not occur.

b. Apologetic

With the growth of knowledge about classes the exploited have acquired the potential of overcoming inequality. First, the goal was scientifically formulated by Engels as the abolition of classes. Then the practical achievements of socialist revolution, in China for example, have begun to realize this goal.

In this situation Kingsley Davis with the collaboration of Wilbert E. Moore undertook to outline a theory of stratification which explained "the universal necessity which calls forth stratification in any social system." (Davis and Moore, p. 242) An opponent of Davis, Melvin M. Tumin, wrote a reply in defense of equality of opportunity, and the two articles, with additional statements and commentaries, have become a famous debate in the field of sociology.

Davis and Moore proved the universal necessity of inequality with a series of propositions that may be summarized as follows:

1. There is "the requirement faced by any society of placing and motivating individuals in the social structure." (p. 242)

2. "some positions are inherently more agreeable than others, . . . and some are functionally more important than others."(p. 243)

3. Some positions require skills "scarce by reason of the rarity of talent or the costliness of training" (p. 244).

4. A society must inevitably have "some kind of rewards that it can use as inducements" on individuals to seek certain positions and to perform their duties. (p. 243, 242)

5. Therefore, there is a distribution of "these rewards differentially according to positions" and the positions which "have the greatest importance for the society" and "require the greatest training or talent" get the best rewards. (p. 243)

These propositions and their terms are so abstract in the bad sense, abstractions used in place of detailed knowledge rather than as summations of it, that they might mean anything. When Tumin tried to deny them or to bend them to allow for equality of opportunity, Davis shifted ground, saying that "the culprit is the family" rather than the stratification system. (Davis, p. 397) But he was very angry, because Davis wants these abstractions, as is clear from the entirety of his remarks and from his political stance, to make the existing order of inequality seem natural, unquestionable, and "functional."

The definite meaning of the generalities can be found in the examples and explanations that Davis and Moore provide. To say it at once, Davis and Moore are employing the occupation-income method of grouping to cover up the facts of class division.

What are "positions"?

"Practically all positions . . . require some form of skill or capacity for performance. This is implicit in the very notion of position, which implies that the incumbent must, by virtue of his incumbency, accomplish certain things." (Davis and Moore, p. 244)[136]

In other words, positions are occupations. The reference is to the concrete labor, the specific tasks performed in the division of labor and the relations of production other than class. Davis and Moore allow for variation in "the degree of specialization," that is, the elaboration and fineness of the degree of occupational differentiation. Positions require training or talent, that is, developed capability to perform certain kinds of concrete labor. The "position of the M.D." (p. 244) is an example of an occupation (not a class, since doctors may be capitalists, petty producers, or salaried workers). There are "purely technical positions" as well as occupations having to do not with the division of labor but with class relations of production, "religious, political, or economic in character." (p. 247) That is, being a priest, a politician, or a top executive is an occupation existing not because of the division of labor, the relation of men as a coordinated army marching on nature to win their needs, but because of class relations of production, the relation of men to men with regard to the surplus labor of the society.

If position means occupation, then reward means income. There are three kinds of rewards.

> "first of all, the things that contribute to sustenance and comfort. . . . second, the things that contribute to humor and diversion. . . . finally, the things that contribute to self respect and ego expansion." (p. 243)

The perspective is clearly on consumption. There are necessary goods and luxury or leisure goods. The highest rewards are "great prestige, high salary, ample leisure" (p. 244). Prestige we may set aside. For the rest, Davis and Moore mean not consumption goods in general but consumption goods acquired by individual purchasing power, by the salary. It is "the amount of the economic return" (p. 246). In the United States the rewards are "monetary income" (p. 249). As for rewards like service to society and collective prosperity as a result (the "reward" for members of a socialist society), Davis, unrestrained by Moore in a reply to Tumin, answers with cynical scorn,

> "Finally, as for the sense of social service, any sociologist [who is ignorant of socialist countries] should know the inadequacy of unrewarded altruism as a means of eliciting socially adequate behavior." (Davis, p. 396)

In other words, consumption must be the result of individual distribution; it is impossible gradually to satisfy needs collectively, without income payments and purchase but simply by supplying meals and homes as parks are provided today.

Davis and Moore's basic terms, position and reward, are simply academic euphemisms for occupation and income. One can substitute these terms in the summary of the five propositions of Davis and Moore on page 207-208. The meaning and the glorification of the existing state of affairs are a little clearer, but the content is not altered.

Davis and Moore say,

> "If the rights and perquisites of different positions in a society must be unequal, then the society must be stratified, because that is precisely what stratification means." (Davis and Moore, p. 243)

Yes, stratification is the traditional word for the division of society according to occupation and amount of income. When they say, "In a sense the rewards are 'built into' the position" (p. 243), Davis and Moore are simply asserting that occupation is the source of income, denying that the sale of labor power is the source of income for workers.

Which are the functionally important positions? On the average they enjoy better rewards, that is, higher incomes, so it is of some interest to know which they are. "Unfortunately, functional importance is difficult to establish." (Davis and Moore, p. 244n.) What a fortunate misfortune! Yet there are some clues.

> "Thus, in most complex societies the religious, political, economic, and educational functions are handled by distinct structures" and within each structure most positions are "clearly dependent on, if not subordinate to, others", "the *key* positions," which may be identified as "of the highest functional importance." (p. 244n.)

In other words, the relations of authority in organizations identify the functionally important positions. This is the theory that he who commands is indispensable or makes a contribution of a different order than anyone else. Exploiting class societies endow authority relations with this illusion; socialist societies break down the differences between organizational labor and direct labor on things.

When pressed by Tumin and not restrained by Moore, Davis became much blunter about the identification of functionally important positions.

> "Rough measures of functional importance are in fact applied in practice. . . . Individual firms must constantly decide which positions are essential and which not." (Davis, p. 395)

Functional importance for Davis is the value of the labor power to the capitalist class. Requiring certain skills to get his machine of exploitation going, a capitalist hires labor powers or inducts lieutenants into the capitalist class, and the reward is the value of this labor power or the sharing of the profits. A position "draws a high income because it is functionally important and the available personnel is for one reason or another scarce." (Davis and Moore, p. 247) This is the capitalist buyer at the labor market speaking.

The assertion that some education "is so burdensome and expensive" that it requires "a reward commensurate with the sacrifice" is simply a general restatement of the correlation between amount of education and income under capitalism. Samuelson mentioned this economic factor, Miller studied the actual numbers, and Davis and Moore endow them with the attribute of eternal necessity.

When Davis and Moore say that "some positions are inherently more agreeable than others," they are saying that occupations must always be divided up as they are in a capitalist society. In socialist societies, duties and rewards are not separated from each other and exchanged; both are transformed. Those in managerial occupations, for example, work on the shop floor a regular percentage of the time, while mass management committees draw floor workers into administration. This narrows differences in the inherent agreeableness of occupations; both occupations become more agreeable.

Translating the abstractions of Davis and Moore into their real content, we see that they are talking about occupation and income, two social relations. Occupation is a person's spot in the division of labor and the relations of production other than class. Income, in societies which display this individualistic form of distribution, is a distribution relation. In a class society, these relations are subordinate to the class relation. In a capitalist society, the categories of occupation and income are fully developed for the first time and reflect the basic relation between the capitalist and the worker. Davis and Moore simply recast some observations on these relations into vaguer, loftier terms that claim to infuse description with necessity.

In a critical analysis of the paper by Davis and Moore, Melvin M. Tumin disagreed with certain parts of their chain of reasoning. He questioned the specific content of functional importance of positions and the determination of it. Davis and Moore had used relations of authority, other production relations, and class relations themselves to assign functional importance. Tumin observed that in a production process, all the roles are necessary to complete it, so it is hard to assign ranks to functional importance. Both the engineers and the unskilled workers are necessary; how are we to say that one is functionally more important? (Tumin, p. 388) Tumin rejected the capitalist content that Davis and Moore put into the concept of functional importance.

Davis and Moore, in proving the inevitability and functional necessity of stratification in any society, had said that some occupations require skills scarce because of the rarity of talent or the costliness of training. Tumin questioned whether stratification systems did not actually end up "foreshortening the range of available talent" (Tumin, p. 393), that is, keeping the poor from developing skills.

"Where, for instance, access to education depends upon the wealth of one's parents, and where wealth is differentially distributed, large segments of the population are likely to be deprived of the chance even to *discover* what are their talents." (Tumin, p. 389)

If this is so, then the functionality of stratification is doubtful at the least. At the most, although Tumin did not insist on the point, if a society is not pressing at the limit to find and utilize all the talent and to impart all the training it can, then the entire argument of Davis and Moore outlining the function that a stratification system performs collapses.

Tumin's most fervent criticism was directed at the proposition built on the concept of rewards for positions, rewards said to be necessary to induce people to seek various positions and perform the duties of the job.

" . . . the emphasis in American concepts of reward is almost exclusively placed on the material returns of positions." (Tumin, p. 390)

Instead, a general theory should recognize that this is

"only one of many variants in the whole range of possible systems of motivation which, at least theoretically, are capable of working in human society." (p. 388)

Four other motivations are joy in work, the satisfaction of the instinct for workmanship or intrinsic job satisfaction, social duty, and social service. (p. 391) Tumin questioned the identification of reward with income.

Tumin attacked the concept of sacrifice which linked individual educational effort to the individual income reward in the resulting occupation. He noted that "the surrender of earning power and the cost of the training. . . . is generally borne by the parents of the talented youth undergoing training, and not by the trainees themselves." (Tumin,. p. 390) Therefore, Tumin rejected the inevitability of such a scheme, proposing instead that "these costs could easily be assumed by the society-at-large." (p. 391)

Then differences in occupational incomes need not be so large, particularly if other motivational systems were employed.[137]

As a result of all this criticism, Tumin questioned the inevitability and functional value of systems of stratification, particularly in the form implicitly understood by Davis and Moore. Still, there is no evidence to suggest that Tumin joined Engels in making his goal the abolition of classes. In fact, Tumin's analysis and remedies have an anti-working class character.

Throughout the analysis, Tumin accepts the occupation-income framework of analysis.[138] He does not like the present system in some respects, but he analyzes it as do Davis and Moore: occupation gives the individual an income, which in turn can be used to purchase such things as education and which generate an atmosphere of success (motivation) that send the children into better paying occupations, too. Tumin never portrays the differences in society as class differences arising out of the class relations of production. Instead, Tumin argues frequently as a petty bourgeois thinker: individual labor should get its own reward, but the individual should not profit from surpluses earned by others, including parents. For example, in his examination of the sacrifice allegedly made to obtain positions which must then be well rewarded, Tumin argues from the logic of fair exchange.

" . . . the parents' ability to pay for the training of their children is part of the differential *reward* they, the parents, received for their privileged positions in society. And to charge this sum up against sacrifices made by the youth is falsely to perpetrate a bill or a debt already paid by the society to the parents." (Tumin, p. 390)

As for the individual himself, who sacrifices earning power for a period of training, Tumin calculates the magnitude of this loss and concludes,

"One might say that the first ten years of differential pay is perhaps justified, in order to regain for the trained person what he lost during his training period. But it is difficult to

imagine what would justify continuing such differential rewards beyond that period." (p. 390)

Tumin feels everyone should think like him in terms of exchanges
of labor versus income between the individual and society as a
whole. But this mode of thinking occurs only in a society of petty
producers and survives only among those who still represent this
point of view. Each individual should contribute labor, or "sacrifice," and receive in return. The view of the individual contracting fairly with society (with others) is a petty bourgeois outlook.
In a modern industrial society, Tumin wants the beginnings of
capitalism without the accumulation of wealth, the differentiation
of petty producers into classes, and the development of inherited
privilege that necessarily result from the individualistic view of
labor and income.[139] Because Tumin emphasized the social good,
the perspective of "society" in these exchanges, he conveyed an
egalitarian and progressive tone. But his views are similar to
nineteenth century petty bourgeois socialists like Proudhon who
outlined schemes for individuals to receive labor certificates for
their work and then draw their consumption needs with them.
The development of individual labor into labor by some for others
was to be forbidden by decree, by schemes of distribution without any attention to property in the means of production, class
relations, and their dominance over other production and distribution relations.

Tumin's ignorance of the history of class relations is apparent
in his acceptance of Davis and Moore's assertion that "Every
known society, past and present, distributes its scarce and demanded goods and services unequally." (Tumin, p. 387) Tumin
does not know what classless tribal society was like, and he does
not realize what changes in class relations socialist societies
make, which must begin to alter distribution relations among the
workers, too, after first altering the distribution between
classes.[140]

The classic remedy of this variety of petty bourgeois thinker is
equality of opportunity. Tumin wants "genuinely equal access to
recruitment and training" (p. 389). But so long as capitalist class

relations and their influence on other production relations exist, schemes to have the state bear the cost of training, to tax estates and inheritances away, and otherwise to break up class privileges and enter each individual in a fair race with others are hopeless. Equality of opportunity is the petty bourgeois answer to the proletarian attack on inequality, to the demand for the abolition of classes.

There is another tendency in Tumin's argument. While paying no attention to real class relations, he dislikes the unequal distribution of income. The result is an attempt to rise above the whole economic situation by moral appeals. What do his other motivational systems mean? "Joy in work" was a favorite slogan of the German fascist-capitalist regime: the workers were to forget about the vulgar chase after material goods, to accept sacrifice and find their joy in the performance of work. They were to console themselves with "the tradition that each man is as socially worthy as all other men so long as he performs his appropriate tasks conscientiously." (Tumin, p. 392-93) Where exploiting classes rule, schemes to enforce social duty or social service mean increased exploitation. Such would be the case, for example, if

"a system of norms could be institutionalized in which the idea of threatened withdrawal of services, except under the most extreme circumstances, would be considered as absolute moral anathema." (p. 388)

In plain words, this means forbidding strikes and outlawing trade unions.

The views shared by Davis-Moore and Tumin prove more important than their differences. Both sides ignore class relations. Both accept the framework of stratification theory, the investigation of phenomena of occupation and income within the context of capitalism. One side defended capitalism outright; the other combined utopian hopes with potentially fascist propaganda.

23. Individual Mobility to Another Class

Individuals may leave one class for another. The study of social mobility concentrates attention on the individual's fate and the degree to which he or she can determine it by self-serving actions in place of collective struggle to change the conditions of one's class as a whole.[141]

The relative sizes of classes limit the amount of mobility that can occur between them. A working class numbering 90 percent of the population can have no practical interest in sending many workers into a capitalist class comprising two percent of the population. This would be the case even if from time to time the entire personnel of the capitalist class changed, which is obviously an extreme assumption. One benefit of belonging to the ruling class is to remain there and to pass on one's membership to at least some of one's children in the average case. Approximate statistics indicate that "since 1801 a majority of prominent businessmen have come from families already well-established economically." (Lipset and Bendix, p. 122) The figures show this majority to range from two-thirds to three-fourths.[142]

Individuals have moved mainly between the working class and the class of petty producers. Mobility from the working class to the petty producers is commonly supposed to be "upward" mobility. This evaluation conforms to the prevailing values of a capitalist society. To a large extent, it has no material truth to it. The income of petty producers is not that much better than the income of workers, particularly on an hourly basis. Small farmers, storekeepers, franchise food operators, and independent truck drivers typically put in many more hours of work than workers. The attraction of the petty producer situation arises from two illusions. First, the petty producer is like the capitalist a propertied person, and the hope is to grow into a small capitalist after becoming a petty producer. As we have seen, this hope is ridiculous in the extreme today. Nevertheless, capitalist propaganda singles out exceptional cases past and present for heavy emphasis. Second, the petty producer escapes the capitalist-worker relation. He is "his own boss" instead of a worker subject to the despotism of capitalist authority in work. At the same time, he loses the discipline of collective production, of having to arrive at the factory at the same time as the rest of the shift, for example, and not when he feels like beginning work. This mobility does not solve the problem of social production fettered by capitalist rule; it is a backward attempt to retreat from collective relations and forces of production.

Statistics now 30 years old suggest that from 10 to 30 percent of the nonfarm labor force launches a business. (Lipset and Bendix, pp. 102-03) Most fail. Between 1900 and 1940, 15,989,000 businesses were started but 14,013,000 closed. (p. 102) Instead of a large amount of mobility from working class to petty producers, there have been a large number of futile attempts to carve out petty producer situations. Since the petty producer class has been shrinking in size and economic strength, current information would indicate even fewer attempts to start businesses and a greater rate of failure. This is one consequence of the changing and now very high ratio of workers to petty producers; the example and possibility of the petty producer situation is exposed much less frequently and with less force to each of the larger number of workers.

In the opposite direction, the proletarianization of petty producers has been grinding on steadily. This direction of mobility is pictured as a dreadful fate in capitalist valuations. The petty producer who enters the working class brings with him a fresh source of resistance to capitalist exploitation and the tyranny of the workplace through which surplus-value is extracted from the workers. Whenever the capitalist mode of production grips a society and converts pre-capitalist relations into capitalist ones, the petty producers mount stiff resistance to proletarianization. The valiant struggles in England by farmers against enclosures, by the Luddites, and by the Chartists are examples. But the petty producer also brings with him the petty bourgeois mentality, an outlook incapable of successful struggle against capitalism. The ideological struggle within the working class between the petty bourgeois mentality and the proletarian outlook goes on simultaneously with the struggle between the capitalist class and the working class, the outcome of each affecting the other. Capitalism may survive the troubles of its introduction. The proletarianization of the petty producers continues for decades more, but without the same importance. In the United States, for example, this vestigial process has been going on with declining significance for about a century. Only now are we at a point at which the petty producer class has probably touched a certain minimum size. Some writers identify the resistance to the initial capitalist assault on a petty mode of production as the only working class struggle against capitalism. This is incorrect, for so long as capitalism exists, the working class exists and is exploited. It is bound to struggle more, freed of many petty bourgeois influences inherent in efforts to resist proletarianization.

The outlines of mobility between classes are bare and stark enough. Individual movements between classes cannot get rid of them. Therefore, capitalist apologists do not study social mobility in terms of class. The individualistic perspective of social mobility is couched in terms of the occupation-income approach. The study of social mobility is 1) defined as individual movement, 2) up or down a rank ordering, 3) usually expressed in terms of occupational groupings, and 4) concerned not with class position but with secondary relations like amount of income, mental or manual labor, and hope for family advancement if not individual success.[143]

Instead of relations of struggle between classes, individuals move "up" and "down" a scale of positions.[144] This scale is almost always an evaluation of various broad occupational groupings, although occasionally an honest methodologist will admit that the justification for ranking one occupational grouping above or below another is weak.[145] All changes in secondary relations are brought in and linked with mobility. Sometimes absurd statements are made that any economic gain is upward mobility, regardless of the relative position of classes.

> "The American working-class has been upward mobile as a group. . . . if we consider only economic gains without making comparisons with the middle classes. This is evidenced by the increasing real income of the working-class group" (Havighurst, p. 107).

Such thoughts betray the attempt to link in the minds of people any improvement in conditions of life at all with the conception of having pulled oneself up.

Apart from such absurd expressions, writers on mobility almost uniformly regard technological progress, with its accompanying change in the mix of occupations, as a source of upward mobility.[146] This trick merely advances the thesis of a large middle class of white collar workers all over again. The income, working conditions, social status, and other minor qualities of nonmanual occupations are taken to be unchangeably better than those of manual occupations. Technology and some other developments have enlarged the number of white collar jobs and shrunk the relative number of blue collar jobs. Hence, there has been net upward mobility to be distributed to U.S. workers. Changes in technique supersede relations between classes as the motor of social development. This confusion is the basis for assertions that, contrary to what we have seen in terms of movement between the working class, the petty producer class, and the capitalist class, "Movement . . . from working class to middle class . . . in one generation is attainable for millions." (Lipset and Bendix, p. 278)

What are the problems with the nonclass analysis of social mobility? For one, researchers usually compare the son's position to that of his father, which is intergenerational mobility.[147] Intragenerational mobility, the mobility of a person during his working life, is rarely studied because it is difficult to research as a practical matter and because there is very little of it. Workers shift jobs and move from one occupation to a technically similar one. But even in terms of occupation, there is a great dividing line that isolates manual and nonmanual occupations, between which there is little permanent movement in one lifetime.[148] In class terms, it has already been shown how insignificant the subject of mobility by individuals is and must be.

Another problem with the conception of occupational mobility is the treatment of women.[149] Women in the labor force pose a problem. Generally, the rank and the change in rank of women is judged not by their own participation in the labor force but by the ranks of their father and husband. Marriages join men and women who differ in participation in the labor force and in occupational grouping; hence the unsolved problems of classification. This problem does not arise for the class outlook, since stable marriages of individuals remaining in different classes are extremely rare. Classes are basic social groups; occupational ranks are not.

In capitalist theorizing about social mobility, the gross amount of mobility is distinguished from the net amount. The latter refers to the net number of shifts from one rank (or class) to another; it is calculated after cancelling out a worker who becomes a petty producer and a petty producer who becomes a worker. Gross mobility refers to the total number of shifts of position. The worker and the petty producer who both move contribute two counts to the total of gross mobility. Sociologists interest themselves in the amount of gross mobility as evidence of the alleged openness of a class society, the supposed absence of barriers between social ranks, and the ability of the individual to achieve a new rank. Yet all the gross mobility in the world cannot change the shape of inequality in a society. If it has a few high ranks, some intermediate ranks, and many lower ranks, then a large amount of gross mobility simply means a large amount of reshuffling that leaves as much bitterness or other reaction to downward mobility as satisfaction with upward mobility. On the other hand, a small amount of gross mobility simply brings home the institutionalized lines of inequality. This dilemma faces academics who avoid the topic of class and study the movement of individuals instead.

Mobility in occupational terms is really not concerned with individuals and their movement up and down ranks. The hard-nosed sociologists study mobility as a problem in the management of the labor supply.

"A high degree of vocational and social mobility (or, looked at in economic terms, the elimination of rigidities in the supply of labor) is, therefore, both a cardinal principle of policy and a condition of survival for the Welfare State." (Floud and Halsey, p. 83)

Careerism, individual action to improve one's position, does not improve the average lot of members of the working class. Few can benefit by careerism, while individual maneuvering against fellow workers only serves to weaken and split the working class in the face of the capitalist class, lowering the average situation of the workers. Class action improves the lot of the working class. Collective action defends working conditions, improves pay, and establishes principles like seniority in place of "individual merit" manipulated by the employer. Such collective action is rudimentary training for revolutionary class action. Its goal is not only the improvement of the conditions of life under capitalism but the abolition of capitalism and exploitation, the substitution of the workers and their state in place of the capitalist ruling class, in a new society, socialism.

24. The Notion of Capitalists as a Superior Race

Capitalists promote attention to occupational and income groupings in order to erase consciousness of class. Production relations are a fact, and it is fortunate if the lesser relations can be emphasized so much as to eclipse the class relation that is principal in any society divided by it. Nevertheless, within this maneuver is concealed a danger. Once the subject of production relations has been raised, people might discover classes. Fur-thermore, apart from these purely instrumental calculations, the capitalists want more than hypocrisy and avarice for a moral outlook; they want to feel that exploitation is justified. When we reach the bedrock of the capitalist view of society, therefore, we discover its own theory of classes. Capitalists think that the working class is biologically inferior and that the capitalist class is a superior race.

Kingsley Davis holds this opinion as part of his stratification theory. He is pretty clearly referring to the ruling class when he writes of "innate talents of such high degree that the persons who fill them are bound to be rare." (Davis and Moore, p. 244) Davis distinguishes between training and innate talent, so he is consciously talking not about those abilities developed by experience and the efforts of society but about a mystical talent which flows in the blood or the genes. It should also be noted that Davis's liberal opponent Melvin Tumin does not reject the view "that some members of any society are by nature more talented than others" (Tumin, p. 389).

The noted economist Joseph Schumpeter, resident for 20 years at Harvard University, embraced the view that the capitalists are a superior race.

> "The ultimate foundation on which the class phenomenon rests consists of individual differences in aptitude. . . . Class structure is the ranking of such individual families by their social value in accordance, ultimately, with their differing aptitudes." (Schumpeter, p. 210)

Schumpeter grants that his view of the capitalist class as a superior race is closely related to the belief that some races are a superior class. His essay

> "is not meant to deny the significance of racial differences in explaining concrete class formations. On the contrary, my early thinking on the subject followed the paths of the racial theory of classes" (p. 134).

The race theory of class and the overt racist view are essentially the same. Superiority and privilege flow in the blood. The ruling class is the race of the race; from there the hierarchy cascades down.

The book in which Schumpeter published these views was graced with an admiring introduction by Schumpeter's student, "radical" economist Paul Sweezy. Sweezy is interested mostly in the structure and plans of the ruling class or elite; he pays little attention to the class struggle and the action of the working class.

His best known scholarly work dissects the interest groups of U.S. finance capital, and in commenting on current events, a session of the Business Advisory Council this month takes priority over a wave of strikes.

The theory that the better off are inherently superior is not only a German doctrine. A confident assertion without evidence is the hallmark of one British sociologist. "I feel it really is necessary to assert that some children are more able than others . . . and that some occupations demand qualities that are rarer than others" (Marshall, 1971, p. 161). Therefore, "The Welfare State is bound to pick the children of high ability for higher education and for higher jobs" (*Ibid.*)[150]

Joining with the British sentiment is a United States sociologist, who claims that there are differences in intelligence between the members of different occupations and that these differences "can safely be ascribed in part also to a 'natural selection' process which has brought those of greater innate ability to the higher positions." (Kornhauser, p. 206) Regarding intellectual ability, "The upper classes are, in this sense, 'superior.' " (p. 209)

Much less scholarly in tone than these men, more virulent and explicit about the same dogma, is John Corbin. He asserts that Thomas Jefferson was wrong, that "some men are destined from birth to higher privileges and opportunities." (Corbin, p. 36) Why? Because "Some men are created taller than others, and stronger; mentally more able, morally more elevated." (p. 37) It is a historical fact that the Greeks and Romans did not know racism, which began only with the rise of capitalism (see Cox, 1970), but Corbin points out the misfortune this was for the ruling classes of those societies. Greece and Rome fell partly owing to "the wasting of the blood of the dominant class in warfare and luxury, and its weakening through intercourse with alien peoples." (p. 50) Just as racism goes along with the race theory of class, so does imperialism. ". . . there are peoples for whom self-government is no blessing—inferior peoples, unequal to the burden of freedom." (p. 41)

Corbin wrote to offer the employers a strategy to split the working class. He suggested that they extend the recognized boundaries of superior racial endowment to those who think of themselves as middle class. It is necessary to tell the members of the middle class that "Very largely they are Americans of the older stock." (p. 47) Corbin is explicit about this strategy of gross class politics: "Today, with class warfare threatening, the blindest employer can see in the middle class a powerful and indispensable ally" (p. 47). He makes an unusually aggressive attack on the concept of social relations, reducing them to instinct. The sense of private property, it seems, arose before the fish climbed onto the land.

"The fox owns his hole; the trout owns his favorite bend in the brook and will fight for it. Among higher animals, of whom man is one, the possession of females is a primordial instinct" (p. 38).

(Sexism is another benefit of this theory.) With more study, Corbin could no doubt extend his insight that the trout fights for his bend in the brook; he will uncover a mortgage market for holes among foxes, sales and repossessions, a class of foxes who build holes and live in the simplest one-chamber burrows while they construct elaborate multi-chamber complexes joined by tunnels for the capitalist fox whose foxblood is a superior tone of blue.

Corbin introduces us to those open reactionaries who bring the race theory of class out of the parlors of mansions into the arena of politics. There they hope to use it as the best possible explanation of class, since it is based not on the confusion of different kinds of production relations but on the absolute denial of social relations. Another race theorist of class along these lines is Arthur Jensen, the statistical charlatan. For Corbin's colloquial terms "blood" and "stock" Jensen substituted the notion of intelligence genes. Where Corbin lauds the superior elements of mankind, Jensen discusses the problems of the inferior. Although he gives the main emphasis to race, Jensen holds to the race theory of class, too. He regards intelligence as genetically determined for the most part and then states that it is a "fact that intelligence is correlated with occupational status" (Jensen, p. 75). (Jensen uses occupation and income as indexes of class.) He speaks of "genotypic as well as phenotypic differences among social classes. It is therefore most unlikely that groups differing in SES [an index of income] would not also differ, on the average, in their genetic endowment of intelligence." (*Ibid.*) With the falsified data go policy recommendations.

> "Unless drastic changes occur—in the population [that is, Jensen recommends genocide], in educational outcomes, or in the whole system of occupational training and selection—it is hard to see how we can avoid an increase in the rate of the so-called 'hard-core' unemployed." (Jensen, p. 89)

According to Jensen, unemployment is a result not of a class relation but of the breeding of inferior classes.

Jensen's own blood or genes must be slightly diluted from the purest superior strain, for he did not prepare his celebrated thesis entirely by himself. Jensen wrote his article following an outline given him by the editor of the *Harvard Educational Review* in April, 1968.[151] It became well known because the ruling class decided to celebrate its own views. The lecture tours, the interviews on talk shows, and the capsule summaries in *Newsweek* and other mass magazines were the routine execution of another propaganda campaign. Dozens of academic figures served as polite foils, never exposing that this house of cards was built on such crude chicanery as the confusion of a number (correlation) and the square of that number (variance).[152]

Jensen's special twist to the race theory of class was pseudo-science.[153] As a politician he was not too skilled. Students at many colleges ran him off campus before he began to speak. The master politicians of this theory were the German fascists. Installed in power by Krupp, Thyssen, Farben and other big businessmen, their ideas were orthodox reproductions of the capitalist race view of class.

"The biological-medical sciences of the past thirty years have taught us that man is conditioned in both his bodily and spiritual qualities much more by hereditary endowment than by all environmental factors. . . . No thinking and feeling can, if they are genuine and profound, overstep their racial boundaries. . . . Blood and soil [stand] as fundamental forces of life" (Quotations from German fascist documents in Brady, p. 51).

What is the most genuine and profound thinking and feeling possible within the racial bounds of the working class? Hitler replied, "The working masses want only bread and circuses, they have no understanding of any kind of ideal" (Brady, p. 149). Let us leave these inferior beings to the National Labor Front, which teaches strength through joy, since even circuses cost money. We can retreat to chamber music in the Bunker. Hitler is joined by Goebbels, in from scribbling more fulminations at the unpleasantly numerous mass of inferior mankind, and by Goering, a little odd in his lace and lipstick. Here are the supreme defenders and the self-proclaimed epitome of the master race. Servants of monopoly capitalism, they drag after themselves the economists, the scientists, and the politicans of the "middle class," who trail in the wake of the fascists' noble descent into oblivion.

PART THREE: CLASS AND REVOLUTION

> *"The coincidence of the changing of circumstances and of human activity can be conceived and rationally understood only as* revolutionizing practice."
> —Marx, Theses on Feuerbach, III

25. Revolution: The Objective Basis in Class

Capitalist apologists obscure class by confusing the class relation with other social relations. To define class out of existence, the apologists use the label of "class" for the production relations of authority, for the division of mental and manual labor, for markets in labor power and other commodities, and for the distribution of income. Class, the relation to surplus labor owing to the particular relation to the means of production, is confused with one or another or a combination of other relations.

All these production relations operate; there is no question of denying their existence, leaving only the class relation on the theoretical stage. But how do they affect each other? Where class exists, it overrides and dominates all other production and social relations. The apologist, after defining class as some relation other than the class relation, attempts to explain something of the makeup and development of capitalist society. But a particular social phenomenon can be understood only in terms of class and its dominance over other relations. Although production relations of authority exist and possess their own specific weight, we see their essence only in light of the class coloration of authority. A class analysis of supervisory and managerial positions is necessary, or the capitalist class appears larger than it really is. Occupations exist, but the history of an occupation, its growth in numbers, its internal restructuring with loss of skill among the mass, and its decline in relative income, can be predicted from the class contradiction. When we examine the power of the various production relations, we find that class, without doing away with other relations, dominates them. Class makes up their essential content, or forces their development in certain directions, or has effects which reduce those of other relations to insignificant amounts. To make a class analysis often means to find out the specific way that class dominates a social relation.

Once classes appear, the inevitable class antagonisms are the substance of the basic political and economic struggles. In a class society, the exploited always live in the round of continual, poorly rewarded work, some of them are denied the basic needs of life, and demands for redress take militant struggle to win. From its beginning, an exploiting class society is headed for revolution. The revolution needed in a society is determined by the basic class contradiction; the goal is to replace one class's mode of production by that of another class. In a capitalist society, the basic class contradiction is the one between the working class and the capitalist class.

So long as capitalism allows the productive forces to develop, the contradiction by itself is not enough for a revolution. Capitalism was progressive in this sense through the industrial revolution of the eighteenth and early nineteenth centuries. With the appearance of monopoly capitalism, the system became opposed to further development of the productive forces. This does not mean that levels of production decline or that technology regresses to more primitive methods; these are even later stages of decay seen, for example, at the end of the ancient world in Europe. The turning point in the life of a class society is passed before that, when the class relation hampers and slows down the development of the productive forces, retarding the introduction of new techniques and restricting the growth of production. In the United States this happened after the Civil War. Monopolies buy up patents and shelve them. They hold production below capacity to maintain higher prices than otherwise possible.

The inevitable result is intensified class struggle. The exploiting class demands more and more surplus labor. At the same time, the battle between the classes over the historical and social standard of necessary labor rages openly. The workers' smallest amenities disappear, situations of modest comfort become lives of worry and bitter choices, and more people are torn by desperation for food and shelter. The exploiters' social system collapses. At every turn, their world is filled with crises, breakdowns, and disasters. Social peace, always superficial, becomes open class struggle; the philistines run for cover, while leaders emerge from among the exploited class which now conducts its war of liberation from the rule of the exploiters.

The revolutionary goal of the working class is to replace capitalism by socialism. The private ownership of the means of production is abolished and replaced by the collective ownership of the factories, offices, and fields by the working class through its state.[154] Surplus labor, exploited from the workers owing to the private ownership of means of production, returns to the working class. This surplus labor can belong to the working class only in forms appropriate to the forces of production and the relations of production. These are collective relations and forces. The large scale of cooperation and the intricate division of labor reached under capitalism become even larger and more finely developed. The various departments of production are necessarily planned on a society-wide scale to achieve the balanced expansion of production. At the same time, the abolition of the class relation to surplus labor still leaves the other relations of production infected by capitalism. The job remains of bringing the division of mental and manual labor, the relations of authority, the wage form of distribution, the family, and all other social relations into their collective, working class forms, purged of capitalist and petty bourgeois influences. This is a long task that goes on under socialism. It is a class struggle. When it is done, society has reached the communist stage, completely free of classes, class influence, and class contradictions.

If a society contains a large class of petty producers, this necessarily affects the kind of revolution that it needs. The revolutions in Russia in 1917 and in China culminating in 1949 are examples. In both countries, the working class was a small percentage of the population, and the mode of production was not capitalist. The largest class was the class of petty producers, mostly rural, farming petty producers. Enslaved in a semi-feudal form of exploitation, they lost their surplus labor not through a wage relation, but through the payment of rent, usurious interest rates on loans, and merchant trade relations. These forms of exploitation reflected the basic economic problem of the petty producers, the lack of complete title to their means of production. Instead of owning their fields, they rented them. Instead of being able to finance their food and seed costs until harvest, they borrowed the goods or the cash to buy them.

The immediate revolutionary goal in Russia and China was not socialism. In these societies, the mode of production was a mixture of landlordism, local capitalism, and imperialist exploitation by the monopoly capitalists of several foreign countries, including the United States. The ruling classes were the landlords, some local capitalists, and the imperialists. The exploited classes were the petty bourgeoisie and the working class.[155] Consequently, the revolution, while not aiming at a mode of production only for petty producers, did give most weight to their needs. In China, this mode of production was called New

Democracy.[156] Its basic economic content was expressed in the slogan of land to the tiller. In revolutionary base areas carved out before 1949 and then in the entire country after liberation, the rural petty producers abolished their relation to the landlords and acquired full, unencumbered ownership of plots of land which they worked themselves. This solved the contradiction for the petty producers. In the Soviet Union, the landlord system was abolished right after the October Revolution of 1917, creating a broad class of middle peasants, petty producers who neither exploited others nor were exploited themselves.

Petty producers cannot achieve their revolutionary goal by themselves. In both Russia and China, as in Albania and other countries that enjoyed New Democratic revolutions, success depended on leadership by the working class, which, to be sure, did socialize the small capitalist sphere. The working class led by its communist party put the greatest emphasis on solving the main contradiction, that between the petty bourgeoisie and its exploiters. As a result, the petty bourgeoisie trusted the working class. The petty mode of production could not last for long. Particularly with the germs of capitalism planted in these countries, a rapid polarization threatened to force most petty producers to mortgage or sell their land and become wage slaves, while a few capitalists, called "kulaks" in Russia, would be at the exploiting end of this new relation. Because of its political record and its ties to the petty bourgeoisie, the working class was able to lead the inevitable collectivization of the forces of agriculture along collective lines in the relations of ownership, too. Small plots must merge or be merged; the working class demonstrated the superiority of collective farming over class polarization in the countryside and persuaded the middle and poor peasants to reject the capitalist road, the freedom to lose one's land by making a doomed individualistic effort. In the Soviet Union, the petty producer and semi-worker peasants joined collective farms and overcame the wrecking attempts of the existing kulak class. In China, with fewer capitalist farmers and with previous Soviet experience to go on, the same process occurred even more smoothly in a number of steps from labor-exchange agreements and mutual aid teams through collective farms to the people's communes, which unite governmental, agricultural, and local industrial functions for tens of thousands of people.

New Democracy is obviously inappropriate to the United States. No large class of petty producers exists, and it would be impossible to convert the working class into a class of petty producers by dividing up the means of production. A factory could not, for example, assign a lathe and a drill press to each worker, so that workers would negotiate the exchange of products to complete the job. Similarly, factories as a whole could not be assigned to the workers employed in each of them, making them business partners who would buy and sell with other factories. The division of labor is so intricate and the scale of production so large that this system would quickly recombine into monopoly capitalist trusts engaged in exploiting most of the "partners." The revolution in a society must reflect the classes in it; the new mode of production must correspond to the needs of the exploited class, including the specific forces and relations of production it represents.

The predominance of the working class in the United States, facing "its" capitalist class alone, defines the revolutionary goal as socialism, and the goal of socialism certifies the overwhelming weight of the working class. Therefore, it is natural for political tendencies that oppose the revolutionary goal of socialism to misrepresent the class structure of the United States, too. If a person or group does not accept a sizeable number of workers as members of the working class, then we expect the group to define the revolution in non-socialist terms. This is the case.

Sham communist parties have dropped the goal of socialism and substituted in its place a so-called anti-monopoly coalition aiming to install an anti-monopoly government. These are parties tied to the Communist Party of the Soviet Union, such as the Communist Party USA, the Communist Party of France, and so forth. Their analysis categorizes many white collar workers as something other than members of the working class. The only logical alternative is the petty bourgeoisie, although the pro-Soviet parties have so far avoided this bald assertion. It is clear that they exclude some workers from the working class, because the parties talk about an alliance between the working class and white collar workers or certain sections of them. When Maurice Thorez, longtime chief of the Communist Party of France, wrote that the "stratum of engineers, managers and technicians" can "range themselves on the side of the proletariat," he was splitting the working class in order to pretend to form an alliance again between its sections.[157] The other parties in this stream of revisionism, of revising the revolutionary and class content out of Marxism, put forward similar programs.[158] In Russia and China, there was an objective basis for New Democracy, for a revolutionary goal between the existing situation and the ultimate socialist goal. If there is no such basis, parties advocating illusionary stages try to create one by inventing new classes. The only source for members of these classes is the working class. Then the parties declare that they will work for an alliance between the remainder of the working class and the unacknowledged petty bourgeoisie they have invented. In this two-step shuffle they get away from socialism. Now we are supposed to unite for an anti-monopoly government. This is an impossible goal. It is an attempt to reform capitalism and would lead to disaster in a revolutionary situation, should such a goal divert many workers from going for socialism. In other words, the anti-monopoly government in unity with the nonexistent, allied, petty bourgeois strata really means more capitalism.

The pro-Soviet parties are not the only tendency that invents a numerous petty bourgeoisie. Among groups which claim in words to reject the Soviet brand of revisionism, a cluster revolves around the notion of a united front against imperialism. On the world scene, this slogan unites a broad variety of forces to oppose foreign big business investments, aggression, and the collusion and contention of the imperialist powers headed by the two superpowers, the United States and the Soviet Union. The slogan has applications within some countries, too. As a fundamental revolutionary program in the United States, however, it is anti-socialist. A number of groups calling themselves Marxist-Leninist adhere to the position of a united front against imperialism within the United States. What is their class analysis? Some programs assert that the petty bourgeoisie is a large class including many different strata and call many workers members of it. Other groups are extremely vague about the analysis of classes; this is similar to the pro-Soviet revisionists' game of talking about an alliance. Marxists always make a clear analysis of classes. Where there is no class analysis, there is no Marxism. One variation of the united front against imperialism tells the working class to ally with the black petty bourgeoisie and even the black bourgeoisie. This fantastic idea is connected with the promotion of nationalism among black workers and the attempt to browbeat communists into forgetting about classes and giving up on white workers as a revolutionary force. The result in class terms is to imply or assert the existence of a large petty bourgeoisie. These groups, while retaining a vague adherence to socialism in words, lack the class analysis that corresponds to it. Like the anti-monopoly coalition, their united front against imperialism can only mean going into a revolutionary situation destined to failure.

What is the relation of the "middle class" to the problem of revolution? The various ways of defining a middle class have nothing to do with class, as we have seen in this book. Occupation, industry, product of labor, and amount of income do not provide grounds on which to define a class. When academic and popular writers conjure up the image of a large middle class, they cannot specify and do not want to specify what mode of production corresponds to it. Unlike tribal and feudal peasants, slaveowners, lords, capitalists, workers, and petty producers, the middle class is the first class without its own mode of production! Therefore, there is no basis for defining a revolutionary change in capitalism. This absurd conclusion demonstrates again the total lack of science in notions of a middle class.

In revolutionary circles, talk about a large petty bourgeoisie where there is none usually means that the speaker thinks of the petty bourgeoisie as the middle class. Ignoring the economic characteristics of the petty bourgeoisie, these persons use the term as no more than a fashionable equivalent for middle class. They introduce the same outlook that is contained in talk of the middle class. One writer in his analysis spoke frankly about the "middle classes (petit bourgeoisie)" in the 1972 edition of a book and revised it to the "petit-bourgeois class" in the 1975 edition.[159] This was merely a change of terms; the text remained largely a study of occupations and income levels. Left groups that talk about a united front against imperialism, if they make any explicit analysis of classes, say that "petty bourgeoisie" is generally used to describe the strata in between the bourgeoisie and the proletariat. That is, it is a middle class. Such definitions open the door to all the usual confusions about how to define classes, so that one may pick and choose criteria as one desires to answer different questions. Sometimes occupational characteristics like the amount of education will be cited, sometimes the amount of income. When a program leans on such varied, secondary characteristics, then the door is open to unprincipled calculations differing from the openly revisionist anti-monopoly coalition only in superficial appearances.

26. Revolution: The Subjective Force in Class

An analysis of classes reveals the basic antagonism in society and the kind of revolution that will resolve it. So much for needs; where is the force to carry through this revolution? The answer can only be that it resides in the class or classes that need the revolution. An apparent obstacle is the fact that the class with the revolutionary duty does not appear to be revolutionary in its outlook and actions. Revolution does not occur as soon as objective conditions demand it. What has to be explained is the temporary absence of class consciousness among the revolutionary class.

Class consciousness is not the same thing as class struggle. Throughout their history, United States workers have waged continual, strong battle against the capitalists for jobs, better wages, shorter hours, equal treatment regardless of race, nationality, or sex, more education, and adequate social insurance and welfare. In the latter 1800's, workers mounted national actions like the railroad strike of 1877, the eight-hour movement of the 1880's, and the Pullman strike of 1894. The Wobblies and the Western Federation of Miners opened the twentieth century with job actions across the West. Many workers opposed the imperialist slaughter of World War I. In the 1930's, workers organized industrial unions and forced acceptance of them on the capitalist class. Anti-racist insurrections marked the later 1950's and early 1960's and flowed into mass working-class marches against the Vietnam war. In between these high points, the workers' struggle always went on here and there, always probing, always testing new fronts. The question is not working-class discontent, activity, militance, and bravery, for workers have poured their energy and lives into class struggle. The needed ingredient is consciousness that would lead to an assault on capitalism itself.

The capitalist class rules by means of force and fraud. Force is used to suppress local rebellions by the working class against its exploitation. Police attack picket lines; martial law is declared. Even fascism is a sign of capitalist weakness requiring the desperate use of force. The fundamental longterm tool of the exploiting class is fraud, the deliberate, systematic inculcation of erroneous ideas in the minds of the exploited classes. The capitalists possess the machinery for putting across this fraud in the educational system, the various political parties and groups it supports openly or covertly, the religious organizations, and in the media of daily information, the newspapers, television, magazines, and so forth. The process of implanting fraud is cumulative; these institutions build on previous results, which become embodied in everyday thinking and habits of action. On the surface, this fraud takes many forms, but essentially it impresses on the exploited classes false pictures of society, misconceptions of their interests, demoralizing evaluations of the prospect for revolution, and erroneous, ineffective suggestions for seeking change.

Fraud is ideology, and an ideology always reflects the outlook of a class. The ideology pushed onto the working class is bourgeois and petty bourgeois ideology. Myths about so-called free enterprise are petty bourgeois. So is a hippie reflection of the same idea, the philosophy of doing your own thing and letting me do mine, letting me exploit other people if I can get away with it. Any idea based on individualism reflects the outlook of the petty producer, who wants to operate his own means of production independently of coordination with others and outside all authority. Large numbers of workers believe petty bourgeois frauds under the pressure of capitalist agencies. The worker lacks the time to combat the propagation of fraud on his own, and workers' organizations, primarily the Marxist-Leninist communist party, can never expose all the fraud to all the workers under the conditions of capitalism. Yet these conditions, important as they are, are not the material basis for petty bourgeois ideas among workers. No idea obtains currency in society unless there is a material basis for it. This basis consists of the relations other than the class relation, relations which bear capitalist and petty bourgeois influences. Everything said in chapter nine about the formation of the petty bourgeois mentality in general applies as well to the question of revolution, a social and political question which is analyzed in terms of one's own view of society, of its classes, and of the interests of oneself and others.

A person's social consciousness may be true to the basic fact of his or her life, the class relation, in which case it is called class consciousness. Otherwise, it is false consciousness. The class relation alone does not determine a person's social consciousness. It is determined by all the relations in which people are engaged, including the secondary relations bearing capitalist and petty bourgeois influences. By a play on words, some writers say that class must determine class consciousness, by which they mean social consciousness; on this basis they revise the definition of class to categorize many workers as middle class or petty bourgeois because their social consciousness is not working class.[160] This theory rejects the concept of false consciousness, of an outlook influenced more by secondary production and social relations than by the basic class relation.

"Variations in class identification have to be related to actual variations in class situations and not attributed to some kind of ideological aberration or self-deception." (Lockwood, p. 203)

Lockwood dumps all the secondary relations into the determination of the objective class position: he defines a person's class by
what position he holds on the labor market (the departments of
the wage relation), whether he exercises authority at work,
whether he is engaged in mental or manual labor, and whether he
works collectively or on his own.[161] With such a definition, the
social consciousness of people appears to flow from their "class
position," requiring little capitalist effort to prevent workers
from learning about classes. This result conveniently obscures
the capitalist machinery for using secondary relations to mislead
people about their class. The game would be acceptable if
people's interests really did correspond to the secondary production and social relations which help shape their consciousness.
But class is primary, it does determine the evolution of the other
relations, and the working class can meet its needs only on the
basis of fighting the class that takes away its surplus labor.

Philosophically, the identification of subjective, inaccurate
ideas with objective realities of class amounts to dropping science
in favor of pragmatism. From the pragmatist point of view, the
objective world, including social relations independent of men's
wills, does not exist. What counts is not the objective world but
the usefulness of attention to various factors in predicting the
consciousness of workers.[162] Furthermore, this prediction is for
the fleeting moment; underlying trends that are bound to emerge
plain to the most obtuse scholar are of no interest. The pragmatist gives the class label to any factor that, accounted for
statistically, appears to correspond to a person's consciousness.

> " 'Class,' like any other sociological concept, is a device by
> which social facts are to be understood, and, in the last
> analysis, the definition of class that is adopted can be justified
> only by its usefulness in the explanation of particular and
> concrete events." (Lockwood, p. 213)

A concept, says the pragmatist, is a device. "Particular and concrete events" refers to the prevailing ideology of everyday life, not fundamental, historical events, among which are revolutions. The use of the term class not to describe the flow of surplus labor in a society, but to serve as a tool of opinion polling is a pragmatist approach without shame.

For a certain historical period the majority of members of society will not recognize the existence of class and its power over other social relations. Still, this power operates. The capitalists' falsehoods run up against the real structure of society at various places and moments, especially during depressions and wars. In the course of political and economic struggles, illusions are shed. Class position is pushed to the fore, particularly in deep social crises, and these arise more and more as capitalism sinks further into decay. Life is getting worse for workers in the United States, not better. The real wage is generally falling, not rising. Those who never had to struggle before must now join in battle. Those who kept their fight within certain bounds are finding that this no longer wins gains. Attitudes become proletarian, and actions deal accurate blows to capitalist social relations. This does not happen automatically, but because class conscious workers organized in a genuine communist party increase their ranks through the course of political struggle. It is not necessary to overcome all petty bourgeois ideas on every subject for the working class to become a revolutionary force. It is enough when many who would defend capitalism in the streets no longer see any reason to put themselves on the line. It is sufficient when some of the workers who thought nothing could be done awaken to the revolutionary current. It is decisive when active workers switch from struggle within the bounds of capitalism to revolutionary struggle against it. Certain truths about the nature of the state and revolution are the crucial ones, on the basis of which the rule of capitalism can be smashed, the working-class state can be set up (this is the dictatorship of the proletariat), and the means will then be at hand to revolutionize all of society over a whole transitional epoch, socialism itself.

27. Revolutionary Policy and Practice

Revolutionary policy and practice uses knowledge of classes objectively in contradiction with each other to assemble the revolutionary force that will smash the exploiters' state, change the mode of production, and build a new society. The struggle for a revolutionary policy goes on between two trends. The Marxist-Leninist trend is based on a correct analysis of classes and of the dominance of class over other social relations. The opportunist trend, appearing in right-wing and "left"-wing varieties, relies ultimately on one or a combination of the anti-class outlooks we have seen in this book.

Marxism-Leninism holds that in the United States today most people are members of the working class, standing in contradiction to a small but powerful capitalist class. The workers are not only our friends; they are the leading and main revolutionary class. While any class has advanced members who enter the struggle first as well as some backward elements, this does not alter the role of the working class as the revolutionary force that will replace capitalism by socialism.

Opportunism acts on the assumption that there is a large petty

244

bourgeoisie in the United States. The difference between academic theorists of a middle class and the opportunist trend is simply that the latter represents itself as wanting a revolution. In its policy toward the alleged petty bourgeoisie, the opportunist trend may take various approaches: an alliance not based on socialism,[163] or rejection of the petty bourgeoisie, or lack of any definite policy for it.

For Marxist-Leninists, the long, patient work of preparing the working class for revolution consists of uniting workers in their struggles, fighting capitalist divisions, and carrying on ideological struggles against petty bourgeois ideas, particularly revisionist ideas about the state and revolution. The opportunist trend is unable to unite workers, often promotes divisions within the working class, and supports petty bourgeois ideas.

A few examples may be mentioned. Marxist-Leninists welcome the increasing level of struggle by public workers. One of the crucial questions in their strikes is that of unity between public and private workers. Many capitalist lies have to be overcome, such as that which would oppose the wages of public employees to the taxes of all workers (similar to the company argument that wage hikes require price rises). The capitalist press tries to charge public workers on strike with depriving us of necessary services, when in fact service worthy of the name can only be maintained by the united struggle of public employees defending their working conditions and workers in general demanding services. The capitalists are the ones who are running down public transit, health services, education, and so forth.

The opportunist trend does not help and often hinders this class struggle. Worries about whether government workers are really workers paralyze revolutionaries who are victimized by the opportunist deviation. Instead of uniting workers, it is likely to play up divisions based on income levels between public workers and the poor who receive many services. By regarding some workers as petty bourgeois, the opportunist trend may end up promoting attacks on them. This splittist activity happened in

New York City in 1975. Some left groups influenced by opportunism in regard to a teachers' strike attacked it for depriving
poor workers' children of an education. Were this argument true,
shifting the blame for inadequate education from the capitalists
to the workers, it could be transferred to all sorts of strikes. The
capitalist Board of Education is responsible for bad education, an
inevitable result of overcrowded classrooms, underpaid and
overworked teachers, and lack of supplies and facilities. The
strike was not a clash of petty bourgeois and working-class
interests, regardless of confused thinking about class and occupation or the criterion of production of surplus-value. The strike
was a battle of workers, both teachers and parents, against the
capitalist government and its servants at the head of the union
bureaucracy.

The opportunist trend covered its position under a show of
criticizing the racism of the union leaders, as if the divisive tactics
of the labor lieutenants of the capitalist class represented the
teachers' interests. Predictably, the leaders sold out the strike.

In general, opportunists sow confusion about the class analysis
of racism. Their confusion prevents revolutionaries from promoting working-class unity in many strikes and other battles, such as
the question of forced busing. The capitalist class introduced
forced busing in Boston to split the workers and draw attention
away from the capitalists' plan to run down the schools even
more. The Marxist-Leninist position was to demand more money
for the schools, for smaller classes, building repairs, an adequate
textbook supply, and so forth. The money should be put where it
is needed most, recognizing that the schools for black children are
most often the worst off. Forced busing added no resources to the
educational system; it only created anger and division. The
opportunist trend helped the capitalists to divide the working
class. One variety attacked white workers as the source of
racism, supported forced busing, and offered no program of class
struggle for better education. Another variety of opportunism
was against forced busing but did not respond at all to racism, to
the systematic discrimination by the Boston School Committee

not only against working-class schools in general but against schools for black children in particular.

An incorrect, non-class analysis of racism is a favorite refuge of opportunism. Sometimes it openly puts class second to this cause of unequal incomes and conditions of life among workers. If pressed for a class analysis, an opportunist could not give one for the Boston busing struggle, particularly with regard to the working class (there might be a lot of talk about wings of the bourgeoisie). So far as "class" appears at all, opportunism defines it on the basis of income and divides workers into the poor and the better off, whom they call petty bourgeois or an aristocracy of labor.

Let us give one more example. Some leftists in the United States-China Peoples' Friendship Association claimed that too few workers and minority people belonged to the organization. One survey counted only seven percent of the members in the working class. What definition of a worker was used in this survey? Surely the association was not composed of 93 percent capitalists and petty producers! Few members of the organization were blue collar workers from large steel mills or automobile factories. A good number were probably laboratory technicians, teachers, retired workers, and so forth. There was no compelling need for the association to have blue collar members rather than white collar members; regardless of occupation and income, they had shown great ability and enthusiasm for reaching all workers with the message of friendship between the Chinese and United States people. But opportunists, interested in a factional battle, were casting around for a diversionary issue. By blowing up occupational differences into the sensitive question of the "class makeup" of the association, they were able to persuade a convention to adopt specific quotas before trips to China and other activities could be launched. As this is written, soon after the convention, the members are already rebelling against such an anti-worker, anti-China friendship position.

These examples are taken from specific cases in a pre-revolutionary period. In general, the Marxist-Leninist trend unites the objective and subjective forces of revolution because it has identified both. The working class is the overwhelming force objectively, and by uniting workers with a proletarian outlook, that force is gathered and directed at the capitalist target. The weight of petty bourgeois ideas to be overcome is heavy, but the actual size of the petty bourgeoisie, with whom there must be at best an alliance for some program other than socialism, is very small.[164]

The opportunist trend generally flies the banner of the united front against imperialism. Sometimes opportunism waters down working-class demands with the excuse of preserving the main thing, the united front. Since the other part of the alliance is really workers, too, who have been mislabeled petty bourgeois, this amounts to telling some workers to adopt a petty bourgeois outlook for the sake of unity with other workers! At other times, a group dominated by opportunism refuses to support the working-class action of people incorrectly identified as petty bourgeois, on the grounds that this struggle is not covered by the united front. In other words, workers who may be taking a step forward in action and consciousness, bringing their politics into line with their objective class position, get no help.

Abandoning the working class or part of it, opportunists try to sell revolutionaries a calculus of political sympathies that will create a revolutionary force that is not quite revolutionary. But the inevitable result of inflating the objective size of the petty bourgeoisie is to dilute the hegemony of working-class ideology, either by unwarranted concessions or by sectarian refusal to work patiently. It takes no great insight to realize that many people do not have a proletarian outlook now. The revolutionary question is the process of change of outlook. A Marxist-Leninist helps workers' outlooks to reflect their class position. And organized political sympathies are always based on principles reflecting some outlook. Without a revolutionary theory there can be no revolutionary movement.

The Marxist-Leninist forces have their headquarters in a genuine communist party, and Marxism-Leninism is the only basis of a real party. It welcomes all workers who step up activities of struggle, and it exposes capitalist and petty bourgeois ideas that hamper the revolutionary movement. The party must do the job of making the workers' struggles the party's struggles and making the party's outlook the workers' outlook. This is the way to spread class consciousness in the course of many struggles. At each phase, those who become class conscious will want to work for socialist revolution, and the communist party organizes them. Wherever this policy is applied (and it is being applied by Marxist-Leninists in the United States), both immediate gains and a base for continued revolutionary work have been won.

In any country, the communist party must know all the classes in the society and their economic basis. Objectively, the class makeup defines the basic class contradiction and the revolutionary goal. It indicates the inherent strength of the leading force in the revolution (the working class) and the main force (the preponderant class among the working people generally). By knowing the essence of every class, the party can recognize the various outlooks in society as reflections and tools of classes. The party can then judge the existing state of objective and subjective revolutionary factors and find the way to propel the situation forward. In the United States, the working class dominates objectively, but the capitalist class has put over petty bourgeois misconceptions. Ultimately, large numbers of workers will become class conscious.

In a revolutionary situation, the crucial forces are located more among the manual workers than among the mental workers, more in big factories than in small shops, and more among the direct producers than the supervisors. But it is not because these workers want to fight that the communist party enrolls them. They want revolution because they have become class conscious, something in which the party has helped them, and the party is the home of the most dedicated, class conscious workers. But all the active workers, not only the members of the communist party, make a revolution. This is a concrete assessment of how secondary relations of production serve the class struggle.

The opportunist trend demands to know, without understanding class, what action various segments of people will take, how much they will contribute to immediate actions. Opportunism winds up defining classes by a number of production relations, not by the class relation alone, and comes up with a sizeable petty bourgeoisie or poorly defined groups, strata, and segments of the working people. The result is that the class relation itself counts for little or nothing with opportunists. This deprives revolutionaries affected by the opportunist trend of a solid basis for the longterm goal; they lose clarity and confidence. Cast adrift in a sea of details, they miss chances to advance the situations that arise. The result of all this can only be to demoralize revolutionaries and hurt the working-class struggle. Conscious opportunists are wreckers and agents of the capitalist class.

The political importance of the correct definition of classes cannot be emphasized too much. Incorrect definitions do more than reject numerous workers as petty bourgeois. The class interests of workers still included in an erroneous definition are inevitably distorted. If the essence of class has not been grasped, even correctly classifying most workers will only lead to anti-working class policies to relate them to other workers. Such things as amount of income, occupation, or industry are not the essence of class. The fundamental point is the exploitation of surplus labor through specific relations to the means of production. Because of technological and other changes within capitalism, anyone who limits the working class to certain images based on selected occupations, industries, or other non-class criteria will be faced with a large group that does not fit the picture. A large group cannot be ignored. What will one do: reject a struggle before one's eyes because it is not familiar enough? capitulate on basic principles and accept capitalist fraud? or maintain the class approach? The answer will determine not only how one places oneself in relation to a large social group but also how one acts as a revolutionary among the more familiar sectors of the working class, too. Only a firm Marxist-Leninist analysis of classes allows one to keep up the revolutionary perspective. The example of the pro-Soviet revisionist parties shows us that the definition of class used by a party reflects not merely the policy toward a specific group but also one's fundamental stance—revolutionary or reformist.

If the party has the Marxist-Leninist outlook and sets up no artificial barriers, it will be united with the working class appropriate to all its degrees of activity and consciousness. This force, led by the most active and conscious workers, can smash capitalism and set up the dictatorship of the proletariat. If revolutionaries keep to the class perspective and reject opportunist calculations based mainly on secondary production and social relations, then they will retain the qualities that make them valuable to the working class—their defense of Marxism-Leninism and their ability to find and go to work on the revolutionary task in every situation. To sort out the two trends, they must ask about any program: what is the class analysis here?

NOTES

1. "In the social production which men carry on they enter into definite relations that are indispensable and independent of their will; these relations of production correspond to a definite state of development of their material powers of production. . . . At a certain stage of their development, the material forces of production in society come in conflict with the existing relations of production, or—what is but a legal expression for the same thing—with the property relations within which they had been at work before. From forms of development of the forces of production these relations turn into their fetters. Then comes the period of social revolution." (Marx, 1904, pp. 11-12)

2. "In the process of production, human beings work not only upon nature, but also upon one another. They produce only by working together in a specified manner and reciprocally exchanging their activities. In order to produce, they enter into definite connections and relations to one another, and only within these social connections and relations does their influence upon nature operate, *i.e.*, does production take place." (Marx, 1933, p. 28)

3. Capitalist writers assert the opposite without evidence.

". . . as soon as technological skills become sufficiently advanced to produce more than a subsistence minimum, the economic surplus tends to be allocated unequally" (Mayer, p. 6).

"Social classes originated with the first historical expansion of productive forces beyond the level needed for mere subsistence" (Bottomore, p. 15). By the context, Bottomore even implies that this is Marx's view.

"As a society becomes larger and as the distribution of wealth, possessions, and prestige begin to differ among its members different kinds of groups become organized around these unequal distributions" (Bennett and Tumin, p. 453). This slippery statement if read closely tells the reader very little, but it is intended to slur over the question of how long a surplus exists without classes appearing.

4. ". . . they cultivated maize, beans, squashes, and tobacco in garden beds. . . . They . . . practiced communism in living . . ."
". . . games . . . were of common occurrence at tribal and confederate councils. In the ball game, for example, among the Senecas, they play by phratries, one against the other . . ."
"Moreover, in the art of government they had not been able to rise above gentile institutions and establish political society. This fact demonstrates the impossibility of privileged classes and of potentates, under

their institutions, with power to enforce the labor of the people for the erection of palaces for their use, and explains the absence of such structures."

"Hunger and destitution could not exist at one end of an Indian village or in one section of an encampment while plenty prevailed elsewhere in the same village or encampment." (Morgan, 1965, pp. 6, 11, 44, 45)

5. "Surplus-labor in general, as labor performed over and above the given requirements, must always remain. In the capitalist as well as in the slave system, etc., it merely assumes an antagonistic form and is supplemented by complete idleness of a stratum of society." (Marx, *Capital*, III, p. 819)

6. Abstract labor as presented here differs from Marx's concept in the first volume of *Capital*. There, he considers only the labor that becomes congealed in value, a category specific to commodity production. We consider all the labor carried out within the relations of production, regardless of whether it becomes congealed in value. Some of it, like the labor of merchandising, does not create value.

7. "This form of free self-managing peasant proprietorship of land parcels as the prevailing, normal form constitutes, on the one hand, the economic foundation of society during the best periods of classical antiquity, and on the other hand, it is found among modern nations as one of the forms arising from the dissolution of feudal landownership. Thus, the yeomanry in England, the peasantry in Sweden, the French and West German peasants."

"The free ownership of the self-managing peasant is evidently the most normal form of landed property for small-scale operation, i.e., for a mode of production, in which possession of the land is a prerequisite for the laborer's ownership of the product of his own labor, and in which the cultivator, be he free owner or vassal, always must produce his own means of subsistence independently, as an isolated laborer with his family." (Marx, *Capital*, III, pp. 806, 807)

8. "The further development of society, and particularly of capitalism, made clear the distinction between the bourgeoisie as a class and the stratum of the intelligentsia." (Ahmati, p. 16)

9. The capitalist "exclaims: 'Have I myself not worked? Have I not performed the labor of superintendance and of overlooking the spinner? And does not this labor, too, create value?' His overlooker and his manager try to hide their smiles." (Marx, *Capital*, I, p. 193)

10. "The control exercised by the capitalist is not only a special function, due to the nature of the social labor-process, and peculiar to

that process, but it is, at the same time, a function of the exploitation of a social labor-process, and is consequently rooted in the unavoidable antagonism between the exploiter and the living and laboring raw material he exploits." (Marx, *Capital*, I, p. 331)

"The labor of supervision and management is naturally required wherever the direct process of production assumes the form of a combined social process, and not of the isolated labor of independent producers. However, it has a double nature.

"On the one hand, all labor in which many individuals co-operate necessarily requires a commanding will to co-ordinate and unify the process, and functions which apply not to partial operations but to the total activity of the workshop, much as that of an orchestra conductor. This is a productive job, which must be performed in every combined mode of production.

"On the other hand—quite apart from any commercial department —this supervision work necessarily arises in all modes of production based on the antithesis between the laborer, as the direct producer, and the owner of the means of production. The greater this antagonism, the greater the role played by supervision." (Marx, *Capital*, III, p. 383-84)

11. Bukharin also says: "*The basic classes of a given social form . . .* are two in number: on one hand, the class which commands, monopolizing the instruments of production; on the other hand, the executing class, with no means of production, which works for the former." (p. 282)

12. The text says "exploiting." This is obviously an error.

13. "Take, for example, the case of Mrs. Horace Dodge, Sr., who, according to *Fortune*, sank her entire $56,000,000 legacy into state and local bonds, the interest from which is nontaxable. At an average yield of 3 percent, Mrs. Dodge could enjoy the comfort of a $1,680,000 annual income, *without even having to bother filing a tax return.*" (Stern, p. 180-81)

14. See Marx, *Capital*, Volume 3, Chapter 21, "Interest-Bearing Capital."

15. U.S. Census, General Social and Economic Characteristics: United States Summary, Table 80.

16. *Ibid.*, Appendix B, p. App-24.

17. U.S. Census, Occupational Characteristics, Subject Report PC(2)-7A, Table 43.

18. "The corporations are the organized centers of the private property system: the chief executives are the organizers of that system."

(Mills, 1959, p. 119) For "private property" should be substituted "capitalist"; capitalist executives do not care for the private property of petty producers.

19. U.S. Census, Earnings by Occupation and Education, Subject Report 8B, Table 1.

20. The number of wage and salary workers earning over $25,000 is given in U.S. Census, Occupations of Persons with High Earnings, Subject Report 7F, Table 14. The distribution of employees of own corporations earning over $15,000 is tabulated in Table 9. Assuming that the distribution of workers earning over $15,000 is the same for employees of any corporation, then 93,794 employees of their own corporations earn over $25,000. Differences of numbers between the experienced civilian labor force and those actually employed are being ignored at these income levels.

21. U.S. Census of Agriculture, 1969, Volume II, Chapter 4, Part 2, Tables 2 and 7, and Part 3, Table 37. Class 1-5 farms (sales of $2,500 and over) were considered; the percentage of such farms with $5,000 in hired labor expenditures as a percentage of all farms was applied to the number of self-employed farmers and farm managers (U.S. Census, Subject Report 7A, Table 43).

22. U.S. Census, Subject Report 7F, Table 14.

23. U.S. Census, General Social and Economic Characteristics: U.S. Summary, Tables 77, 78, and 80.

24. All figures are for 1970 and, except as noted, are taken from U.S. Census Bureau, *Statistical Abstract of the United States: 1974*, Tables 598-609.

25. $89.8 billion stands in the same proportion to the total of $116.3 billion in personal tax and nontax payments as the sum of $623.9 billion stands in proportion to the gross personal income of all classes of $808.3 billion. (An allowance has been made for tax-free income, basically welfare income.)

26. U.S. Census Bureau, *Statistical Abstract 1972*, Table 651.

27. The steps followed in analyzing the 1970 Census data in chapter four are applied as follows:

For 1960:

CLASS OF EMPLOYED WORKERS (AGE 14 AND OVER, 1960)

"Class"	Number of persons
Private wage and salary earners	48,202,492
Government workers	7,860,565
Self-employed workers	7,902,068
Unpaid family workers	674,231
Total	64,639,256

(From U.S. Census, Volume I, Part I, Table 206)

Step 1. Combine all wage and salary earners into one group of 56,063,067.

Step 2. Divide unpaid family workers in half, forget one half, and assign 377,116 to wage and salary earners.

Step 3. Data not available.

Step 4. The $15,000 threshold must be used. Move 533,109 wage and salary earners to capitalist class (Report 7A, Table 27).

Step 5. Using the criterion of $5,000 per year expended to hire labor, move 65,153 farmers from self-employed to capitalists (1959 Census of Agriculture, Volume II, Chapter IV, Table 4, and 1960 Census, Volume I, Part 1, Table 206).

Although $15,000 is too low, this cutoff point will be used to move 521,457 self-employed persons to the capitalist class (Report 4C, Table 26).

Step 6. Add 3,434,827 unemployed to the working class (Volume I, Part I, Table 194). Arbitrarily add 200,000 to the capitalist class.

CLASSES IN THE UNITED STATES, 1960

Class	Number of persons	Percent
Working class	59,301,901	87
Petty producers	7,315,468	11
Capitalists	1,319,719	2
Total	67,937,088	100

For 1950:

CLASS OF EMPLOYED WORKERS (AGE 14 AND OVER, 1950)

"Class"	Number of persons
Private wage and salary earners	40,032,797
Government workers	5,506,236
Self-employed workers	9,573,337
Unpaid family workers	1,112,970
Total	56,225,340

(From 1950 Census, Volume II, Part I, Table 128)

Step 1. Combine all wage and salary earners into one group of 45,539,033.

Step 2. Divide unpaid family workers in half, forget one half, and assign 556,485 to wage and salary earners.

Step 3. Data not available.

Step 4. The $10,000 threshold must be used. Move 305,250 wage and salary earners to the capitalist class (Volume IV, Part 1, Chapter B, Table 22).

Step 5. Using the criterion of $2,500 per year expended to hire labor, move 182,799 farmers from self-employed to capitalists (1950 Census of Agriculture, Volume II, Chapter 14, Table 8). Since there were more farmers than commercial farmers, no reduction was made as previously, when it was assumed that farmers were operating more than one farm.

Although $10,000 per year is too low, this cutoff point will be used to move 300,845 self-employed persons to the capitalist class (Volume II, Part I, Table 143).

Step 6. Add 2,832,206 unemployed to the working class (Volume II, Part I, Table 50). Arbitrarily add 200,000 to the capitalist class.

CLASSES IN THE UNITED STATES, 1950

Class	Number of persons	Percent
Working class	48,622,474	83
Petty producers	9,189,693	15
Capitalists	988,894	2
Total	58,801,061	100

For 1940:

CLASS OF EMPLOYED WORKERS (AGE 14 AND OVER, 1940)

"Class"	Number of persons
Private wage and salary earners	30,120,692
Government workers	3,844,567
On public emergency work	2,529,606
Employers and own-account workers	9,757,736
Unpaid family workers	1,443,088
Total	47,695,689

From 1940 Census, Volume III, Part 1, Tables 1 and 2)

Step 1. Combine the first three categories into one group of 36,594,865.

Step 2. Divide unpaid workers in half, forget one half, and assign 721,544 to wage and salary earners.

Step 3. Data not available.

Step 4. The $5,000 threshold must be used. This is obviously too low, and the number of persons counted will be reduced 40 percent. Move 242,097 wage and salary earners to the capitalist class (Volume III, Part 1, Table 72).

Step 5. Data are not available. As one looks at the censuses, a larger percentage of the remaining self-employed are capitalists. Therefore, the series will be started in 1940 by arbitrarily moving three percent of the self-employed, or 292,732, to the capitalist class.

Step 6. Add 5,093,810 unemployed to the working class (Volume III, Part 1, Table 1). Arbitrarily add 200,000 to the capitalist class.

CLASSES IN THE UNITED STATES, 1940

Class	Number of persons	Percent
Working class	43,168,122	81
Petty producers	9,465,004	18
Capitalists	734,729	1
Total	53,367,855	100

As a check on the reasonableness of the above transformations of census data, we may compare the percentage weight of the self-employed among the employed given by the census and the percentage weight of petty producers among classes as finally calculated. The comparison, shown below, is fairly constant and, the transformation being small, a reasonable one.

RESULT OF CALCULATIONS, 1940-1970

Year	Self-employed as percent of employed	Petty producers as percent of classes
1970	7.7	8
1960	12.2	11
1950	17.0	15.6
1940	20.5	18

28. This threshold, while not uniform and perfectly accurate, is the one available in statistics.

29. We have the following table:

DISTRIBUTION OF CORPORATIONS BY SIZE OF ACTIVE ASSETS

Capitalist's assets	Number of corporations (000)	Total assets ($ billion)
$100,000 - $999,999	599.1	178
$1 - $10 million	87.0	240
$10 - $25 million	9.8	153
$25 - $50 million	3.9	135
$50 - $100 million	2.1	145
$100 - $250 million	1.4	222
$250 million and over	1.2	1,530
Totals	704.5	2,603

This data and the data on the 200 largest manufacturing corporations are taken from U.S. Census Bureau, *Statistical Abstract: 1974*, Tables 792 and 799.

30. *Business Week*, raw steel production and price of finished steel composite, weeks of December 1, 1973 and July 13, 1976. The increase in price in the face of declining production and sales demonstrates the monopoly power of the steel corporations. "What about our costs?" the owners always cry. Statistical research will show that wages rarely keep up with price increases, so the working class is neither the cause nor the beneficiary of inflation. As for raw materials (which in the case of steel companies controlling their ore supplies is largely an irrelevant question), to cite price increases of these commodities is merely to pass the buck in a monopoly economy.

31. *The Fortune Double 500 Directory*, 1971. The entire payroll of each corporation is counted, and the figures are compared with the unadjusted total of all wage and salary earners.

32. One panacea favored by demagogues in Congress is to divide a big corporation into four or five companies to restore competition. While this is technologically possible, since capital is centralized even beyond the technological minimum of concentration, the result, if it were politically feasible, would re-create neither the petty bourgeoisie nor competition. It would only increase the expense of hiding the fixing of output and prices among the new firms. This was shown before World War I by the "breakup" of Rockefeller's Standard Oil Trust into the various Standard Oil companies. Yet the trust busters are back again, promising heaven on earth if Big Oil is broken up.

33. This history is taken from Lanzillotti.

34. 1970 Census, Report 7C, Table 5.

35. For example, when Gulf Oil Corporation's $12 million in bribes to United States and foreign politicians became public, the Mellon family decided that some officers would have to be sacrificed. The latter were unwilling to leave but could not stand up to a special, three-man audit committee including top Wall Street lawyer John J. McCloy and Nathan W. Pearson, the financial advisor to the Paul Mellon family. (Robertson, pp. 121, 209) Gulf's chairman and three other officers resigned.

36. G. William Domhoff studied these capitalists in *The Higher Circles*, New York, Random House, 1970.

37. The feudal lords had feudalism. At first the peasantry had tribal society, then became individual producers going for the petty mode of

production. See Furey, *The Disintegration of Feudalism in England in the Thirteenth and Fourteenth Centuries.*

38. Capitalists extract some and at times all of this surplus labor through trade relations when the petty producer buys his materials and sells his product, and through credit relations. This can undermine and ruin petty producers, but the basis of the capitalist class overall remains the exploitation of wage and salary labor power.

39. See Part III for a discussion of alliances with the petty bourgeoisie.

40. See Morgan, *Ancient Society,* and Engels, *Origin of the Family, Private Property, and the State.*

41. "The commodity owner can, by his labor, create value, but not self-expanding value. He can increase the value of his commodity, by adding fresh labor, and therefore more value to the value in hand, by making, for instance, leather into boots. The same material has now more value, because it contains a greater quantity of labor. The boots have therefore more value than the leather, but the value of the leather remains what it was; it has not expanded itself, has not, during the making of the boots, annexed surplus-value." (Marx, *Capital,* I, p. 165)

42. See Lenin, *What Is To Be Done?,* section II.B.

43. See p. 67 and note 41 on the error of this view.

44. "But in different stages of society, the proportions of the whole produce of the earth which will be allotted to each of these classes, under the names of rent, profit, and wages, will be essentially different; . . . . To determine the laws which regulate this distribution is the principal problem in Political Economy" (Ricardo, p. 1).

45. "In the price of commodities, therefore, the profits of stock constitute a component part altogether different from the wages of labor, and regulated by quite different principles." (Smith, p. 49)

46. "The natural price itself varies with the natural rate of each of its component parts, of wages, profit, and rent" (Smith, p. 62).

"These, then, are the laws by which wages are regulated, and by which the happiness of far the greatest part of every community is governed." (Ricardo, p. 61) These laws are the following: the goods needed by habit for the working class to subsist, the state of agriculture, supply and demand, and the laws of population.

"The natural tendency of profits then is to fall; for, in the progress of society and wealth, the additional quantity of food required is obtained by the sacrifice of more and more labor." (Ricardo, p. 71)

47. "As soon as stock has accumulated in the hands of particular persons, some of them will naturally employ it in setting to work industrious people, whom they will supply with materials and subsistence, in order to make a profit by the sale of their work" (Smith, p. 48).

"As soon as the land of any country has all become private property, the landlords, like all other men, love to reap where they never sowed" (p. 49).

48. "Long before me bourgeois historians had described the historical development of this class struggle and bourgeois economists the economic anatomy of the classes." (Marx and Engels, 1936, Marx's letter to Weydemeyer, March 5, 1852)

49. "Classes I define as social collectives composed of persons in like or similar class position; class position is determined by a person's property relation to the means of production, or, stated differently, by a person's function in the economic system and consequently by the (predominant) source of his income. In this I adhere to the tradition from pre-Marxian British social theory to Max Weber." (Heberle, p. 18)

"The capitalist method of distribution has important social consequences. It is clear that such a method of distribution must create two groups, or classes, of persons, the first of which receives its income from payments for its work, and the second of which derives its income from payments in respect of its ownership of property in the means of production. The first of these two groups or classes of persons are commonly called workers and the second capitalists." (Strachey, p. 96) Never more than a semi-Marxist, Strachey became a fascist.

50. "I take it that it is best for all to leave each man free to acquire property as fast as he can. Some will get wealthy. I don't believe in a law to prevent a man from getting rich; it would do more harm than good. So while we do not propose any war upon capital, we do wish to allow the humblest man an equal chance to get rich with everybody else." (Abraham Lincoln, quoted by Schlüter, p. 172)

51. "But his [Weber's] analysis is not Marxian, for he emphasizes economic distribution instead of production." (Cox, 1950, p. 223)

52. Weber's section heading here reads, "Determination of Class-Situation by Market-Situation" (Weber, 1946, p. 181). "Class situations, in turn, can be primarily *determined by markets*, by the labor market and the commodity market." (*Ibid.*, p. 301)

53. "By 'class situation,' in contrast, we shall understand the opportunities to gain sustenance and income that are primarily determined by typical, *economically* relevant, situations; property of a certain kind, or

acquired skill in the execution of services that are in demand, is decisive for income opportunities." (Weber, 1946, p. 301)

54. Weber retracted this position; see Weber, 1946, p. 301.

55. ". . . the performance of manual labor is the function of one group in society, whereas it is the function of another group to own, direct, and control the means of production." (Briefs, p. 237)

Another example of this view, this time by a sham Marxist, is the following: "The proletarian is a man who is unprotected from the extremes of exploitation by any special qualifications which would prevent him from being replaced by another worker with equal physical strength. According to Marx's intentions [which Ossowski has mystically divined], this criterion would exclude the [hired] engineer or doctor from the class of the proletariat." (Ossowski, p. 79)

56. ". . . the occupational structure is the foundation of the stratification system of contemporary industrial society. . . . class differences comes to rest primarily on occupational positions and the economic advantages and powers associated with them." (Blau and Duncan, p. vii)

". . . the body of statistical information likely to provide the greatest amount of indication of the class structure in any advanced society is to be found in the classification of occupations" (Cole, 1955, p. 6).

"The backbone of the class structure, and indeed of the entire reward system of modern Western society, is the occupational order. Other sources of economic and symbolic advantages do coexist alongside the occupational order, but for the vast majority of the population these tend, at best, to be secondary to those deriving from the division of labor." (Parkin, p. 18) Parkin simply ignores the capitalists, who are outside the "vast majority."

"Occupation, or occupational grouping, has been a common indicator of position with respect to the means of production. Let it be said that this secularized derivative of Marxist theory is the meaning assigned to class in this book" (Birnbaum, 1969, p. 6). Birnbaum's implication that Marxist theory is a religion, since it must be secularized, gives away the seriousness with which he wants to study relations to the means of production.

"Marx maintained that every productive system established a limited number of types of work roles—a man could raise food, make tools, be a merchant who traded goods, or perhaps be an owner of land or other property. Each group of men who stood in the same relationship to the means of production formed a class. They not only did the same kind of work, but had basic interests in common" (Kahl, p. 2). Here is another anti-Marxist concerned to teach us botched up Marxism.

"According to Marx, ... The forms of ownership of the means of production, and the forms of labor of nonowners, give rise to the formation of the principal social groups—the social classes." (Matras, p. 64) Weber's influence is apparent.

"If class is linked with production, then occupation must be its chief index. But we find that, in study after study, occupation is used only as an index of social status." (Marshall, 1956, p. 5) Marshall sets up the occupational definition of class as a straw man, so that he can attack the whole concept of class.

At least one capitalist sociologist sees that something is wrong. "Most stratification studies that depend upon occupational prestige as a measure of class reach an uncomfortable denouement; one sentence ends on a reference to occupation and the next picks up with a reference to class." (Reissman, p. 160) ". . . the use of occupation as an index of class often becomes a means to avoid taking a clear stand on one's theory of class and social stratification. In a great deal of research, occupation is depended upon not so much to index class as to define class entirely" (*Ibid.*, p. 161). Reissman has no answer to this dilemma, because he cannot see surplus labor. He rejects the theory of surplus-value (p. 409).

57. "The small proprietor who is a farmer belongs to the same *class* as the manufacturer, or the small proprietor who is an artisan, and as the small proprietor who is a shopkeeper; there is no class distinction between them, they are distinguished only by their *occupations*." (Lenin, 1968b, p. 39)

58. ". . . the *career of an occupation* consists of changes of its internal organization and of its place in the division of labor of which society itself consists." (Hughes, p. 9)

59. The owner of his own rig supervises himself while the employee is supervised, but this difference in a production relation is usually ignored in defining the occupation of truck driver. It is taken into account when defining a specialized occupation arising out of this relation of authority, the occupation of manager, trucking line.

60. Edwards himself used "white-collar" to refer only to clerical and kindred workers.

61. This is regardless of whether they create surplus-*value*.

62. The new "middle class is composed of bureaucratic officials and private employees working on a salary" (Meusel, p. 412).

63. "Nevertheless, the fact that we do speak of a class system suggests that we can distinguish some significant 'break' in the reward hierarchy. In Western capitalist societies, this line of cleavage falls between the manual and non-manual occupational categories." (Parkin, p. 25) The white collar group is such a mixed bag that Parkin here uses only the negative term "non-manual" to identify them.

64. "Some jobs fall in a gray area between these two poles. These are, in general, the lowest level clerical positions." (Levison, p. 21)

65. One authority says, "In the long run the relative prestige of office jobs, set over against shop jobs, is based on the potential upward mobility of the white-collar worker." (Caplow, p. 44) Another says that "the traditional compensation of routine clerical work disappears: that of a reasonable chance of promotion." (Westergaard, p. 95) In other words, the biggest advantage of a clerical job is nothing definite, merely a chance. This says more about the remuneration of the clerk than it does to prove that promotion occurred frequently.

66. Here is the answer of the militant leader of a clerical trade union: "Clerical workers, like the manual workers, are in the grip of a declining capitalist system which, in obedience to its own law that the motive force of industrial activity and the clerical processes associated therewith is profit, and faced with the necessity of trying to overcome the tendency of profit to fall, seeks at every stage to restore the level of profit by reducing directly and indirectly the standard of life of the worker by hand and brain alike." (W. J. Brown, preface to Klingender.)

67. Coyle, p. 31. The figures that Coyle quotes from Paul H. Douglas include lower salaried managers with clerical employees, but this does not hurt the relative comparison over these decades.

68. "In one city machines have been bought at the insistence of the local Office Managers' Association and installed in the schools in an attempt to meet the rising demand for office machine workers." (Coyle, p. 18)

69. Klingender, pp. 4-10, 15-23. Although Klingender proves and recognizes the "complete economic proletarianization" of clerical workers, by which he means their descent to the working-class average in pay, benefits, working conditions, and job security, he still calls them lower middle class on the basis of the unexplained assertion that they perform "no specific economic function." (p. xi)

70. Doctors include physicians, surgeons, dentists, chiropractors, optometrists, osteopaths, and veterinarians. Nurses include professional

nurses, student professional nurses, dietitians, and therapists. Technologists and technicians include clinical lab, dental, health record, radiological and other technologists and technicians.

71. 1970 Census, Report 7A, Table 43, and 1950 Census, Volume 14, Part 1B, Table 12. The 1970 figures exclude those persons, primarily doctors, who were employees of their own corporation. The bias introduced by this difference in definition does not change the conclusions drawn.

72. Blank and Stigler, p. 25. These authors set the ratio of engineering salaries to the earnings of full-time wage and salary employees at 100 for 1929, regardless of what the actual ratio was. Then by 1954 this index had contracted to 67.9.

73. The same $25,000 boundary was used among self-employed managers to separate capitalists from petty producers.

74. For example, see Reich, p. 175.

75. "In many great works, almost the whole labor of this kind ["inspection and direction"] is committed to some principal clerk." (Smith, p. 49)

76. The median wage and salary earnings of all male wage and salary earners and of male managers were recalculated, using interval interpolation, after excluding earnings of $25,000 and over (1970 Census, Report 7A, Table 24).

77. If we diagram the lines of authority as a tree with five lines emanating from each manager to managers below him, then the total number of managers in a tree of n levels is

$$\frac{5^n - 1}{4}$$

and the number of managers at the lowest level is 5^{n-1}. The ratio of the latter to the former tends to 4/5 from above.

78. This is the case for about one chief executive in five, and it helps to distinguish top executives from middle managers. "A hundred and three of them [chief executives]—over 15 percent of those covered by the survey—joined their present companies at the very top. . . . One in five of the chief executives, as opposed to about one in ten of the other executives, is now employed by a firm with which his father was once associated." (*Fortune*, p. 307)

79. "The 'managers' are merely representatives of the capitalists and

carry out their will. They themselves are usually large shareholders, ensure great privileges and high incomes from their posts, and appropriate a part of the surplus value created by the workers." (Papajorgji, p. 46) In other words, these men are simultaneously a top manager subordinate to the owners and a capitalist, too.

80. Magnates who begin with nearly complete ownership of the stock draw in the capital of others without losing control by means of as little as two percent of all shares. The dispersal of stock into insignificant lots of one or even many hundred shares makes a farce of the notion that small shareholders, including top executives, own a company. They merely have a claim ticket on such surplus-value as the true owners decide to pay in dividends. (Battles between large financial groups over companies are another matter.)

81. ". . . the salary of the manager is, or should be, simply the wage of a specific type of skilled labor, whose price is regulated in the labor-market like that of any other labor" (Marx, *Capital*, III, p. 436).
". . . the wages of superintendance do not enter [into the] average rate of profit at all." (Marx, 1971, p. 505)

82. That is, the fully mature application of education to work. In socialist societies, education and work are mixed from the start. This is impossible for capitalism, with its unemployment, wage and profit relations, and divorce of theory and practice.

83. "From about the middle of the nineteenth century there began an extensive increase in the number of salaried workers, office workers, managers and superintendants of branch stores or shops or departments of larger enterprises. This group of 'white collar' and salaried workers, most of whom are technically wage earners, are, because of their education and character of work, more nearly allied with the property-owning and intellectual workers than with industrial wage-earners. Hence, usually they are regarded, and regard themselves, as middle class." (Fairchild, definition of "middle class," p. 193)

"These social changes created and enlarged the 'new middle class' of salaried and highly trained people—chemists, engineers, factory-managers, teachers, nurses, and office workers." (Havighurst, p. 109)

Reissman refers to "The white-collar and professional groups of the middle class. . . . The working class is also still identifiable." (Reissman, p. 217)

"Managers of junior and middling grades in private and public enterprise; executive and technical staff of equivalent levels; members of such lower-tier professions as teaching, trained welfare work, nursing and other medical auxiliary occupations: these and others in similar positions can be crudely described as 'middle class'." (Westergaard and Resler, p. 349-50)

"The great shortcoming of Marx was of course not to foresee the development of the 'new middle classes' of salaried employees." (Heberle, p. 21)

". . . a new middle class has been rising, a class of technicians, white-collar workers and minor executives in the large industrial establishments." (Ossowski, p. 183)

"The growth of the new middle classes—comprising office workers, supervisors, managers, technicians, scientists, and many of those who are employed in providing services of one kind or another . . . manifests the greater complexity of social stratification in modern industrial societies" (Bottomore, p. 24).

84. "But added to the traditional working class must be the 'new working class,' or the white-collar personnel who work in production-related scientific and technical jobs." (Anderson, p. 125; the original is entirely in italics.)

". . . we shall include in the new working class virtually all of the hired professional and technical workers." (*Ibid.*, p. 127)

85. "Often enough, groupings within the technical intelligentsia experience a contradiction between their capacities and insights and the imperatives visited upon them from above." (Birnbaum, 1968, p. 357)

Anderson speaks of "the contradiction between *(a)* the level of educational preparedness and innovative ability possessed by knowledge workers and *(b)* the restricted scope of daily work activity and decision-making authority that is actually theirs." (Anderson, p. 173)

"Even on the professional levels of white-collar work, not to speak of wage-work and the lower white-collar tasks, the chance to develop and use individual rationality is often destroyed by the centralization of decision and the formal rationality that bureaucracy entails." (Mills, 1956, p. 226) Mills like the others protests against authority, which he can conceive only in a bureaucratic form, but he is not so elitist as the other writers, recognizing the feeling among all workers, not only highly educated ones.

86. Lumpenproletarians are people who, under the impact of prolonged unemployment, have turned to crime, semi-legal small business, or hiring out as agents of any bidder in order to get an income.

87. Most writers on alienation try to force a choice between alienation and exploitation. "In recent years there has been an increasing interest in the concept of alienation. In the advanced industrial societies an absolute increase in wealth and a relatively more equal distribution of income has pushed economic problems into the background." (Blauner, p. 1) In advanced capitalist societies (including those of the Soviet bloc), the inequality of income between classes has been increasing, and now the absolute income of the workers is beginning to diminish, too.

88. "The tendency toward hierarchy and centralization reduces individual and social responsibility, thereby destroying the basis both for freedom and for a practice and ethic of voluntary cooperation." (R. Edwards, p. 524)

89. France has always had a larger class of small farmers than other capitalist countries. It is no accident that Andre Gorz, Serge Mallet, and other theorists of the new working class grew out of this soil.

90. Anarcho-syndicalism in its pure form is the view that the workers in each factory should own and operate it. Preferably, these are small factories in which all the workers can meet frequently as a whole to guide their business. The state should not exercise control over their business activity, such as by a collective plan. Anarcho-syndicalism arose among farmers who entered factories, transfering the petty producer outlook to their new situation. It has flourished particularly in capitalist countries with a large population of small farmers, like Spain, Italy, and France, and in Latin countries generally.

91. Wage and salary workers (not employees of their own corporation and earning less than $25,000) make up 93.9 percent of blue collar occupations and 87.6 percent of white collar occupations. See note 20 for method used to deduct both employees of their own corporations and employees earning $25,000 or more from the working class without double counting.

92. 1970 Census, Report 7A, Table 43. These are wage and salary workers not employed by their own corporations, counting the craftsmen, operatives, nonfarm laborers, and nonhousehold service workers.

93. 1970 Census, Report 7C, Table 5. These are the wage and salary earners in manufacturing, construction, transportation, communications, utilities, and automobile and other repair.

94. 1967 Census of Manufactures, Volume 1, Chapter 2, Table 3. The Census counts as production workers those "workers (up through the working foreman level) . . . closely associated with . . . production

operations" (Appendix, p. A-1). It excludes employees in sales and delivery, advertising, credit, clerical (except recordkeeping for production), and staff functions, and separate plant construction workers.

95. This is a correction of writers like Bell and Stodder who equate the growth of white collar occupations with the service sector of the economy. There are many blue collar service workers, and there are also a growing number of white collar managers, technical staff, and clerical assistants directly associated with industrial production.

96. By comparing the experienced unemployed workers to the employed workers in the 1970 Census, we find an unemployment rate of 3.3 percent among clerical and sales workers and 6.1 percent among all operatives (Report 6B, Table 11). The overall unemployment rate shown by this Census tabulation was 4.1 percent.

97. Family dependents suffer from not participating in production. This is a source of petty bourgeois consciousness, as noted in section 9.B. They are, nonetheless, dependents of workers. Some analysts cite housework as the qualification for membership in the working class. This is to view labor outside the class relation. To what class does the housewife of a petty producer (for example, a tailor with his own shop) belong? If she were called a worker, this would make the husband a capitalist exploiter of surplus labor; but he is a petty producer.

98. 1970 Census, Report 6A, Table 5.

99. If one spouse is a capitalist, then the other almost always has no need for an income through the sale of labor power, so the family counts strictly as a capitalist family. The working spouse represents an infiltration of the ranks of the working class by the capitalists. The number of such instances is extremely small.

100. 1970 Census, General Social and Economic Characteristics, Table 90, and Report 6A, Table 12.

101. U.S. Labor Department, *1969 Handbook on Women Workers*, Table 15. A 1960 study found a similar percentage, 38 percent (Watson and Barth, p. 14).

102. So degenerate is Stodder's analysis that this split is not along occupational lines but along two alleged constellations of orientations and values, one supposedly consisting of workers who support imperialist manufacturing, anti-human technological rationality, and other hobgoblins that haunt the petty bourgeois intellectual, the other camp being that of "holistic human development and self-actualization." Stodder is moderate enough to note that there are decadent tendencies

among the latter. The whole scheme has nothing to do with class analysis.

103. For Corey personally, attacking the thesis of polarization seems to be a way of confessing the error of his view that wage workers would always outnumber the salaried. In 1935 he had written, "Salaried employees have not displaced the wage-workers, and they cannot." (Corey, 1935, p. 275)

104. Most of Marx's writing on this subject is contained in his *Theories of Surplus-Value*, a three-volume work written in 1862 and 1863. It follows the writings of the so-called early Marx as well as the *Grundrisse* of 1857-58 and the *Contribution to the Critique of Political Economy* (1859), whose views it therefore supersedes. On the other hand, *Theories of Surplus-Value* was written before *Capital*.

105. "The use-value of the commodity in which the labor of a productive worker is embodied may be of the most futile kind. The material characteristics are in no way linked with its nature" (Marx, 1963, p. 158).

106. "As the co-operative character of the labor-process becomes more and more marked, so, as a necessary consequence, does our notion of productive labor, and of its agent the productive laborer, become extended. In order to labor productively, it is no longer necessary for you to do manual work yourself; enough, if you are an organ of the collective laborer, and perform one of its subordinate functions." (Marx, *Capital*, I, p. 508-09)

"And Adam Smith treats services, in so far as they directly enter into production, as materialized in the product, both the labor of the manual laborer and that of the manager, clerk, engineer, and even of the scientist in so far as he is an inventor, an indoor or outdoor laborer for the workshop." (Marx, 1963, p. 295)

107. As will be seen, the application of the definition of productive labor to monopoly capitalism is misleading.

108. Smith is engaged in the "glorification of the *industrial capitalist* in contrast to landlords and such moneyed capitalists as live only on their revenue." (Marx, 1963, p. 271)

109. "Political economy in its classical period, like the bourgeoisie itself in its *parvenu* period, adopted a severely critical attitude to the machinery of the State, etc. At a later stage it realized and—as was shown too in practice—learned from experience that the necessity for the inherited social combination of all these classes, which in part were totally unproductive, arose from its own organization." (Marx, 1963, p. 175)

"Bourgeois society reproduces in its own form everything against which it had fought in feudal or absolutist form. In the first place therefore it becomes a principal task for the sycophants of this society, and especially of the upper classes, to restore in theoretical terms even the purely parasitic section of these 'unproductive laborers,' or to justify the exaggerated claims of the section which is indispensable. The *dependence* of the ideological, etc., classes on the *capitalists* was in fact proclaimed." (*Ibid*)

110. The Soviet edition is defective, having the single quotation mark before "necessary."

111. "Although the bourgeoisie was originally very thrifty, with the growing productivity of capital, i.e., of the laborers, it imitates the retainer system of the feudal lords. According to the latest report (1861 or 1862) on the factories, the total number of persons (managers included) employed in the factories properly so called of the United Kingdom was only 775,534 while the number of female servants in England alone amounted to 1 million." (Marx, 1963, p. 200-01) See also *Capital*, I, pp. 445-47.

112. See *Capital*, I, pp. 593-95.

113. For example, "employees and workers form a stratum and a class distinct one from another because only the second participate effectively in the process of production." (Bouvier-Ajam and Mury, p. 65) By employees the authors mean salaried workers who do not produce surplus-value.

114. 1970 Census, Report 7A, Table 43, counting wage and salary workers except employees of their own corporations.

115. In the middle of the eighteenth century, a number of Continental merchants became nobles by purchase rather than feudal inheritance of title. "As today's newly rich tycoon might fill his living-room with music from a costly high fidelity phonograph because it is fashionable (and costly), so Vienna's new nobility populated their salons with live musicians." (Harman, p. 86)

116. Industrial products are more often exchanged directly between the capitalist who produced them and the capitalist who uses them as input to his production activity, or through a shorter network of brokers.

117. ". . . there has arisen a tremendous overlay of purely superfluous white-collar workers who contribute in no way to the maximization of surplus value, are totally unproductive, and live entirely off the surplus value created by the working or producing classes. The functions which

they perform make sense only within the limits of capitalism and are completely dispensable to the material and social well-being of the society from a noncapitalist perspective. Insurance, real estate, credit institutions, advertising, and much of the entire financial apparatus must be so classified." (Anderson, p. 54) According to this view, the clerk in the Prudential Insurance building in Boston or the keypuncher at the Bankamericard center in San Francisco is not part of the "working or producing classes." Furthermore, if a worker must not only find a job but make sure that it allows him to add to social well-being viewed from a noncapitalist perspective, there are very few workers indeed.

118. U.S. Census Bureau, *Statistical Abstract 1974*, Tables 424 and 427. The figures are as of October 1973. Table 427 was used only for welfare agency employment, which was deducted from "all other" in Table 424.

119. ". . . surplus consumers are extremely important and indispensable precisely for the reason that they consume the surplus" (Anderson, p. 55).

About women raising families by themselves on welfare, one writer said, "Also the bourgeoisie needs people who can be the source of sales without having to be paid wages." (Hill, p. 77)

120. In 1967, Nicolaus also published his translation of Gorz's *Strategy for Labor*. An active year!

121. ". . . the 'middle' classes—the 15 million-odd American families that enjoy, in the mid-1970s, incomes of more than about $10,000 but less than about $15,000—" (Heilbroner, p. 29).

122. "An English sociologist (D'Ett) has gone so far as to draw a table of classes: the first and lowest class (paupers) have a budget of eighteen shillings per week; the second class, twenty-five shillings; the third, forty-five shillings, etc. This conception is . . . naive and erroneous." (Bukharin, p. 277)

"Finally, in a *class* system, the social hierarchy is based primarily upon differences in monetary wealth and income." (Mayer, p. 7-8)

"We shall also discover the outlines of the actual American class structure that emerges from the inequalities of income, wealth, and economic power." (Kolko, 1964, p. 6)

123. One writer summed up the Weberian view. "What we are arguing for is the reintroduction of property as the central variable in social class analysis, assisted mainly by income analysis and secondarily by occupational analysis." (Anderson, p. 134)

124. "The so-called distribution relations, then, correspond to and arise from historically determined specific social forms of the process of production and mutual relations entered into by men in the reproduction process of human life. The historical character of these distribution relations is the historical character of production relations, of which they express merely one aspect." (Marx, *Capital*, III, p. 883)

125. "Husband, wife, and children . . . are always in the same unit. Other relatives in the household are separate units if they earn more than $15 a week and do not pool their incomes. Persons living in institutions, military reservations, hotels, or large rooming houses are excluded." (Kolko, 1964, p. 12)

126. Kolko, 1964, p. 14.

127. Kolko rejects the view that we are all one group, the theory of mass society, as well as the class view. ". . . contemporary theories of occupational and class behavior and mobility based on apocalyptic Marxist analyses and status quo-oriented theories of mass society are equally inadequate in interpreting economic mobility and social relations." (Kolko, 1957, p. 38)

128. See Marx, *Capital*, I, chapter 25, sections 1 and 3.

129. The nuclear family is the unit of the reproduction of labor power under capitalism, and individual consumption is simply the maintenance and reproduction of labor power. The family, among the working class, is thus the unit of production of labor power.

130. Marx, 1972, p. 16-17. Marx was discussing not only capitalism, but also the first phase of socialist society, which necessarily bears the marks of capitalism in many respects.

131. For example, consider a childless family in which only the husband works versus a working husband with a wife and two children. In 1969, the couple-only family was twice as likely to earn under $3,000 per year. The same probability holds for the $4,000 ceiling. On the other hand, more couple-only families received $25,000 or more than families with two children. Since the average income of the two kinds of families is approximately the same, this shows the tendency to find couple-only families more often at the extremes of income. 1970 Census, Report 8A, Table 2.

132. "If the various groups can be seen in a relationship to one another which may be symbolized on paper as a layer-cake diagram, the society is said to be stratified." (Bennett and Tumin, p. 453)

"A social stratification in this sense [of social class] cuts horizontally through the population." (Mombert, p. 532)

"The term 'social class'—often shortened to 'class'—is used by sociologists to refer to the horizontal stratification of a population by means of factors related in some way to the economic life of society." (Gordon, p. 3)

"Social stratification means the differentiation of a given population into hierarchically superposed classes." (Sorokin, p. 11)

"The specific character of the relation between social classes is hierarchy." (Speier, p. 20, original all in italics)

133. "One of the basic facts which characterizes the nature of human association is the existence of rank differences between individuals and groups in all human societies . . . In our own society the ranking system takes the form of a class structure" (Mayer, p. 1).

134. Lenin quotes the summary of an English philosopher who, although an idealist, describes the issue accurately.

135. "By social class . . . is understood the totality of individuals whose occupational, economic, and socio-political status (rights, and privileges, duties and disfranchisements) are closely similar." (Sorokin and Zimmerman, p. 61)

"Differences in income, property, and occupation divide the members of modern societies into several strata or *classes*." (Mayer, p. 23)

136. Notice the style of argument, which extracts conclusions from the definition and manipulation of a word. Davis and Moore are dressing up what they mean with an air of necessity about it.

137. The weakness which Davis caught was that although the family and not the trainee paid for the education, the family makes the sacrifice to get a good position for its child. This is not an argument against Tumin's system, but it is a defense that the present system works as Davis and Moore explained it.

138. Reviewing the debate years later, Moore praised Tumin's non-class approach. "Tumin in his suggested desiderata for the next steps in analysis of social inequality happily does not use the term 'class,'—which unfortunately our neighboring social scientists think is one of our most useful analytic tools—and his way of putting the questions does not presuppose that conceptual category. Can we get anyone to join the joyful march to sensible investigation?" (Moore, p. 28)

139. See *Capital*, I, chapter 24, section 1.

140. Tumin wrote in 1953, when new distribution relations among workers still had to be understood from the progress made toward them in the Soviet Union. China is now altering all relations, not just ownership.

141. "The term 'social mobility' refers to the process by which individuals move from one position to another in society. . . . When we study social mobility we analyze the movement of individuals" (Lipset and Bendix, pp. 1-2).

"The core of the general investigation is the study of social mobility in Britain—of the extent of movement in social status or social position by individuals of diverse social origins." (Glass, p. 5)

"Probably the crucial characteristic of a social-class system is individualism. Although it is still true that we explain poverty or wealth by stereotyping large groups with certain attributes, individuals are nonetheless assumed to have willingly chosen the course leading to their station in life. . . . Individualism presumes also that one person is as free as another to achieve advantageous social position. It acclaims ambition, progress, and, above all, success." (Cox, 1970, p. 148)

142. Since the capitalist class has been shrinking and concentrating since 1801, these figures reflect the origin of surviving members. At the same time, more than one-third or one-fourth of the existing capitalists may be mobile out of the capitalist class.

143. "The term 'social mobility' refers to the process by which individuals move from one position to another in society—positions which by general consent have been given specific hierarchical values. When we study social mobility we analyze the movement of individuals from positions possessing a certain rank to positions either higher or lower in the social system." (Lipset and Bendix, pp. 1-2)

"For the purpose of this paper we must define individual socio-economic mobility as mobility in a scale of occupational prestige" (Havighurst, p. 105).

"Occupational mobility is studied as an index of the relative 'openness' of a social structure. This refers to the ease with which individuals or groups can acquire goods and positions which are the objects of competition. . . . as income, honor, and power" (Rogoff, p. 19).

"We have been using the term 'social mobility' to mean movement, either upward or downward, between higher and lower social classes" (Barber, p. 356).

". . . higher or lower ["class position"] are defined in terms of the prestige ratings of the occupations." (S. M. Miller, p. 148)

"There is a notable tendency in studies of social mobility to treat occupation as an adequate single index of social class and to employ the terms social mobility and occupational mobility interchangeably." (Westoff et al., p. 378)

144. Commenting on Malthus, Marx says, "Thus there must be lower classes in order that the upper ones may fear to fall and there must be upper classes in order that the lower ones may hope to rise. . . . What it all boils down to is that a worker may hope to exploit other workers some day." (Marx, 1971, p. 62-3)

While the poor "ought to be kept from starving, so they should receive nothing worth saving. If here and there one of the lowest class by uncommon industry, and pinching his belly, lifts himself above the condition he was brought up in, nobody ought to hinder him" (Bernard de Mandeville, quoted in Marx, *Capital*, I, p. 614).

145. "The terms 'upward' and 'downward' are used in connection with a measuring technique that is somewhat difficult to justify. . . . To use the [Alba] Edwards categories in this way is to attribute virtues to them which they never claimed to have." (Rogoff, p. 24)

"Movement into white collar work from factory work has been commonly regarded as mobility. In the United States at least, the economic differentiation between factory and white collar workers has lessened. . . . On point after point, the advantages which once marked off white collar from factory work are diminished or overturned." (S. M. Miller, p. 148)

146. One writer gives as a source of net upward mobility, "A shift in occupational distribution so as to increase the proportion of middle and higher status occupational positions." (Havighurst, p. 107)

"Technological progress, immigration, and differential fertility have heretofore contributed to a great excess of upward over downward circulation in American society." (Sibley, p. 381)

". . . the increase in the proportion of professional, official, managerial, and white-collar positions and the decline in the proportion of unskilled-labor jobs creates a surge of mobility, which is upward—provided these positions retain their relative standing and income." (Lipset and Bendix, p. 57) The authors forget this last proviso as they go on.

"It is the expansion of the nonmanual sector of the labor force that has made possible the preponderance of upward mobility over downward mobility." (Lipset and Bendix, p. 88)

147. "The most useful general index of the extent to which mobility exists is some measure of the propensity of children to enter and remain in occupations of the same or similar grade as those of their fathers." (Floud and Halsey, p. 83)

148. Lipset and Bendix found in one study that 75 to 80 percent of a man's worklife was spent on one side of the dividing line between manual and nonmanual work, and that when the line was crossed, the move was temporary and without significance for a man's career as a whole in most instances. (Lipset and Bendix, p. 165)

"As far as mobility between the blue-collar class and the white-collar class is concerned, the conclusion of Lipset and Bendix is essentially confirmed by the OCG data." (Blau and Duncan, p. 432)

149. ". . . we make the assumption that a move from manual to nonmanual employment constitutes upward mobility among *males*." ". . . the most nearly relevant data deal with intermarriage across class lines by contrasting the occupations at marriage of husbands and wives" (Lipset and Bendix, pp. 14, 42-43).

150. In the novel *Europa*, a German Marxist says to an English student: "So, my young friend, can it be bewondered that your biologists mit good academic positions tumble the one over the other to prove the immutable, predetermined heredity? *Natürlich!* Your landlords, they believe in the heredity of real property; your noble lords, they believe in the heredity of blue blood; the powers by the Grace of God established, which call themselves nations, such as your thief England, they believe in the heredity of superior races. We also, of course, believe in the hereditary *Tugenden* of the big Aryan race of German donkeys. All the peoples mit good banking accounts and expectations by heredity transmissible, believe in the excellence of heredity and in the hereditary stupidity of the lower classes. The individual mit an immutable immortal soul by heredity transmitted, that is the corner stone, the *Grundanschauung* of all the thoughts of an immutably rascally thief society. Were that not so, would it not evidently appear that the high-respectable opinions of the immortal thieves one bloody pack of lies are?" (Briffault, p. 150)

151. *New York Times*, August 31, 1969.

152. See Jensen, pp. 50-1 for an example.

153. Jensen is not the only academic supporter of innate differences.

"Although the observed differences in IQ tests of children born of parents from different classes admittedly are attributable in part to cultural variations, the findings are at least equally predictable from a genetic theory of intelligence." (Eckland, p. 180)

"Even today achievement and native endowment play in the formation of classes a role whose social significance should not be lightly estimated." (Mombert, p. 535)

". . . the discussed physical and mental differences of the upper and lower classes are the result of both factors: heredity and environment, selection and adaptation." (Sorokin, p. 317, original all in italics.)

154. State ownership of operations by itself means nothing. The capitalist state represents only the capitalist class, so nationalization of a company or industry by this state is a matter between the particular owners of the works and the rest of the capitalist class. Usually they arrange terms at the expense of the working class. Only state ownership of the entire means of production by a working-class state, the product of a proletarian revolution, constitutes socialist, collective ownership.

155. "What classes are there in present-day Chinese society? There are the landlord class and the bourgeoisie. . . . And there are the proletariat, the peasantry, and the different sections of the petty bourgeoisie other than the peasantry, all of which are still the subject classes in vast areas of China.

"The attitude and the stand of these classes towards the Chinese revolution are entirely determined by their economic status in society. Thus the motive forces as well as the targets and tasks of the revolution are determined by the nature of China's socio-economic system." (Mao, 1967, p. 319)

156. In Russia, Lenin called for the revolutionary-democratic dictatorship of the proletariat and the peasantry. See Lenin, 1967.

157. Quoted by Bouvier-Ajam and Mury, p. 62-3, from *Cahiers du Communisme*, July-August 1959, p. 30.

158. "The question is to *what degree* the workers engaged in the new or modified forms of productive labor are drawing closer to the proletariat and what section of them is beginning to merge with the working class proper?" (Timofeyev and Chernyaev, p. 333) "Workers" here is clearly a general term like "labor force." Confusion is rampant, the authors implying that there is a working class improper. The problem is "the problem of the alliance between the working class and the intelligentsia." (p. 335) See also Fedoseyev, p. 61.

"An important implication of the changing status of intellectuals in relationship to the working class is the possibility for a powerful alliance between the working class and intellectuals and professionals in the anti-monopoly struggle and for socialism." (Ristorucci, p. 58)

159. Hill, 1975, p. 2.

160. "Meanwhile, the class structure itself has been transformed: a new intermediate stratum of administrative, technical and service personnel, often possessing a considerable degree of education, has emerged. Objectively dependent upon those who command great concentrations of property, including state property, this stratum has in general refused to align itself politically with the working class." (Birnbaum, 1968, p. 349-50)

161. "Under 'class position' will be included the following factors. First, 'market situation,' that is to say the economic position narrowly conceived, consisting of source and size of income, degree of job-security, and opportunity for upward occupational mobility. Second, 'work situation,' the set of social relationships in which the individual is involved at work by virtue of his position in the division of labor. And finally, 'status situation,' or the position of the individual in the hierarchy of prestige in the society at large. The experiences originating in these three spheres may be seen as the principal determinants of class consciousness." (Lockwood, p. 15) Notice the switch from class position in the first sentence to class consciousness in the last one.

162. "In sociological terms, the 'falsity' of the class consciousness of the clerk can only mean that his attitudes and actions tend to deviate from those which are most frequently to be found among individuals of the 'propertyless' class." (Lockwood, p. 212)

163. An ultra-left trend holds that the petty bourgeoisie can be won directly to socialism.

164. It will be easy enough to leave a few petty producers in an otherwise socialist economy. Unlike capitalist property, theirs should not be forcibly reorganized. Braverman

References

Ahmati, Muzafer, "Intellectualism—a totality of counter-revolutionary concepts and practices," *Albania Today*, Sept.-Oct. 1975.

Anderson, Charles H., *The Political Economy of Social Class*, Englewood Cliffs, Prentice-Hall, 1974.

Barber, Bernard, *Social Stratification*, New York, Harcourt, Brace and Co., 1957.

Barbour, John, "Middle Class Fed Up," *San Francisco Examiner*, April 11, 1976, p. 1.

Bell, Daniel, *The Coming of Post-Industrial Society*, New York, Basic Books, 1973.

——, "The Coming of the Post-Industrial Society," *TWA Ambassador*, Jan. 1976.

Bell, Spurgeon, *Productivity, Wages, and National Income*, Washington, D.C., Brookings Institution, 1940.

Bennett, John W. and Melvin M. Tumin, *Social Life: Structure and Function*, New York, Alfred A. Knopf, 1949.

Birnbaum, Norman, "The Crisis in Marxist Sociology," *Social Research*, 35, Summer 1968.

——, *The Crisis of Industrial Society*, New York, Oxford University Press, 1969.

Blank, David M. and George J. Stigler, *The Demand and Supply of Scientific Personnel*, New York, National Bureau of Economic Research, 1957.

Blau, Peter M. and Otis Dudley Duncan, *The American Occupational Structure*, New York, John Wiley and Sons, 1967.

Blauner, Robert, *Alienation and Freedom*, Chicago, University of Chicago Press, 1964.

Bottomore, T. B., *Classes in Modern Society*, New York, Random House, 1966.

Bouvier-Ajam, Maurice and Gilbert Mury, *Les classes sociales en France*, 1, Paris, Editions Sociales, 1963.

Boyte, Harry and Frank Ackerman, "Revolution and Democracy," *Socialist Revolution*, 3, July-Aug. 1973.

Brady, Robert A., *The Spirit and Structure of German Fascism*, New York, Citadel Press, 1971.

Briefs, Goetz A., *The Proletariat: A Challenge to Western Civilization*, New York, McGraw-Hill Book Co., 1937.

Briffault, Robert, *Europa: The Days of Ignorance*, New York, Charles Scribner's Sons, 1935.

Bukharin, Nikolai, *Historical Materialism: A System of Sociology*, New York, International Publishers, 1925.

Caplow, Theodore, *The Sociology of Work*, Minneapolis, University of Minnesota Press, 1954.

Cole, G. D. H., "The Conception of the Middle Classes," *British Journal of Sociology*, 1, 1950.

———, *Studies in Class Structure*, London, Routledge and Kegan Paul, 1955.

Corbin, John, *The Return of the Middle Class*, New York, Charles Scribner's Sons, 1922.

Corey, Lewis, *The Decline of American Capitalism*, New York, Covici-Friede, 1934.

———, *The Crisis of the Middle Class*, New York, Covici-Friede, 1935.

———, "American Class Relations," *Marxist Quarterly*, 1, Jan.-March 1937.

———, "Problems of the Peace: IV. The Middle Class," *Antioch Review*, 5, Spring 1945.

Cox, Oliver C., "Max Weber on Social Stratification: A Critique," *American Sociological Review*, 15, April 1950.

———, *Caste, Class & Race*, New York, Monthly Review Press, 1970.

Coyle, Grace L., *Present Trends in the Clerical Occupations*, New York, The Woman's Press, 1928.

Davis, Kingsley, "Reply," *American Sociological Review*, 18, Aug. 1953.

Davis, Kingsley and Wilbert E. Moore, "Some Principles of Stratification," *American Sociological Review*, 10, April 1945.

Dobb, Maurice, "The Economic Basis of Class Conflict," *On Economic Theory and Socialism: Collected Papers*, London,

Routledge and Kegan Paul, 1955.

———, *Studies in the Development of Capitalism*, New York, International Publishers, 1963.

Eckland, Bruce K., "Genetics and Sociology: A Reconsideration," *American Sociological Review*, 32, April 1967.

Edwards, Alba, *A Social-Economic Grouping of the Gainful Workers of the United States*, U.S. Census Bureau, Washington, D.C., 1938.

Edwards, Richard C., Michael Reich and Thomas E. Weisskopf, eds., *The Capitalist System*, Englewood Cliffs, Prentice-Hall, 1972.

Engels, Frederick, *Herr Eugen Dühring's Revolution in Science: (Anti-Dühring)*, New York, International Publishers, 1966.

———, *The Origin of the Family, Private Property and the State*, New York, International Publishers, 1971.

Fairchild, Henry Pratt, ed., *Dictionary of Sociology*, Totowa, Littlefield, Adams and Co., 1965.

Fedoseyev, P. N. and others, eds., *The Science of Communism and Its Falsifiers*, Moscow, Novosti Publishing House, 1972.

Floud, Jean and A. H. Halsey, "English Secondary Schools and the Supply of Labour" in A. H. Halsey and others, eds., *Education, Economy and Society*, New York, The Free Press, 1971.

Fortune, "1,700 Top Executives," 60, November 1959.

Fortune Double 500 Directory, New York, Time, Inc., 1971.

Furey, Joseph Carroll, *The Disintegration of Feudalism in the Thirteenth and Fourteenth Centuries*, Ph. D. thesis, University of Maryland.

Glass, D. V., ed., *Social Mobility in Britain*, Glencoe, The Free Press, 1954.

Gordon, Milton M., *Social Class in American Sociology*, Durham, Duke University Press, 1958.

Gorz, André, *Strategy for Labor*, trans. by Martin A. Nicolaus and Victoria Ortiz, Boston, Beacon Press, 1967.

Harman, Carter, *A Popular History of Music*, New York, Dell

Publishing Co., 1956.

Haug, Marie, "Social-Class Measurement: A Methodological Critique" in Gerald W. Thielbar and Saul D. Feldman, eds., *Issues in Social Inequality*, Boston, Little, Brown and Co., 1972.

Havighurst, Robert J., "Education and Social Mobility in Four Societies," in A. H. Halsey and others, eds., *Education, Economy and Society*, New York, The Free Press, 1971.

Heberle, Rudolph, "Recovery of Class Theory," *Pacific Sociological Review*, 2, Spring 1959.

Heilbroner, Robert L., *Business Civilization in Decline*, New York, W. W. Norton and Co., 1976.

Hewes, Amy, "Clerical Occupations," *Encyclopedia of Social Science*, 3, New York, Macmillan, 1930.

Hill, Judah, *Class Analysis*, Emeryville, Class Analysis, 1975.

Hughes, Everett Cherrington, *Men and Their Work*, Glencoe, The Free Press, 1958.

Jensen, Arthur R., "How Much Can We Boost IQ and Scholastic Achievement?" in Harvard Educational Review, ed., *Environment, Heredity, and Intelligence*, Cambridge, Harvard Educational Review, 1972.

Kahl, Joseph A., *The American Class Structure*, New York, Holt, Rinehart and Winston, 1967.

Keat, Paul G., "Long-Run Changes in Occupational Wage Structure, 1900-1956," *Journal of Political Economy*, 68, Dec. 1960.

Klingender, F. D., *The Condition of Clerical Labour in Britain*, London, Martin Lawrence, 1935.

Kolko, Gabriel, "Economic Mobility and Social Stratification," *American Journal of Sociology*, 63, July 1957.

——, *Wealth and Power in America: An Analysis of Social Class and Income Distribution*, New York, Praeger, 1964.

Kornhauser, Arthur W., "Analysis of 'Class' Structure of Contemporary American Society—Psychological Bases of Class Divisions" in George W. Hartmann and Theodore Newcomb, eds., *Industrial Conflict: A Psychological Interpretation*,

New York, Cordon, 1939.

Kuhn, James W., "Engineers and their Unions" in Albert A. Blum and others, eds., *White-Collar Workers*, New York, Random House, 1971.

Lanzillotti, Robert F., "The Automobile Industry" in Walter Adams, ed., *The Structure of American Industry*, New York, Macmillan Co., 1961.

Larner, Robert J., "The Effect of Management-Control on the Profits of Large Corporations" in Maurice Zeitlin, ed., *American Society, Inc.*, Chicago, Markham, 1970.

Lenin, V. I., *Materialism and Empirio-Criticism* (Collected Works, Volume 14), Moscow, Progress Publishers, 1968, a.

——, "The Trudoviks and the Worker Democrats," *Collected Works*, Volume 18, Moscow, Progress Publishers, 1968, b.

——, *Two Tactics of Social-Democracy in the Democratic Revolution*, Peking, Foreign Languages Press, 1970.

——, *What Is To Be Done?*, Peking, Foreign Languages Press, 1975.

Levison, Andrew, *The Working-Class Majority*, New York, Coward, McCann and Geoghan, 1974.

Lipset, Seymour Martin and Reinhard Bendix, *Social Mobility in Industrial Society*, Berkeley, University of California Press, 1959.

Lockwood, David, *The Blackcoated Worker: A Study in Class Consciousness*, London, George Allen and Unwin, 1958.

Mao Tsetung, "The Chinese Revolution and the Chinese Communist Party," *Selected Works*, 2, Peking, Foreign Languages Press, 1967.

Marshall, T. H., "General Survey of Changes in Social Stratification in the Twentieth Century," *Transactions of the Third World Congress of Sociology*, 3, London, International Sociological Association, 1956.

——, "Social Selection in the Welfare State" in A. H. Halsey and others, eds., *Education, Economy and Society*, New York, The Free Press, 1971.

Marx, Karl, *A Contribution to the Critique of Political*

Economy, Chicago, Charles H. Kerr and Co., 1904.

————, *Wage-Labour and Capital*, New York, International Publishers, 1933.

————, *Theories of Surplus-Value: Part I*, Moscow, Progress Publishers, 1963.

————, *Capital: A Critique of Political Economy*, three volumes, New York, International Publishers, 1967.

————, *Theories of Surplus-Value: Part III*, Moscow, Progress Publishers, 1971.

————, *Critique of the Gotha Programme*, Peking, Foreign Languages Press, 1972.

Marx, Karl and Frederick Engels, *Correspondence: 1846-1895*, New York, International Publishers, 1936.

————, *Manifesto of the Communist Party*, Peking, Foreign Languages Press, 1968.

Matras, Judah, *Social Inequality, Stratification, and Mobility*, Englewood Cliffs, Prentice-Hall, 1975.

Mayer, Kurt B., *Class and Society*, New York, Random House, 1966.

McConnell, John W., *The Evolution of Social Classes*, New York, Russell and Russell, 1973.

Meusel, Alfred, "Middle Class," *Encyclopedia of the Social Sciences*, 10, New York, Macmillan, 1933.

Miller, Herman P., *Income Distribution in the United States*, Washington, D.C., Bureau of the Census, 1966.

Miller, S. M., "The Concept and Measurement of Mobility," *Transactions of the Third World Congress of Sociology*, 3, London, International Sociological Association, 1956.

Mills, C. Wright, *White Collar: The American Middle Classes*, New York, Oxford University Press, 1956.

————, *The Power Elite*, New York, Oxford University Press, 1959.

Mombert, Paul, "Class," *Encyclopedia of the Social Sciences*, 3, New York, Macmillan, 1930.

Moore, Wilbert E., "Rejoinder," *American Sociological Review*, 28, Feb. 1963.

Morgan, Lewis H., *Houses and House-Life of the American Aborigines*, Chicago, University of Chicago Press, 1965.

Nicolaus, Martin, "Proletariat and Middle Class in Marx: Hegelian Choreography and the Capitalist Dialectic," *Studies on the Left*, 7, Jan.-Feb. 1967.

Ossowski, Stanislaw, *Class Structure in the Social Consciousness*, New York, The Free Press of Glencoe, 1963.

Papajorgji, Harilla, "The Working Class in Capitalist Society Today," *Albania Today*, Jan.-Feb. 1975.

Parker, Richard, *The Myth of the Middle Class*, New York, Liveright, 1972.

———, "Fact and Fancy About America's 'Classless Society,' " *Business and Society Review/Innovation*, Summer 1974.

Parkin, Frank, *Class Inequality and Political Order*, New York, Praeger, 1971.

Quinn, T. K., *Giant Business: Threat to Democracy*, New York, Exposition Press, 1953.

Reich, Michael, "The Evolution of the United States Labor Force" in Richard C. Edwards and others.

Reissman, Leonard, *Class in American Society*, New York, The Free Press, 1959.

Ricardo, David, *The Principles of Political Economy and Taxation*, London, Dent, 1965.

Ristorucci, Donna, "The Changing Status of Intellectuals and Professionals," *Political Affairs*, 52, Nov. 1973.

Robertson, Wyndham, "The Directors Woke Up Too Late at Gulf," *Fortune*, 93, June 1976.

Rogoff, Natalie, *Recent Trends in Occupational Mobility*, Glencoe, The Free Press, 1953.

Samuelson, Paul A., *Economics*, New York, McGraw-Hill Book Co., 1970.

Schlüter, Herman, *Lincoln, Labor and Slavery*, New York, Socialist Literature Co., 1913.

Schumpeter, Joseph A., *Imperialism and Social Classes*, New York, Augustus M. Kelley, 1951.

Sibley, Elbridge, "Some Demographic Clues to Stratification" in

Reinhard Bendix and Seymour Martin Lipset, eds., *Class, Status and Power*, Glencoe, The Free Press, 1953.

Sloan, Alfred P., Jr., *My Years With General Motors*, Garden City, Doubleday and Co., 1964.

Smith, Adam, *An Inquiry Into the Nature and Causes of the Wealth of Nations*, New York, Modern Library, 1957.

Sorokin, Pitirim A., *Social and Cultural Mobility*, Glencoe, The Free Press, 1959.

Sorokin, Pitirim and Carle C. Zimmerman, *Principles of Rural-Urban Sociology*, New York, Henry Holt and Co., 1929.

Speier, Hans, *Social Order and the Risks of War*, New York, George W. Stewart, 1952.

Stern, Philip M., *The Great Treasury Raid*, New York, Random House, 1964.

Stodder, Jim, "Old and New Working Class," *Socialist Revolution*, 3, Sept.-Oct. 1973.

Strachey, John, *The Theory and Practice of Socialism*, New York, Random House, 1936.

Sturmthal, Adolf, ed., *White-Collar Trade Unions*, Urbana, University of Illinois Press, 1967.

Szymanski, Albert, "Trends in the American Class Structure," *Socialist Revolution*, 2, July-Aug. 1972.

———, "Response," *Socialist Revolution*, 3, Sept.-Oct. 1973.

Timofeyev, T. and A. Chernyaev, "Some Aspects of the Study of the Modern Proletariat," *Marxism Today*, 17, Nov. 1973.

Touraine, Alain, *The Post-Industrial Society*, New York, Random House, 1971.

Tumin, Melvin M., "Some Principles of Stratification: A Critical Analysis," *American Sociological Review*, 18, Aug. 1953.

U.S. Census Bureau, Washington, D.C. The following censuses were used: *Census of Population: 1970*, General Social and Economic Characteristics: United States Summary, and Subject Reports: Final Reports PC(2)-6A, -6B, -7A, -7F, -8A, and 8B; *Censuses of Population: 1960, 1950*, and *1940*, various reports. *Censuses of Agriculture: 1969, 1959*, and *1950. Cen-*

sus of Manufactures, 1967.

———, *Historical Statistics of the United States, Colonial Times to 1957,* Washington, D.C., 1960.

———, *Statistical Abstract of the United States: 1972,* Washington, D.C., 1972.

———, ———: *1974,* Washington, D.C., 1974.

U.S. Labor Department, Women's Bureau, *1969 Handbook on Women Workers,* Washington, D.C., 1969.

Wall Street Journal, "Recession, Cost Cuts Don't Dim Splendor of Executive Offices," June 1, 1971, p. 1.

———, "Tax Laws Encourage Companies to Reward Officials With 'Perks', " July 15, 1971, p. 1.

Watson, Walter B. and Ernest A. T. Barth, "Questionable Assumptions in the Theory of Social Stratification," *Pacific Sociological Review,* 7, Spring 1964.

Weber, Max, *From Max Weber: Essays in Sociology,* New York, Oxford University Press, 1946.

———, *Economy and Society: An Outline of Interpretive Sociology,* New York, Bedminister Press, 1968.

Westergaard, John H., "The Withering Away of Class: A Contemporary Myth," in Perry Anderson and Robin Blackburn, eds., *Towards Socialism,* Ithaca, Cornell University Press, 1966.

Westergaard, John and Henrietta Resler, *Class in a Capitalist Society,* London, Heinemann, 1975.

Westoff, Charles F., Marvin Bresler and Philip C. Sagi, "The Concept of Social Mobility: An Empirical Inquiry," *American Sociological Review,* 25, June 1960.

Wright, Carroll D., *Outline of Practical Sociology,* New York, Longmans, Green, and Co., 1900 and 1902.

Index